WHAT YOU SEE IN CLEAR WATER

WHAT YOU SEE IN CLEAR WATER

Life on the Wind River Reservation

Geoffrey O'Gara

Alfred A. Knopf
New York
2000

This Is a Borzoi Book
Published by Alfred A. Knopf

Copyright © 2000 by Geoffrey O'Gara
All rights reserved under International and Pan-
American Copyright Conventions. Published in the
United States by Alfred A. Knopf, a division of Random
House, Inc., New York, and simultaneously in Canada
by Random House of Canada Limited, Toronto.
Distributed by Random House, Inc., New York.

www.aaknopf.com

Knopf, Borzoi Books, and the colophon are
registered trademarks of Random House, Inc.

Library of Congress Cataloging-in-Publication Data
O'Gara, Geoffrey.
What you see in clear water : life on the Wind River
Reservation / Geoffrey O'Gara.— 1st ed.
    p.   cm.
ISBN 0-679-40415-5 (alk. paper)
    1. Shoshoni Indians—Social conditions.   2. Shoshoni
Indians—Government relations.   3. Arapaho Indians—
Social conditions.   4. Arapaho Indians—Government
relations.   5. Indians, Treatment of—Wyoming—
Wind River Indian Reservation.   6. Wind River Indian
Reservation (Wyo.)—Social conditions.   7. Wind
River Indian Reservation (Wyo.)—Environmental
conditions.   I. Title.
E99.S4.O38 2000
978.7'63–dc21   00-034913

Manufactured in the United States of America
First Edition

*Wyoming Law partners Andrew Baldwin and
Berthenia Crocker helped me understand many
of the issues discussed in the book, and while they
played roles during parts of the legal battle over
the Wind River, they've been rendered largely invisible
in this book. This is because one of them, Berthenia,
is my life partner, and I could show little objectivity in
portraying someone I admire and love so much.*

What we call man's power over nature turns out to be a power exercised by some men over other men with nature as its instrument.

—C. S. Lewis, *The Abolition of Man*

Contents

Introduction

Writing about real events, one sometimes strains to accelerate the plodding tempo of everyday life and discourse to a more dramatic pace. In the case of the Wind River Valley, though, such frustrations are rare. If anything, the shorthand of hurriedly scribbled notes and the decorum of restrained storytelling may have on occasion reduced colorful speech and events to something less expressive than they were in real life.

I gathered material for this book over a period of fourteen years: first as a newspaper and magazine reporter; then as a friend of people in the valley, with no particular mission; and finally, with the more focused aim of producing this book. As a result, I reach into an enormous grab bag of material to bring forth a handful of story. Just as a historian must wrestle with the professional urge to include and footnote every last item of historical minutiae unearthed, I have struggled with what to put in and leave out of a book that might otherwise meander like a river that has spilled from canyon onto open plain.

This is a work of nonfiction—a declaration that seems more necessary today than it might have been a few decades ago. For brevity's sake, I have sometimes compressed the chronology of events, but only when such modifications have no bearing on the narrative that constitutes the larger historical record. In one instance I have changed the name of a family, at their request, and some identifying characteristics in their story, to protect their privacy. The stories recounted represent my own research and experience, the accounts of others, and gleanings from historical records.

Few residents of the Wind River Valley have ever sought the spotlight; if anything, we who live here share a happy secret in our lack of notoriety, which helps to sustain the delicate natural beauty of the surrounding wildlands. If one can assign a lesson to a book like this (a hopeless task), mine would be: Every watershed in the country, even those straddled by urban sprawl, has its own particular and subtle order, its own vying cultures, its own imprinted past and imagined future, waiting to be discovered. So I would hope in the end that the people exposed in this book can find in it some worth to ease their discomfort, and then will be allowed to retreat into the community that owns them to continue with their private toils and affections.

WHAT YOU SEE IN CLEAR WATER

Prologue

Seventeen years ago I drove a forest green Land Cruiser towing a U-Haul trailer from Washington, D.C., to Wyoming, two thousand miles horizontally and one mile up in elevation. Like a lot of people traveling west, I came with a joyful noise, opening the window now and then to shout hosannas at the prairie dogs in the badlands and the antelope in the bunchgrass. The plains emptied out around me and the mountains loomed ahead, and urban irritations fell away as the challenge of bad weather and chancy geography took their place. Antelope! by God, lifting their pronghorns to chew skeptically as we went shouting by. A river with geese on it, and the sky above the tent barnacled with stars!

My way into Wyoming was along the Bighorn River, which began farther west and higher up as the Wind River in the mountain range of the same name. The Bighorn joins with the Yellowstone River in Montana and flows to the Missouri and the Mississippi and the sea, but I was heading *upstream* on the two-lane highway that runs beside the river. It cuts through a small range called the Owl Creek Mountains, and here the name changes: everything above is Wind River, everything below is Bighorn. No one remembers why, but perhaps the Name Givers were influenced by the river's illogical decision to cut through the mountains and go north, instead of taking the easy route east across the plains. The Owl Creeks enclose the lower end of a basin that, followed upstream, curves south, east, and then north, draining the towering Wind River Mountains in the west.

Entering the bottom of the steep canyon through the Owl Creeks, still seventy miles shy of the town where I would begin a new job, I passed a nondescript green sign that might well have marked merely the transition from one county to the next. But this one read ENTERING THE WIND RIVER INDIAN RESERVATION.

Throughout the West, that's all the indication you get that you've crossed the border of an Indian reservation. You may feel, as I did, an uptick of curiosity—oh, I hadn't realized there were Indians just *here*—but after a few moments of glancing about for something different, you're simply in the West again, stunned by the scenery. There are no border guards, no sudden changes in pavement or roadside vegetation, no people in odd habitation or colorful dress.

The upper end of the canyon is sealed by a small dam that backs up a big blue reservoir with only a few power boats on it, and farther up the road I came to a little town with a Conoco gas station and a drugstore that made "the world's finest" malt shakes. Things you find anywhere.

But much of this land was an Indian reservation, a place that has its own rules, a place created by a treaty between nations over a century ago, before Wyoming was a state.

To most Americans, reservations have faded from the everyday landscape, all but unseen except for those unobtrusive signs we pass occasionally along backroads west of the Mississippi. Reservations today rarely fit the expectations of the latter-day immigrants who are moving West, and what doesn't fit becomes invisible.

Thanks to John Ford movies, we picture Indian country as high, open plains, a landscape both beautiful and bleak, populated thinly by traditional people on horseback and wearing braids; or we see it through occasional television news reports that highlight the poverty and despair on reservations. Traditional crafts and jewelry are sold at roadside shops, and sometimes tourists can attend powwows featuring dancing and drums and costumes. That's about as much contact as a visitor without introductions can expect.

The federal government is in charge, sort of, and assists the people with various programs. As one drives through, it might seem that not much is going on around the rundown prefab housing in these little reservation towns. There is no "downtown," no business district. The children are cute, but the teenagers and adults avoid eye contact with strangers. Generally, reservations are labeled "undeveloped," and some parts may be considered dangerous. There are few signs telling you where to go.

One romantic notion about Native Americans is that they're connected to the land in some sacred sense forever inaccessible to non-Indians. More plainly, an Indian's link to the reservation is historical and indissoluble. An Indian can move from house to house, or to a faraway city, but his roots in the land of his tribe's reservation will never be cut, because the reservation is not to be bought and sold.

It's worth remembering, at the same time, that reservations are an unhandy accommodation set up by the grandsons of European immigrants for a conquered, darker-skinned people, where the conquerors still act as a "trustee" of tribal resources. While it is helpful sometimes to recite that reservations are "domestic dependent nations" with special status in the U.S. Constitution, they are also entangled in the laws and lives of their non-Indian neighbors, some of whom also have been there a long time, at least by non-Indian standards. Only in a few instances—the Shoshone at Wind River are one—were reservations demarked on a people's ancestral homeland. And "home" was a seasonal concept for nomadic tribes before the European conquest: the Shoshone passed through the Wind River Valley like birds through a field.

Despite this adulterated origin, reservations are one key to the differences between whites and Indians. As an Indian, you're part of a community interminably grounded in a place. For better or worse, it was the land of your parents and will be the land of your children, whether they live there or not. By your lineage, you share in its ownership with thousands of others, share in its responsibilities, its past, its suffering, its future. The minerals, the soils, and the water—that most essential resource in the West—are as mutual as ancestral blood. For the rest of us, it's rarely so: We buy and sell property in widely various places, and drive our Land Cruisers from home to home.

      A newcomer to the West is unlikely to arrive thinking about this. I certainly didn't. The publication that had hired me covered environmental and resource issues throughout the Rocky Mountains, and the copies I'd studied made no mention of the reservation that began on the outskirts of Lander. I forgot the reservation boundary sign almost the moment I'd passed it. The map in my head was all peaks and alpine valleys, without subdivisions or boundaries or many people. The gleaming river that emerged from Wind River Canyon had begun its journey on the flanks of a 14,000-foot mountain, a bulging vertebra on the spine of the Rockies; it dropped down to a valley famous for its sunshine and good soil, then departed through this canyon. It was a smallish river, magnified by the twisting severity of the canyon it had cut, muscling over boulders and scouring trout holes beneath the drops. Eventually, blended with other rivers, it would pour out across the Mississippi Delta and become an insignificant drop in the Gulf of Mexico. But in the high basin that emptied through this canyon, the Wind River was something else. Fortunes would be made, history would be recast, hearts would be broken, all over this little cataract. On that first look, though, I only wondered: canoe or kayak?

    There are certainly bigger river systems in the world than the Wind, rivers that have carried the ships and powered the turbines of great empires. But this small watershed has its unique historic knots to unravel, and its twists and turns lead the way through a struggle that has been going on for centuries, since the first European settlers came to the Americas. It is the unfinished struggle between Native Americans and the whites who surround and threaten to subsume them—once a military conflict, now a cultural war, complicated after all these years by the fact that neighbors, even antagonistic neighbors, know one another in intimate and sometimes affectionate ways. Stories about people who live along the river, taken together, help explain how the West became itself, and how it's still taking new shapes, like a meander in spring runoff.

I drove my green Land Cruiser along the Wind River, impressed with the steep canyon walls, longing to dip my face in the tumbling water, thinking ahead to the valley where I would soon live. Travelers in the arid West have always followed its waters, from the ancient people who carved their stories in sandstone cliffs above springs to the immigrants who steered close to trickling draws as they crossed the desert in Conestoga wagons. In the years that followed my entrance through the canyon into the Wind River Valley, a landmark struggle would take place between Indians and non-Indians over the small river that plunged beside me, a struggle that would affirm what the explorer John Wesley Powell wrote in 1870: "In the whole region [of the West], land as mere land is of no value. What is really valuable is the water privilege."

Following the river, I've found stories to tell—some old, some new. Rather than follow a time line, I've followed the river, pursuing an upstream journey that began in Wind River Canyon and will end at the headwaters near the Continental Divide. There are others who live along the Wind River who know much more. I hope they'll tell their own stories when they're ready.

CHAPTER 1

Wind River Canyon

A century ago, when a journey from the Union Pacific depot in Rawlins, Wyoming, to the Shoshone Indian Reservation meant 150 miles in a hard saddle across windy tablelands set with waist-high sagebrush, Indian Inspector James McLaughlin trekked to Wind River Canyon. On the long trip north, he rarely looked up at the tall skidding clouds, or down at the sudden draws that dropped through the floor of the plains. It was spring, but barely spring, and scalloped ridges of snow still snugged against the lee sides of the hills. The creeks were mostly still dry, deep cracks blistering across the dun-colored plain. The ground was as cold as a corpse, but in places where the sun could soften it, gnarls of dust rose behind the horses. Then the clouds would collide in the huge sky, and the whitened bone of parched land would be suddenly drenched. Bentonite in the soil would turn it to a paste that coated the wheels until they looked like gray balloons, so heavy and slippery that the horses couldn't pull. McLaughlin would wait it out patiently. He was a twenty-five-year veteran of the Indian Service, and he'd made trips like this before into harsh corners of the plains that had been left to the Indians. The government recognized his knack for parleying with tribes, and it sent him all over the West. With experience and the trust he felt he'd earned among the Indians, he found these negotiations were not difficult; it was getting there that was hard.

The high desert McLaughlin crossed was the bottom of an evaporated ocean that once thinly covered the belly of the continent. Uplifted and emptied, the ocean bottom was turned back like a sheet and smoothed by wind. Along McLaughlin's route were hogbacks of red sandstone and scatterings of jade on the ground, but only an avid rockhound would want to linger. Now and then spikes of granite poked through, including a pinkish hump like Split Rock, a landmark westward immigrants still looked for in McLaughlin's time. West of the Rawlins uplift, the creeks drained into a desert bowl with no outlet—the Great Divide Basin, where the Continental Divide forks into west and east branches.

At night, if the wind wasn't whistling, the coyotes howled; now and then, as the party headed north, they found a fire ring and grass munched down by pack animals. But there were more signs of death than life: the curled ribs of an antelope carcass, a collapsed homestead cabin with a fallen wooden cross over a child's grave. An experienced traveler accepted the monotony, hardened himself to the artifacts of past suffering, and prepared for the unfriendliest weather. McLaughlin kept his gaze low and forward. This kind of open vista, this nakedness, had driven people mad.

Several days into the trip, the plateau suddenly dropped away. They couldn't see the escarpment as they approached it, because the world had been flat for miles, but by then they had spotted the white peaks of the mountains rising above the long curve of horizon and knew the ordeal would end soon. They dropped off Beaver Rim and the world began to change.

The desolate prelude made the natural beauty of the Wind River all the more stirring. The valley is a small concavity of warm, still air and braided river bottom that would seem to have no place in the midst of the high desert. The plains form a huge moat to the east and south—much more intimidating distances in McLaughlin's time than now—and on the other two sides rise knifelike peaks that only a fool, or an explorer like John Frémont, would scale. The basin was not without its own scabby draws and sagebrush snags, but the natural ramparts provided a sense of security missing on the trip north. The travelers were relieved, though no one said so. Thickly forested lake-dotted foothills sloped up to the west, and a weave of rippling water lined by cottonwoods etched the broad valley below.

McLaughlin had been the agent at Standing Rock in the Dakotas, a much bleaker post, where the Sioux leader Sitting Bull had been killed during McLaughlin's tenure. Wind River, with its generous portions of lakes and timber and arable land, was unusually rich in resources for a reservation. He looked into the steep cut where the Wind River plunged through the Owl Creek Mountains and was particularly impressed. "It is really such a grand work of nature that I believe, when the transportation problem has been solved in that country, it will rival the Yellowstone Park and the Grand Canon [sic] of the Colorado as an attraction for lovers of scenic grandeur."

McLaughlin's mission to Wind River in 1896 did not directly concern the canyon, but an area just downstream. He was meeting with leaders of the Northern Arapaho and Eastern Shoshone tribes to discuss an enormous hot spring that flowed from a red sandstone outcrop over a white travertine shelf into the Bighorn River just north of the canyon. McLaughlin, who had been called "White Hair" by the Sioux during his years in South Dakota, came to negotiate the sale of the hot spring. Among the largest in the world, it poured out nearly 19 million gallons of scalding water daily, and frontier entrepreneurs were diverting it in crude ditches to tent-walled spas with names like the Hotel de Sagebrush. They had visions of a Saratoga-like health resort. First, though, there was the problem of land title: the spring and the surrounding lands belonged to the tribes.

McLaughlin considered himself sympathetic to Indians—his wife was part Santee Sioux—but he shared the prevalent view that white dominance of Indians was "natural law." His role in dismantling the Sioux reservation had made him no allies among Sitting Bull's followers, but he titled his memoirs *My Friend, the Indian,* and in them he sounded sympathetic indeed. "The Indian," he wrote, "has been made the object of speculative persecution by every white man who felt that he needed what the Indian possessed." Perhaps he touted the beauty and tourism potential of the canyon—which would remain in Indian hands—to distract attention from his role in relieving the tribes of the hot springs. The springs never became a western Saratoga, but today they are piped through commercial pools and resort motels in a state park.

Nowadays you will rarely see an Indian face at the hot springs, but once a year Native Americans turn out in force, and in costume, for a pageant called the Gift of the Waters. While local farm girls in moccasins and greasepaint sing praises to the hot spring, the legendary Shoshone chief Washakie raises his arms in welcome to the tourists and reads from a script: "I Washakie freely give to the Great White Father these waters beloved of my people that all may receive the great blessing of bodily health in the bathing. Red man or white, the difference lies only in outward appearance, our father knoweth his children by their hearts, and knowing them, loves them. . . . May we meet with no line a boundary, save that of mountains majestic and rivers of pure flowing water, receiving a kind benediction of love from the One Dama Upa."

The old chief is played by Starr Weed, a white-haired Shoshone dressed in a feathered headdress and buckskin decorated with colorful beading and quillwork; he smiles fixedly at the camera-wielding tourists, who are dressed in Ray-Bans and Bulls T-shirts and sun block. The script is, well, *pageantlike,* and Weed recites his lines stiffly but affably, stumbling now and then in the purple rhetoric, squinting at the paper before him. The crowd doesn't seem to mind, or pay much attention to what Weed says: they've come more for the dancing and costume. When it's over, they turn away and head for the pool or the camper, talking about which resort has the better water slides or where they'll rendezvous for dinner.

Weed had some pageant cash in his pocket and a smile on his face when we shook hands beside the hot spring. "The Shoshone came here on a hunt, from way over on the other side," he said with a gesture west, "and they saw something up there." He pointed to a ledge of tan sandstone that forms a bed-sized platform in the rock above the green-bottomed pool where the water emerges. Weed speaks slowly and gestures with his hands, smiling always. The hot springs in this basin were homes to monstrous serpents, and the Shoshone were warned by the Nimimbe—an elusive race of dwarfish mountain people—to respect them or suffer consequences. This is not mentioned in the pageant script, but an elder like Weed knows all about it. "That's where the lizard was, bigger than a man, and when the people came, he rolled off the ledge and plunged down into the spring. Scared them bad. The old people tell me that."

Weed is a descendant of Chief Washakie, the warrior who according to some stories cut the heart out of a Crow chief in a fight over which tribe would control the hunting grounds of the Wind River Valley. Weed was a latter-day warrior himself, spending months in a German prison camp during World War II; he has served on the Shoshone ruling council, and is a rancher who trains horses and riders for bareback races at Indian rodeos. He could have told the hot springs story more easily, and surely differently, in Shoshone or sign language.

Nearly a century after McLaughlin admired the canyon upstream from the hot springs, few tourists find their way to the steep gorge where the Wind River drops through the Owl Creeks. They pass through on a highway cut into the cliffs along the river, usually on their way to Yellowstone National Park. That trip is often broken up by a stop in Thermopolis, where the hot spring is now harnessed for water slides and spas, owned by non-Indians. At the top of the canyon is a dam built by the U.S. Bureau of Reclamation, so the flows through the canyon fluctuate less than they did in McLaughlin's time. Fishermen may have heard that there are big trout in the canyon's pools—big, but hard to catch—and some stop to cast a line, though others find it too much trouble to buy a reservation fishing license on top of their Wyoming permits. Kayakers often ask if they can run the canyon's rapids, but are refused by the tribes (a few have run them anyway). At the bottom of the canyon, where the walls drop away and the river smooths out, is a site called Wedding of the Waters, where the Wind River becomes the Bighorn River, for reasons no one can remember.

Recently, though, Darren Calhoun has begun taking adventurous visitors on whitewater raft trips down the canyon. In an eddy near the top of the canyon, not far below Boysen Reservoir, he stands thigh-deep in the water and steadies a rubber raft loaded with me and a group from Iowa. Heavyset and long-haired, Calhoun is an Eastern Shoshone whose ancestors were present at the

McLaughlin negotiations. He and his college roommate spent a few fun years in Jackson Hole after graduation, and at one point he took his father, Pete Calhoun, on a raft trip down the Snake River. Calhoun *fils* and *père* decided to approach the tribes about setting up an Indian-run business in the canyon. Calhoun spends most of the year in graduate school in Montana, while Pete ranches on the upper reaches of the Wind River—and some of the water passing through the canyon today might first have crossed his fields, a hundred miles away.

In June, the river is swollen with snowmelt from the mountains in the west, raising some of the rapids close to a difficult, Class V rating. Calhoun asks the passengers in the raft if any have whitewater experience. Where the river is not whipped into foam, it is pale brown, partly from eroding sandstone far upstream and partly from irrigation runoff that carries soil from the fields into the river. Patches of moss, torn from hot springs rising in the streambed, float in the water. The river has good-sized trout, but they're invisible this time of year.

Darren normally has a dry sense of humor—as he backs his trailer full of rafts toward the river, he cackles a little at his own erratic steering and mutters "back-paddle!"—but not once he's in the water. He was affected deeply when a rafter died after a boat overturned earlier in the summer, though the cause of death was a heart attack, not a boatman's mistake. He went to a traditional Shoshone sweat afterward, and as the cedar fumes and steam filled the lodge he felt a panicky impulse to flee, imagining in the darkness that everyone was looking at him, the way tearful people looked up at him on the riverbank after the man didn't respond to CPR.

Growing up on his father's ranch along the Upper Wind, Darren rode horses from boyhood. These were not trail-plodding plugs but working horses, smart and agile. A boy sitting atop a powerful animal would not be there long if he was inattentive or cruel. Now, pushing off from the riverbank, he encouraged his guests in the canyon to approach the river the way he had a horse—with respect. "You can't just yahoo down this river," he said, "when the water is this high"—more than 4,000 cubic feet per second, pushing up standing waves taller than a man. With an edge in his voice to keep their attention, he explained how to pull a passenger back on board if someone took an unscheduled "swim." He was much more earnest than any stewardess as he gave the rafting equivalent of make-sure-your-seat-belts-are-securely-fastened. But as he listened to the unconcerned giggles from the front of the boat, he wondered if his clients these days came from a world so conditioned by the artificial thrills of amusement parks that a truly wild river was inconceivable.

To date, no amusement park has been able to create this sort of geological sculpture: a steep-walled incision into dark metamorphic rock laced by veins of pink and white quartz, with towering sandstone walls looming hundreds of feet above. Below, tapering down to the river, gentler talus slopes are anchored by grasses and juniper. A sparse fringe of conifers spikes the canyon rim, atop a vertical wall where only bighorn sheep can find footing. The stratigraphy of rock visible in the walls of the canyon is not horizontal but tilts downward south to north more steeply than the grade of the canyon itself, creating a dizzying sensation of going up when you travel down the canyon, and vice versa. In the wall are dips and shadows like the features of a face, where boulders have broken loose and tumbled down to the river. Some of those rocks, as big as small houses, now clog the riverbed and force the water to take odd twists and turns.

The jumble of colors and formations is typical of Rocky Mountain geology, where thrusting and faulting tilt the strata laid down in ancient seas and ridges. It's not unusual for pre-Cambrian rock to be found folded over Flathead sandstone two billion years younger, or to find ocean-bed fossils on a peak of igneous basalt.

The mountains the canyon cuts through are actually an older range than the towering peaks along the Continental Divide to the west. The Owl Creeks were buried beneath a huge load of sediments that eroded rapidly from the younger and taller Rocky Mountain ranges that thrust up 100 million years ago. For millions of years they lay in a tomb of silt. Then the region as a whole lifted again, and the streams pouring off the Rockies got faster, cut deeper.

Eventually, the Wind River resurrected the Owl Creeks, and cut its own difficult route north through this canyon.

The group now pushing off from the banks near the top of the canyon knows little of this, and they get only snippets of more recent history from their hosts. Indian bands—Crow, Sioux, Arapaho, Shoshone—used to cross the Owl Creeks in both directions on hunting expeditions, and many of the toughest rapids in the canyon have been named after leaders of the tribes that eventually settled here. " 'Black Coal,' " says one rafter, looking at the black shale boulders that squeeze the river channel ahead of the raft. "Is that really coal?" No, Calhoun explains, Black Coal was an Arapaho chief. "Cool," says the passenger, and then he thinks of the name of another rapid further down the river. "What about 'Sphincter'?" But today Calhoun isn't amused, even though he named that nerve-racking rapid himself.

"We're not selling culture," Calhoun told me along the river. But the names attached to the landmarks in the canyon figure large in the history of the two tribes who live on this reservation, the Northern Arapaho and Eastern Shoshone. Though you rarely see an Indian in the canyon today, there was a time when hunting parties regularly traveled back and forth from one basin to another. The vision of Yellow Hand, who brought the Sun Dance to the Shoshone, might have occurred here, according to tribal members.

The Black Coal rapid is a good paddling warm-up, a fifty-yard stretch of fast, narrow water that gives all the passengers a chance to try their strokes and feel how the raft takes standing waves. Black Coal, one of the last recognized chiefs of the Arapaho, over a century ago, is a distant relation of Calhoun's mother's family. Black Coal was a handsome man, with a broad face and a wide, expressive mouth. As a young warrior, he rolled in the ashes at a battle site where the Arapaho had fought the Utes, and earned his name. Before they were officially residents of the Wind River Indian Reservation, his people often allied themselves with the Sioux, and shared some of their claim to Black Hills territory. The tribe also had relatives in Colorado, the Southern Arapaho, and hunted now and then around the Owl Creeks. Before they settled here, they frequently were accused, along with the Sioux, of stealing from and even murdering white ranchers and miners in the Wind River country. Their historic role in some of the attacks on whites is debatable, but no one denies that they sometimes raided the settlements of an enemy tribe that lived in the area—the Shoshone.

In the 1870s, the Arapaho were still wandering, running out of places to go, pinched by encroaching white settlement, conflicts with other tribes competing for dwindling game, and the U.S. Army's increasingly firm hand against independent tribes. In 1863 and 1868, the Shoshone had signed treaties accepting the Wind River country as a reservation. The Northern Arapaho had signed a treaty in 1851 and had been promised a reservation too, but proposed sites along the North Platte and Sweetwater Rivers had never materialized.

On the morning of the Fourth of July in 1874, Black Coal's band was camped in the steep-gulleyed hills east of Wind River Canyon, along Nowood Creek. They were no sentries to spot the soldiers who were moving through the ghostly hills under cover of night. The soldiers dismounted back from the rim and approached on foot, looking down into a deep gulley. In the first glimmer of morning light, two hundred tepees cast sharp shadows alongside the small creek, with the fires smoldering, the dogs sleeping, and the horses clustered around a nearby spring. Revenge was in the hearts of some of the soldiers: Two white women living near the army post had been recently killed and mutilated by Indians, and such depredations were generally assigned to the Sioux or Arapaho. The troops advanced down the hills, and the Shoshone who were with them sang out their war cries, precipitating disorder in the ranks. The camp dogs barked. Bullets ripped the tepee hides, and the flaps of the lodges flew open. Children crawled toward the bush and men rushed out with Spencer carbines. Black Coal mounted his horse, but it was shot out from under him; he was wounded in the chest. The gulch filled with smoke, gunfire cracked all around; an elder sang his death song. A doctor accompanying the soldiers saw an Arapaho boy, shot in the leg, pull himself into a sitting position, fold his arms, and stoically face the oncoming soldiers, who finished him. In the confusion, Black Coal and several warriors made their way to the top of a sandstone butte north of the camp, and from there they fired back at their attackers, who chased off the horses and then retreated. One contemporary account described the battle as lasting minutes; another said four hours. The stories told by Arapaho elders describe the battle as a victory, and indeed, the army and the Shoshone had to retreat once the Arapaho began firing from the butte. But the Shoshone chief Washakie had called the retreat, standing below the butte with his white hair free in the wind, shouting, "Don't kill 'em any more! We have whipped them! We've set them a-foot! Don't kill 'em anymore!" At least twenty-five Arapaho were dead, their horses were gone, and other tribes would later refer to 1874 as "The Year They Killed the Arapaho." An Arapaho woman who was a child during the battle told her grandchildren that afterward, when she went to shear sheep in the Owl Creeks, she could still hear the cries of her people as they ran.

There is a long, smooth stretch of river before the next rapid, Sharp Nose, one of the toughest in the canyon. There are some big holes. When the water is low, a rock appears on the right side shaped like the probiscus of a giant floating on his back. When the water is high, rafters must stay in the middle and paddle hard.

Following the ambush in the Owl Creeks, the Arapaho tried to win friends among the whites by scouting and fighting for the army against other rebellious tribes. Sharp Nose, a younger leader, helped Black Coal in the endless negotiations with the U.S. government—at one point they met with President Rutherford B. Hayes in Washington—and when Black Coal died in 1893, Sharp Nose became head chief. The qualifications and the role of a chief had changed significantly by the time the Indian Wars drew to a close at the Wounded Knee massacre in 1890. Many of the tribal leaders of the early twentieth century were elevated more for their ability to deal with white men than for their military prowess or leadership within the tribe. They were secular, not spiritual, leaders, a distinction among elders that remains significant today. Sharp

Nose was exceptional, qualifying as a chief in both the old and new sense: he was a courageous and resourceful fighter, and his recorded speeches are eloquent, and moving to whites who heard them. An army officer who served with Sharp Nose in later campaigns against Sioux and Cheyenne bands under Crazy Horse and Dull Knife described him as "dignified and commanding, coming nearer to the Fenimore Cooper style of Indian than any I have seen since my visit to [Cochise]." What good, though, was nobility during a period of enormous decline and loss? The tribes were sinking into poverty, and disease was taking many more lives than carbines; whites were chipping away at the reservations from the moment their boundaries were surveyed. The first treaty signed by the Shoshone, in 1863, described vaguely a reservation extending far into Utah, comprising as much as 44 million acres. An 1868 revision reduced the Shoshone land, and there were more cuts to come. The Wind River Valley was the Shoshone Reservation (it would later be renamed Wind River), and the Shoshone did their best to make their traditional enemies, the Arapaho, feel like second-class citizens. The hot spring downstream from the canyon—where rafters these days usually go after whitewater trips, to relax the stress out of their bodies—was part of the original reservation. Once the white settlers began dreaming of a spa resort, McLaughlin embarked on his mission, offering $50,000 for the spring and 64,000 acres surrounding it.

It was an opportune moment in history to take advantage of the Indians. An 1894 special report to the U.S. Census indicated that while the Shoshone and Arapaho had made a good-faith effort to become farmers, they were starving, and the government had failed to deliver the food, the seed, or the tools it had promised. The feds would offer fencing materials to get the Indians to enclose their fields and livestock. Then, after the backbreaking posthole digging was done, no wire would be provided, and hundreds of acres were "fenced by posts alone." The annuities tribal members received under the Shoshone's 1868 treaty were due to expire in two years, in 1898. The venerable Washakie, now eighty-eight years old, wanted money fast; the Shoshone lived mostly on the west side of the reservation, and Washakie considered the area around the hot springs—on the east side—worthless now that the bison had been exterminated. He resented the presence of the Arapaho at the negotiations, and for that matter their presence on the reservation at all.

When Sharp Nose took his turn to speak, he disagreed with Washakie, asking that the tribes not be given money; rations and cattle would be more useful, he said, and less likely to be squandered. Then Sharp Nose digressed, and his peculiar speech seemed to come right from his despairing heart. He had spent a lifetime serving his people, leading bison hunts, fighting for his tribe and later the U.S. Army, and now he was negotiating with the Arapaho's conquerors. But he rose in the smoky room and declared he had never done any "work," and didn't know how—a criticism of Indians that is echoed in coffee shops around the West today. "I think I am too old myself to learn how to *work*," he said. "When I was young, I hunted the buffalo and I was a soldier for the Great Father. Our women did the 'work' such as we had. Now our young men will learn to work, as the Great Father wishes us to do. I do not know whether the money that the Great Father will give us for the spring is enough. When I heard of it, I tried to count it but I could not do it." McLaughlin, the Indian agent and friend, raised the ante to $60,000—still a steal, the non-Indians knew.

In the middle of the canyon there is a long stretch of flat water, some of it fast and smooth, rising in humps only during high water. This section is called Sacajawea Straits, after the Shoshone "bird woman" who guided the Lewis and Clark expedition through the West, carrying her newborn child on her back.

Near the bottom of the canyon, when floaters can look ahead and see the steep walls open out into green fields and red sandstone, comes the biggest rapid of all. Calhoun barks commands, but he avoids the nervous glances from the bow of the raft—his eyes are on the water ahead. It's late in the day now, and some close calls in earlier rapids have earned the paddlers' respect. There is no easy way over Washakie Falls, which drop abruptly at least five feet across the entire river. The key is to get over without dipping the bow or turning sideways, because you meet a series of tall standing waves that will swamp you if they aren't met head on. To the right is a deadly hole, and two enormous rocks on the left. "You ready?" Calhoun asks. He should smile in reassurance, but he doesn't. "Paddle ahead!" His passengers dig for their lives as they plunge over the falls.

In October 1874, before the tribes gave up the hot spring, Chief Washakie led his people over the Owl Creeks for a fall hunt in the Bighorn Basin. Washakie, then in his seventies, was already the stuff of legend. He was tall among his tribesmen, easy with command, and graced with a sense of humor. He had scouted and fought with the U.S. Army against the rebellious Sioux, and negotiated for the Shoshone perhaps the finest reservation in the West. The tribe was "rich": there were bison herds and elk and fish abundant on their land, gold in the mountains and seeps of oil that hinted at greater wealth underground. But the scope of Shoshone life had been diminished—once they ranged as far north as Canada and south to Mexico—and as they made the adjustment to reservation life, the people became more subdued. The fall hunt was a return to the old ways, an escape from schools, farming, and a domestic life in which the warrior class no longer held much sway. Nearly two thousand Shoshone went with Washakie over the Owl Creeks in the fall of 1874, struggling through early snow to achieve the crest of the range, where the cloud cover below spread across the valley like "a wonderful ocean of pure milk." An Episcopal schoolteacher who had accompanied the hunt to provide a "roaming school" (and keep his own paycheck coming) was astonished by the singing and drumming and wild joy in their mountain camp. Young boys grabbed flaming sticks from the bonfires and ran at one another in mock combat. In a cacophony of drums and rattles, the old men sang songs of hunting and war, and medicine men prayed for success. An ecstatic Washakie strode through the camp "like another being," his white hair streaming behind him and his voice exhorting strong and clear. The teacher stayed long enough to note the Shoshones' speed and skill bringing down bison, then, realizing no one was interested in his lessons, rode back to the government school.

Just over the crest of the Owl Creeks, he happened on a small herd of buffalo that were rolling in the dust to rid themselves of vermin. To find any bison this close to the reservation settlements was increasingly rare. All over the Great Plains, they were being pushed toward extinction by hide hunters, who were killing over a million animals every year in the early 1870s. Watching the plumes of dust rise from the wallow, schoolteacher James Patten felt a premonitory chill: The great beasts would be gone, as early as next year, and Washakie would probably never again lead a fall hunt.

Indeed, as the game diminished, Washakie lost interest in the Owl Creeks, and the Bighorn Basin to the north, and the huge hot springs that poured into the river. When he made the deal with McLaughlin twenty years later, he said he had become "afraid to stay there when there was nothing to eat." His only condition was that the springs remain free to all—a wish the state of Wyoming honors still in a small public facility sandwiched by two commercial pools. Today, a handful of tribal members still go into the Owl Creeks to fast and pray. Participants in the Sun Dance, a spiritual rite practiced by both Arapaho and Shoshone, gather sweet sage in the canyon. But this is the eastern corner of the reservation, far from the Indian communities off to the west.

Below the last rapid, the river smooths and slows, and paddlers drop backward off the raft to float on their backs in calm water— blithely unaware, or forgetful, of whose place this really is.

When Jeff Fassett made his first visit to Wind River Canyon, in 1978, the question of whose place it is was very much on his mind. He looked at the water in the canyon with a very different eye from a paddler's. The state of Wyoming was suing the Shoshone and Arapaho tribes, challenging the tribes' assertion that they had rights, based on the 1868 treaty, to the water that flowed from the Continental Divide to the canyon within the reservation. That was a long and circuitous journey, and it was Fassett's job to figure out what happened along the way: how much water there was, who was using it, where it went. His Colorado engineering firm would develop a computer model of the basin—a kind of plumber's schematic, on a large scale.

But on his first visit, Fassett was like a wide-eyed tourist, smitten by the beauty of the canyon as Agent McLaughlin had been a century before and Calhoun's passengers would be years later. The geology, in particular, fascinated him. Whenever he saw the brown-and-white Highway Department signs identifying the geological formations, he would pull over, get out of the car, read the dates on the signs, and stare awestruck at cliffs of Precambrian rock 2 billion years old, Paleozoic limestones 300 million years old, and red Triassic sandstones once trod by early dinosaurs.

Fassett is short and has a round, choirboy face, framed by a full head of black hair. He is quick to smile. He was in his twenties when he first visited Wind River, but could have passed for a teenager. That he was not native to this country might have added to his openmouthed beguilement; he grew up in New Jersey, and had come West seven years earlier to enroll, sight unseen, at the University of Wyoming. He was restless; his father sold cars in New Jersey, and he didn't see his future there, but he had no plans. Fassett found his academic home in engineering, a domain of "logic and common sense" far removed from the "creative stuff" that made him less comfortable in the fine arts or the sociology building.

In the 1970s, when he got his undergraduate degree, engineers were being snapped up by energy companies before the ink was dry on their diplomas. But Fassett balked at "the big rooms of people sitting at their drafting tables" and chose a different route; he went to work first for the Denver water department, and then for a Colorado consulting firm that specialized in water engineering and water rights. This firm was hired by Wyoming to help prepare for the Bighorn Basin water adjudication. Though he'd taken only one elective water-law course in college, Fassett was destined to play a key role in the battle between the state and the tribes over the Wind River.

In 1978, on that first trip, Fassett drove all over the basin, pulling together data on how much water came down from the mountains, who took it out of the river, how much was diverted to beet and alfalfa fields, how much was returned. The basin collected the drippings of hundreds of alpine lakes, snowfields, and glaciers, and in Wyoming, as throughout the arid West, nothing is quite as valuable as water. Its scarcity here gives it an ineffable luster sometimes lost on observers from the rain-soaked East and South. The one-armed Civil War hero John Wesley Powell recognized it over a century ago, after harrowing explorations down the Colorado River, when he argued that society in the West should be organized—economically, politically, and socially—around watersheds. Western states spurned Powell's suggestion, but Wyoming at least recognized the value of water in its Constitution, where it declared that all water within its boundaries belonged to the state. That radical and farsighted move to centralize water management in state government occurred in 1890—twenty-two years after the treaty that created the Wind River Indian Reservation. A century later, those dates would have great significance.

Fassett was visiting farms and wading in creeks in order to translate the business of shoveling mud from ditches and broadcasting water through pivot irrigation systems into number-crunching acre-feet and cubic-feet-per-second for the courts. But back in 1978, he had let the Wyoming landscape sink in. Like many newcomers, he was ill prepared for the unviolated openness of the reservation, the distances between people, the sense of a prehistoric world. "This was still wide-eyed country," said Fassett. "The canyon was something I'll never forget . . . and there was a vastness." He stopped to visit farms and look at their irrigation systems, talked to officials in the U.S. Bureau of Indian Affairs and the Wyoming State Engineer's office, waded into streams to gauge the amount of water flowing past.

He does not remember meeting an Indian on that trip.

When Fassett reached the top of the canyon, he stopped at the dam and looked south across Boysen Reservoir. After the tumble of canyon whitewater, the reservoir seems as still as a painting—a spill of turquoise water fingering its way amidst the treeless tableland of the lower Wind River Valley. If the river had continued east, instead of making its sudden cut north through the Owl Creeks, it would have meandered slowly into the open plains like so many other fatigued rivers coming out of the Rockies. Looking west, you can see the valley grow tight and green as it reaches up into the Wind River Range toward the Continental Divide. But down here, the 800,000 acre-feet of water contained behind the dam has done little to change the sagebrush desert that surrounds it. A few lonely powerboats wander the reservoir's surface, and plumes of dust rise here and there where trucks drive the dry dirt roads.

Down one of those roads in the summer of 1978 drove another engineer who was seeing the Wind River Valley for the first time. Woldezion Mesghinna was born in North Africa, about seventy miles north of Asmara, the capital of Eritrea. A young civil engineer with a freshly minted doctorate, he was working for a large San Francisco firm that consulted for the federal government and Indian tribes. Like Fassett, Mesghinna was following the streams, visiting farms and ranches, talking to people, trying to figure out how water had been used in the past, who was using it today and how it might be used in the future. But their purposes, like their backgrounds, were as different as their clients: Mesghinna was there to help the reservation tribes make a case that the water in the Wind River Valley belonged to them.

Mesghinna could not have been farther from home. His friends, the young men and women with whom he'd gone to school, were fighting a protracted civil war against the Ethiopians for control of Eritrea. He was not a warrior himself—a septic knee injury suffered when he was seven had turned him into a bookish child—but his thoughts about the struggle in North Africa were a constant distraction.

Riding with Mesghinna was Harry Sachse, a red-haired lawyer from Washington, D.C., who worked for the Shoshone tribe and was sizing up both the landscape and his companion. In a court fight over resources, the experts you hire to testify are crucial. Mesghinna would cut an unusual figure in a Wyoming courtroom: he dressed and groomed himself impeccably, and was a man of color in a region where the colors were either white or Indian. His manners took some getting used to—such politeness could be mistaken in these parts for servility—and his lilting, accented English seemed to have a childlike quality.

The expert had to have the number-crunching, jargon-munching expertise to provide good data in a complex argument about how the plumbing of the basin worked and how it could be put to use. And the expert needed to come across to the judge as more trustworthy, articulate, and front-porch-friendly than the opposing expert. This was a lot to ask of a young man from the other side of the world who had never testified in court.

At the east end of the valley, Sachse and Mesghinna were looking through a dust-smeared windshield at the lands that nobody wanted—the colorless, windblown flats away from the river where the silvery sagebrush grew like witchy cauliflower. The object was to convince the courts that by diverting water, the tribes could make something of this land, though for a hundred years they'd shown little interest in it. Sachse had to wonder what the natty, watchful Eritrean was thinking as they drove along the dirt roads. Sachse, who came from the green, wet South, was thinking, Oh, my God, look at this desert, we're going to *lose* this one. All that sagebrush. You can't irrigate this land, you can't grow *anything.*

Shaking his head in discouragement, he looked over at his companion and found Mesghinna's head pivoting around, his eyes shining. Smiling, the Eritrean spoke in his musical voice: "Oh, my friend, if we had this land in Ethiopia, we could feed . . . ten thousand people!"

As they turned back toward Riverton, Sachse relaxed. He knew they had the right man.

CHAPTER 2

The Community Hall

When Mesghinna and Sachse finished touring the eastern side of the Wind River Valley, they drove west, upriver, toward the little towns set along the banks of the valley's rivers. The dam at the top of Wind River Canyon is the spout where the bowl of the valley tips and pours, releasing the mountain-steeped water into the merging veins of the Bighorn, the Yellowstone, the Missouri, and ultimately, the Mississippi. Above the canyon, the Wind River travels a crescent path that follows the curve of the valley, a smile on the map with the corners lifted at the west and east ends. To the west are the white-peaked Wind River Mountains, to the north are the high meadows of the Absaroka Mountains and, bending east from them, the Owl Creeks. South of the basin rises the tableland that McLaughlin crossed a century ago, some of the most empty and wind-scoured high plains in the West. Across this terrain pioneers on the Oregon Trail crawled to the Continental Divide, climbing over South Pass into the Great Basin of Utah and Nevada, with perhaps one last, longing look northward, across the backs of oxen and through the dust of the rutted trail, at the meadows and tumbling streams of the Wind River Basin.

The Shoshone, who were here much earlier, called it the Warm Valley. *Youa die.*

In 1990, as I drove upstream from Boysen Reservoir, west toward the mountains, for a few miles I was still more on the plains than in the foothills. The draws were empty late in the year, but their jagged banks and eroded beds indicated violent floods in other seasons. There was a yellowy desert tinge to the ground. A fringe of cottonwoods in the distance described the river's path, wandering like a curled ribbon across a floodplain of gravel and sand brought down from the towering Rockies eons ago. Then the river disappeared behind soft, low hills as I went south onto Highway 789. I turned off the highway onto a county road, across the heart of the basin, toward an old, steepled building of red-painted logs.

I was on my way to a meeting, and so was Catherine Vandemoer, who swung her Dodge pickup onto this road around twilight on a June day. The gentle indentations between the hills she passed were sometimes cultivated—young fields of alfalfa as cool and smooth as green, freshly tucked sheets—and sometimes fallow, streaked white here and there where irrigation had left salts on the surface. The days were beginning to lengthen, and there was a sweet breath of wet sage in the air. In these parts, June was more spring than summer, or so she had learned since arriving in Wyoming. The mountains were still impassably clogged with snow, and that alpine snow might yet be deepened by a last howling blizzard hurtling in from the Northwest. That never hurt: The glaciers and snowfields up near the Divide were the water "bank" that kept the fields green. Water was Vandemoer's business, and she was always taking its measure. As she turned off the highway, she looked west, where the valleys began constricting into canyons as they climbed the slopes of the mountains, and guessed at the altitude of the lowest snowfields.

It was a warm day in the valley, and Vandemoer had rolled her sleeves up. Her usual dress was jeans and an open-necked flannel shirt, the kind of clothes you'd wear to go out into these fields and get mud on your boots, not the sort of outfit farm wives once wore when they came to socials here at the community hall. And though it was Vandemoer's birthday, the ranchers she would be meeting with shortly were unlikely to bake her a cake. Most of them were members of the Midvale Irrigation District, the beneficiaries of a federally funded irrigation project, the Riverton Unit, that sits near the center of the Wind River Basin. The project is surrounded by the historic borders of the Wind River Indian Reservation, but the influence and presence of the tribes—a ghostly presence, since few Indians farm on the project—was rarely acknowledged.

Not, at least, until recent years. Vandemoer was a hydrologist working for the tribes. Like Wold Mesghinna, she had come to Wyoming to help the Shoshone and Arapaho manage the water in the basin they believe belongs to them. She had helped draft a tribal water code that these farmers didn't like at all. Their lands had been excised from the reservation almost a century ago, yet here the Indians were claiming most of the water that flowed through the valley, and suggesting that non-Indian farmers, who had irrigated these fields for generations, might now want to buy that water at what they felt would be extortionate prices. The state, represented by the young engineer Jeff Fassett, had reassured them that all water in the basin belonged to the state—as proclaimed in its constitution—and the state would decide who had rights to use it. But the state courts, to pretty much everyone's surprise, seemed to be siding with the Indians. The farmers were starting to wonder if the state could back up its big talk. And they wanted a closer look at this short-haired, tough-minded woman who, from what they read in the newspapers, seemed to be putting these ideas in the Indians' heads.

Dennis Horton of the Fremont County Farm Bureau was impressed that Vandemoer was willing to appear in such a potentially hostile environment. She agreed only after several members of the tribes' Joint Business Council said they would accompany her. Horton made a point of telling Bureau members beforehand that they should be polite and keep this a civil exchange of information. He wasn't really expecting trouble—during the farmers' busy summer season attendance was generally low at these meetings.

There was another reason Vandemoer expected the farmers to be especially touchy. In April, the Joint Business Council of the Shoshone and Arapaho tribes had issued a permit dedicating 252 cubic feet per second of the Wind River to instream flow. That meant they expected that much water to stay in the river, and not be taken out by farmers for their fields. The U.S. Fish and Wildlife Service, which had an enrolled Eastern Shoshone named Dick

Baldes in charge of its Wind River office, had recently planted fingerling trout in the river. Baldes and his agency seemed to be daring the farmers to drain the river—as they sometimes had in years past—and kill the fish. Some of these farmers would have taken that challenge, because they considered the tribal water code a sham, a gimmick that allowed the tribes to start charging them for water. But the fight over the Wind River was attracting the press— even national media, thanks to Baldes and Vandemoer—and the Midvale farmers were uncomfortable in the spotlight. As one of them put it, "When we've got a problem, we go sit out on the ditch bank and take care of it." They didn't want to play the villains in a television news bite that ended with rainbow trout flopping in a dried-out riverbed.

Kate Vandemoer knew they were riled. So when her mother, who was visiting from Arizona for her daughter's birthday, offered to come to the meeting, Vandemoer suggested it would be a tedious affair. That answer would have sufficed, except that Vandemoer left without Honey, her dog. Honey was a gray, white, and gold border collie who attended her mistress with fanatic devotion. Wherever Vandemoer went, Honey would wait in the truck. The rest of the world was just a distraction, and when she was separated from Vandemoer she fell into a fidgety state of mourning. When Vandemoer left for her meeting without Honey, her mother knew this was not a mission without some danger.

An irrigation ditch ran along the right side of the road to Pavillion, brimming with water. Vandemoer had a better sense than most of where she was—cupped in the deep curve of the Wind River and its major tributaries, the Popo Agie River and the Little Wind River, which carried their snowmelt south and then east and then north. Even a century ago, it was obvious that this topography was ripe for an irrigation project: You could pull the water from the river at the higher elevation on the northwest side, spread it east around the valley floor north of that big curve, then pour it all back into the riverbed at a lower elevation on the east side. But here was the same problem encountered at the hot spring: Most of the irrigable land was part of the Wind River Indian Reservation. It was not the custom, a century ago, to build federal water projects for the improvement of Indian reservations.

There were dozens of trucks at the fire hall, a red log building (formerly a church) with a small steeple on its peaked green roof. Vandemoer looked around for Wes Martel, one of several tribal leaders who'd promised his moral support. Martel was a "Sho-rap," with relatives in both tribes; he was a singer in a drum group and had a powerful voice that could take over a meeting. He jokingly called Vandemoer "The Mermaid," because of her immersion in the science of water. But she didn't see his rooster head of black hair in the parking lot, and for a moment she fought the urge to bolt . . . just pull back onto the road and drive away.

In the parking lot, the scene was not unlike the prelude to numerous meetings she'd attended on the reservation. The pickup trucks, overflowing the small parking area, had shovels in the back, extra tires, fencing tools, and sometimes a muddy set of rubber ditch boots. Farmers leaned in the windows of open truck doors and chatted, kicking at the dirt with sharp-toed boots. Many of these men and women had come from a long day moving irrigation pipe or getting the harvester ready for the first cut. But they found time, because it was the custom, to put on clean clothes before coming to the Community Hall.

Vandemoer had been spotted, and there would be no escaping. Bill Brown, a farmer who also managed Midvale, greeted her with a smile. He was a big, swarthy man with stubby hands that often held a Winston. "How are you, Kate?" he asked, and she thought he meant it. They talked often on the phone, sharing information about the river, and it was his nature to warm to people as he spent time with them, whatever their differences.

But most of these people were strangers, and she could feel their eyes in the parking lot and the meeting hall. She was not likely to be mistaken for a Midvale farm wife, though many of them, too, wore jeans and rolled up their sleeves when they worked in the fields. Vandemoer, though, had short, jet-black hair and dark, freckled skin; she leaned forward when she walked, as if she were about to dive into a football scrimmage. Though not tall, she still had the sturdy build of her athletic career at Smith College; when she squared her shoulders and narrowed her eyes, an interlocutor felt fully engaged.

One of the fellows looking her over was Carroll Riggs, who had been attending these community gatherings for fifty years. He was a gentle-faced man, white-haired and slightly bent, and moved among his neighbors with an unassuming smile. He took a seat at the front of the meeting room.

Riggs had arrived at the Riverton Project from Oklahoma after World War II, "looking for greener pastures" and lured by advertisements that promised abundant water, a beautiful home, and cheap land. Promotions like these had been kicking around since 1906, when the north portion of the Wind River Indian Reservation was first opened to white homesteaders. One of the last land rushes in the West, it brought trainloads of would-be settlers to survey the area before lots were drawn. In all likelihood, there wasn't an Indian in sight as more than half the reservation—nearly 1.5 million acres—was put up for grabs. A claim would cost you only $1.50 an acre and sweat. The land sale was supposed to benefit the tribes, too: Some of that money was assigned to construct irrigation ditches for Indians on the reservation south of the river.

But the talk among the homesteaders who put in for plots near the Wind River was about an irrigation system planned for the new settlers north of the river—a project much bigger than anything envisioned for the reservation. A private company promised gold, coal, and copper; fertile land; "a sweet prosperous home" that could be "Obtained Cheap"; and of course, the "Greatest Irrigation System in the Country," covering over 300,000 acres. The Union Pacific Railroad was coming, too, and a new town would spring up near the juncture of the Wind, the Little Wind, and the Popo Agie Rivers. Hopeful farmers and merchants snuck onto townsite lands ahead of time, went hungry, and slept with their guns to fend off other squatters.

But after that first gleeful rush, only a small stretch of ditch materialized, and the expected fortunes did not. Private water projects like this were failing all over the West, and when they did, stranded settlers would next turn to the federal government. By

1928, the ditch company and its grandiose promises had evaporated and the federal government had taken over. Only sixteen settlers were on the project, living in hovels.

The first federal money invested in the Riverton Unit came from Indian appropriations bills in 1917 and 1918—though the very point of this project was that it was *not* Indian, that whites would homestead the lands north of the river while the Indians made do with reservation lands on the south side. When the secretary of the interior, Franklin K. Lane, complained that the Riverton Unit shouldn't be paid for with Indian appropriations, Wyoming Representative Frank Mondell rebuked him:

"I have been told that the Indian Office objects to having this project carried on the Indian Bill on the ground that it is not an Indian Project. . . . Just why this should be the case when Congress has deliberately and definitely adopted the project I do not know, for I assume that the Indian Office does not intend to take an attitude of opposition to the expressed will of Congress in matters of this kind."

That congressional harrumph quieted Lane down, and after its first few years the project was transferred to the U.S. Reclamation Service. That agency went to work on the key structures of the irrigation system: a diversion dam on the Wind River and a canal to the farms. The United States was entering the "go-go" era of reclamation, with plans for big concrete plugs on the Colorado and Columbia Rivers to generate cheap electricity and green the desert. But the Riverton project, small as it was, was not a pet project of the service, and the farmers continued to falter. The diversion dam was completed in 1923, a power-generating reservoir went in by 1926, and the Wyoming Canal began inching its way through the sagebrush. But it took the Great Depression, the Dust Bowl, and World War II finally to stock this project with farmers.

When Carroll Riggs returned home to Oklahoma after the war, his wife, Mayme, a schoolteacher, handed him a column in the *Daily Oklahoman* that offered free information to veterans on projects in the West being developed by the U.S. Bureau of Reclamation. For a penny postcard, Riggs got a packet from the BOR describing projects in Idaho, Wyoming, and California. But when

he visited the Riverton Project in January, it didn't match the glowing description in the brochures. During the most bone-chilling
weeks of winter, "Everything was brown and dark. I kind of
thought it was the jumping-off place of the world."

The latest round of homesteads were chosen by lottery, and
Riggs got the twenty-seventh pick. A BOR panel interviewed him to
see if he met the criteria for a homesteader, and he did. He had
farming experience and some money in the bank and was prepared
to live on the land most of the year and put it into production. Then
he went back to his motel room to see if the soil of these homesteads met *his* criteria. He took frozen cores of soil he'd chiseled
from the ground on the project lands and dissolved them in the
bathroom sink to see if the soil was permeable, and it was.

The Riggses drove a trailer up from Oklahoma, arrived at sundown, and parked on their 160 acres of sagebrush. "The next morning, I rolled up my sleeves and went to work," Riggs said. "And by
the second sundown we had an outhouse. A two-seater." In March
they drove north to a World War II internment camp for Japanese
near Heart Mountain and earned some free lumber by helping to
tear the barracks down. A wall fell on Mayme during the demoli-
tion. When they returned to their homestead, Mayme went into
the hospital and Riggs went to work with a hay rake, and when he'd
cleared the mountainous sagebrush he planted seed potatoes.

Today Riggs, in his late eighties and widowed, still spends his
days surrounded by 150-pound seed sacks at the seed-cleaning business he built from that original homestead. He keeps a rack of
leafcutter bee larvae (the bees pollinate alfalfa by cracking the blos-
soms and tracking pollen to other plants) in the bathroom. He wanders through experimental plots of salt-tolerant alfalfa that he's
spent decades developing, adjusting his spectacles, tottering just a
little bit. Like a nurse turning babies in a nursery, he stops now and
then to finger a bud or pull some weeds. Where many farmers
think the universe ends at their fencelines, Riggs thinks of the
world as he walks the furrows: He figures that with the population
growing endlessly, all the world's best farmland will eventually be
required solely to feed human beings, and forage crops like alfalfa
will have to survive in harsher, saltier soil. Alkalinity has always been

a problem in Wind River, despite the brochures' glowing descriptions. Trading alfalfa strains with academic researchers throughout the West, he still hasn't found a plant that can survive 2000-parts-per-million alkalinity, but he hasn't stopped trying.

The Episcopal cross atop the Community Hall brings back memories to Riggs and some of the other old-timers. In the 1940s, when visiting with your neighbors was the primary form of recreation, regular meetings at the hall included sandlot baseball, horseshoe contests, carry-in dinners, and a lot of talk. Men sat on one side and women on the other, and the children were everywhere ("It was the one sure crop we produced," said Riggs). Roy Haggerty sometimes pulled out his fiddle for a square dance, or they played 78 records like "Tickle Toe" by the Hot Spring Band and "Donkey Serenade" by Billy May. "Maybe it was that way because we hadn't gotten television," said ninety-five-year-old Ruth Neal, laughing, "or better cars that could go farther." She had lived on the Riverton Project for fifty years. A small town named Pavillion grew within the project, and everyone except the storekeepers was a farmer. Nobody was getting rich, but farmers don't expect to get rich. Many of them had endured years of drought on dryland farms in Nebraska and Oklahoma, where, as one said to me, "all you could do was look at the sky." Here they had a ditch, and the assurance that water would never be a problem; even when it was still treeless rabbitbrush, it felt like the Promised Land.

Then fifty years had gone by. Instead of talking about farming, Catherine Vandemoer came to talk to Riggs and his neighbors about the tribes' plan to protect "instream flow" for fish. The crowd was mostly men—old and young, with white foreheads and beaky red noses—dressed up in clean pants and boots for the evening. Some of the men kept their hats on, as they did in restaurants and at movies. It was an overflow crowd, with some standing packed in behind the chairs. People glanced at Vandemoer and kept talking, and for a moment she thought she could be just another person in the shadows at the back of the hall, listening. There was no sign of anyone from the tribal council. The few who greeted her were polite; by now she was used to a show of courtliness, though she knew the feelings beneath the surface were something else. "That's

what Wyoming men are like: I'm a lady, and they're very cordial."
She chuckled when she told me this. "You've got to give the tribes
credit for hiring a woman—this way, nobody gets hit in the face."

Ushered to the front of the hall, she introduced herself, tried a
smile, and began pacing back and forth, putting the tips of her fingers in her jeans pockets. When she first began studying the basin,
she figured she had to educate the residents about the hydrology
of Wind River—the fourteen inches of annual precipitation, the
complex groundwater system, the huge glaciers that melted into
the streams. But in her early meetings with ranchers, Indian and
non-Indian alike, she found they knew all that stuff from years of
observation.

So that night she talked about the courts, and how state and
federal judges now recognized the tribes' right to more than half
the water flowing through the basin. "The Shoshone and Arapaho
want to make this lower stretch of the Wind River into a good fishing stream again"—she saw some heads shaking dismissively—"the
way the elders of the tribes remember it." Smiling to ward off the
shaking heads, pacing, keeping it nice, she told them that if they
used their water efficiently there would be enough for everyone.
Then she explained that if it came down to their fields or the tribes'
needs, the tribes' water would come first.

For years, the farmers on the project had worried about crop
yields and drainage and alkalinity as they scratched out a living on
lands that had defeated others. The altitude was high here, the
growing season was short, the soil wasn't great—they had lots of
hurdles to overcome. They had stuck with it while neighbors had
gone for easy wages in the oil patch, while uranium miners and city
folk had bought up country places to be weekend cowboys with
the kind of money farmers never expected to see. Now a young
woman who'd been in their valley only a short while was telling
them they didn't know how to irrigate efficiently. She was telling them that she and the tribes had a plan to manage water that
differed radically from how the State of Wyoming had been doing it
for a century. They heard her place herself above the state's water
engineer—that Fassett fellow from Colorado or New Jersey, whom
they weren't sure about either—and suggest she might upset the

delicately balanced system of rights and distribution that watered their crops.

"Oh, she was stirring the pot," said Bill Brown, shaking his head later with a mixture of amusement, admiration, and puzzlement. "She exaggerated some pretty important stuff, and she was stoking these guys pretty good. She had some guts."

It was obvious to Vandemoer that these ranchers had rarely spoken with tribal leaders—perhaps never. It was obvious to the ranchers that she had not listened to the Midvale people, who had wrested a livelihood from this difficult land with water she now had other plans for. When she noted the high unemployment and poverty on the reservation, she saw those heads shaking back and forth again. This was when she needed Martel. The tribes, she said, have lands they want to irrigate with their water, but no dams and ditches like yours. They want to help their people, so they hope to use some of their water to bring fly fishermen who will come a long way to catch a trout. The economist who had calculated the tourist-dollar benefits of restoring the river was sitting in the audience, but didn't rise. The air in the hall felt close, and the smell of the fields was supplanted by the mingled breaths of sixty people. Some hands went up. It was question time.

"I'll tell you and I've been here, that there ain't been any fish in that river," said one farmer. "What it comes down to, anyway, is money, not fish." Vandemoer tried not to be argumentative, but she talked a little about the research the biologists had done.

"You want to drive us off? Drive us off these farms we've made?"asked another farmer.

There was enough water for everyone, she said, managed right.

"You think it's easy to get a good crop out here? It takes a lot of work. It's tough already."

In the back, a rancher I knew turned to me: "The truth is—and I've hired Indians myself—they work like hell until the first paycheck. Then you don't see them again."

A voice from the audience: "Why don't you people stop looking for another handout and just get to work? You could've done what we did."

Later, Vandemoer would remember the question as "Why don't

you people stop looking for another *fucking* handout?" I missed the adjective, if it was said. Vandemoer was furious, but once the first open hostility had been voiced, she no longer felt in jeopardy, like a foot soldier whose busy mind surrenders to reflex once the bullets start flying. She felt surrounded by a protective shell, and though she was trembling, she kept a thin smile on her face.

She took a deep breath. "Let's talk about handouts," she said. "The biggest handouts are going to reclamation projects like this one."

She spelled it out. It's a subject that makes farmers squirm, because they pride themselves on being self-reliant, living off the land and feeding the world while city dwellers soak up the cheap food and welfare programs. The Bureau of Reclamation released statistics in the 1980s showing that while the government had poured over $70 million into the Riverton Unit, farmers had never repaid a cent of the cost of constructing the project's dams and canals and had covered only the operation and maintenance costs. According to BOR calculations in 1988, the unpaid debt amounted to a $73.40 per year taxpayer subsidy for each acre on the project. Though it's dwarfed by boondoggle reclamation projects elsewhere in the West, the Riverton Project is by far the biggest federal agricultural subsidy in Wyoming. The usual defense, repeated that night at the meeting hall, is that irrigation projects boost the economy and generate taxes in all kinds of other ways, in addition to providing wetland habitat for wildlife and reservoirs for water skiing.

When Vandemoer was finished, it appeared that minds hadn't been changed but hardened. She saw a hand go up in the front row and pointed to a white-haired man, though her mind felt too drained to make another answer.

It was the inventive, worldly, mild-mannered Carroll Riggs. He asked, "You say you got seventy percent unemployment out there? Why don't you get those guys each a shovel and put them to work in those ditches out there? That'd take care of a lot of problems." He glanced around at the approving nods of his neighbors.

Dennis Horton had heard enough. He stood up and raised his hands to quiet the crowd. "We didn't bring her in to lynch her. We said this was going to be polite. You remember, she's doing this work for someone else."

Later, Riggs told me, "I think I got her with that one."

In another meeting, almost a century before, Indian leaders gathered in council chambers to talk about these very lands with James McLaughlin, "White Hair," who had negotiated the sale of the hot springs. This time, a much bigger chunk of the reservation was under discussion: the lands that would eventually become the Riverton Unit. McLaughlin's views were more pacific now in 1904, and he expressed great respect for some of the Indian leaders, like Washakie and Black Coal, with whom he'd parleyed.

These meetings were big social events on the reservation, and everyone came: elders, mixed-breeds, women, and children, traders, soldiers, schoolteachers. Indian tepees were set up outside, and aromas from the cooking pots wafted through camp. In the boxy meeting room, white government officials sat at a table at one end, while the Indians crowded on benches or leaned against the walls. The smell of smoke-tanned buckskin and sage lifted in the close air.

For years, the government had tried to talk the tribes out of the northern half of the reservation, and a smaller portion of the southern end, too. In 1872, they bought a large parcel south of the Popo Agie River, which included some small non-Indian settlements in South Pass where gold had been discovered. In 1896, they got the hot springs. Now they focused on the lands north of the Wind River, where fewer Indians lived and whites saw the potential for farming. The tribes were willing to listen because their situation had worsened, and they needed money more than they needed land. Their federal rations were chronically short; the northern portions of the reservation were overrun with the cattle of non-Indians; and the Shoshone, in particular, were rudderless after the death of Washakie in 1900. By then, illnesses like measles and the flu, food shortages, and the demoralization of failing, so far, at this new agrarian way of life had dropped the reservation's Indian population to only 841 Shoshone and 801 Arapaho. Washakie's death, after his fifty years of leadership, inspired more than a hundred Shoshone to sign a plaintive letter asking the government's Indian agent to appoint a new chief: "It is now with us like a man with many tongues all talking at once and every one of his tongues pulling every which way."

The latest land deal, designed largely by a Wyoming congressman doing the bidding of his white constituents, was this: 1.4 million acres north of the Wind River would be opened to homestead; the tribes would get a portion of the money from land sales, to be used for schools, cattle, payments to individual tribal members, irrigation ditches, and the purchase of water rights from the State of Wyoming. Government officials said the tribes could realize $2.2 million from the deal. In the end, they got nowhere near that.

Grace Coolidge wrote a mildly disguised account of the meeting in her 1910 book *Tipi Neighbors*. The daughter of a Boston hotel owner, she came west to visit the family of a friend from her private school outside of Philadelphia, then met and married an Arapaho man, Sherman Coolidge, with whom she lived on the reservation. In her description of the parley with McLaughlin, the agent insists over and over that the land must be sold so the tribes can buy water rights for their remaining land from the state. White men, he said, were using the water downriver, off the reservation, and filing claims to it.

The water-rights question puzzled the older tribal members. An old man invited the negotiators to "see the river that flows down our valley and waters our land. It is there. It is ours. It is born in these mountains above us."

McLaughlin responded with a long speech acknowledging that when the 1868 treaty was written, the government meant to give the tribes the water as well as the land. But he warned that the state was taking over water regulation, and no one knew for certain whether the Indians' claims would hold up in a court of law. Money from the sale of these lands, said McLaughlin, could both resolve this legal uncertainty and provide for irrigation on the remaining reservation.

Then a younger tribal member rose, in Coolidge's account, and talked about how strangers had come into the Shoshone country "like a flood" and compensated the Indians for what they took with seed, wire for fences, and money. Coolidge described the intensity of the Indian's voice, "subdued, as if on a leash." He went on: The Indians squander the money, because "we are like children. This the Great Father in Washington understands, and also that our ears are dull, that our eyes cannot read his written words. Therefore, in his kindness, he sends to us this man to speak to us face to face."

The mockery in these words seems to have been lost on McLaughlin. Or maybe he was sharp enough to sense a divide in the Indian ranks, a desperation on the back benches more urgent than the speakers expressed. He jumped to his feet and called on the crowd to seize the opportunity he had put before them— sign the deal, right now!, for the good of their children. They must seize the opportunity. His emotional outburst struck a chord, and the Indians began to come forward. With heads lowered, they came to the table, and with trembling hands enough of them made their marks to clinch the deal, looking up as they did at White Hair, who watched them with sympathetic gravity from behind the table. He had earned their respect . . . and he had certainly earned his salary.

The deal seemed to make practical sense. The tribes were failing as farmers, and no one paid them for the trespassing livestock that grazed their lands north of the river. Why not take the money White Hair promised, by letting the homesteaders buy reservation land that had already slipped out of tribal control?

But when the 10,000 would-be settlers got out onto the reservation, only the best property sold, and the murky records of the Indian Service are inconclusive about the tribal revenues. If there was any money at all, it was much less than anticipated—not enough, certainly, to install the promised ditches to every Indian farm. One researcher concluded that less than $500,000 was actually received, and the government's jumbled files reveal nothing of how it was spent. The bill for building irrigation systems on the reservation over the next few years was much higher, which led to charges to the "customers" and effectively drove cash-poor Indian farmers out of business. As a result, not only the best farmlands north of the river were turned over to non-Indians, so were other productive lands on the reservation, deeded to Indians under a federal allotment program and later sold to whites when the Indians couldn't meet their irrigation costs.

The non-Indian irrigation system north of the river that became, after private efforts failed, the BOR's Riverton Project, was bigger and costlier than anything they'd attempted on the reservation, and got under way, as noted, with Indian appropriations. Lands in the opened portion that proved unarable were returned to the tribes in the 1930s—a million acres of mostly useless real estate restored to the reservation.

When the meeting finally broke up, it was nearly midnight. The farmers applauded Vandemoer at the end, though more out of reflective Western decorum than a change of heart. Through all the hydrology and legal jargon and rhetoric, they clung to what they knew: They had bought this land, 'proved it up, and now the Indians were trying to wrest it from them.

As she left the meeting, Vandemoer's thoughts were less reductive; she felt as if a world that had only recently become familiar to her was again, suddenly, unfamiliar. She wondered if the farmers had heard what she heard—the ignorance, racism, and fear in their voices. She doubted whether her lecture about water law and management had done much good; she feared she might've sounded arrogant, and imagined that maybe she was. She wondered why, after she'd mentioned with a chuckle that she was visiting Midvale on her birthday, no one had wished her happy birthday.

She wondered, too, why no tribal leaders had shown up. She knew she had enemies on the reservation, and some of the elders didn't like the way her name cropped up in the papers. Had she gone too far—stepped out on the plank alone, just a shove away from the deep? Should she fear the farmers or the people who'd hired her? How long could a Mermaid swim in these waters?

Instead of returning to Lander on the highway, she took a longer, more northerly route through the project lands. Farm homes in the Riverton Unit are few and far between, and the small clusters of houses on the reservation are separated by long uninhabited stretches. The drive took her west through Pavillion and south across the river to Ethete, then on to Lander. The colorless landscape was comforting, and the stars shone like a spray of crystals through the thin air above.

She was new enough that the sky still astonished her, but familiar enough to be comforted by it. Her roots were far from Wyoming. She had been born in Mexico, her blood a mix of Dutch and *Mayflower* and Zapotec ancestry. Her father had been a mining engineer. Her schooling was Ivy League. Straddling these different traditions wasn't always easy, and she remembered her confusion at Thanksgiving during her years at Smith College. Do I sit down for a plump turkey in memory of my *Mayflower* ancestors or join the Indian protestors spitting on Plymouth Rock?

She had arrived at Wind River in the fall from California and first saw the reservation during a blinding snowstorm. After the initial shock of the whiteout—*my God, my God, what am I doing here?*—she began to feel at home, though she didn't really know why. Maybe she'd been less happy in California than she realized. She had no private life here, no romance, and only a few friends to confide in. There were nights when she returned after dark to her empty house and felt afraid that someone might break in.

But she sensed an opportunity at Wind River. It wasn't just the chance to be in charge, to actually set up and run programs instead of consulting or working under someone else, but also her belief that there were solutions to these conflicts, though she hadn't found them yet. And in the dark, alone with her thoughts, she felt something else moving in her, something she would hesitantly label spiritual.

She had come to Wind River on a mission that was only beginning to make itself clear. This was a place where the persistent problem of water scarcity in the arid West came together with the equally enduring problem of Indian and non-Indian relations. This was a chance to build a model. For the West, maybe even for the world.

Driving in the dark, Vandemoer laughed. She wasn't sure

whether it was at her own pretension—changing the world at the
Pavillion Community Hall—or just the unraveling tension. And
when she got home, her mother was holding a cake, and Honey
was dissolving with wagging joy at her return.

They'd waited up. After all, it was her birthday.

CHAPTER 3

Riverton

Highway 26 runs upriver, a smooth stream of asphalt carrying the Winnebago bound for Yellowstone, the powerboat with peeling decals dripping home from Boysen Reservoir, the lumbering tractor with hay spilling off its trailer. Driving west of the Pavillion turnoff on the highway, you can't see the Wind River but you are within its grasp, as it bends around the south edge of the basin behind some hills to your left and then flows north into Boysen Reservoir and Wind River Canyon.

The landscape is a quilt of sagebrush hills and green cultivated fields fed by the canals and lateral ditches of Midvale. The crescent path of the river cups an ideal plot for irrigation, as good as farming gets in Wyoming. But I've seen, we've all seen, bigger and richer farms in states to the east, south, and west. Even Wyoming's best will never match the deeper soils and gentler climate at lower elevations. The season is short, the winters are cruel, and the water table sometimes rises too high, leaving white streaks of alkaline on the surface. That's the deal you make with Wyoming: in exchange for a stunningly beautiful, uncrowded world, so compact that you can know it intimately, you must accept its unfriendliness to settlement, its marginal sustenance.

If you could rise above this landscape for an eagle's-eye view of the valley, the streams would look like a budding branch of silver sagebrush, flattened on its side: a thick but twisty trunk at the eastern end of the valley where this journey began—the Wind River where it enters Boysen Reservoir—branching rapidly as you look west into thinner and more numerous tributaries, the smallest and most western of them topped by swollen terminal buds, the alpine lakes. Where the largest limb joins the trunk—where the Little Wind River pours into the "Big" Wind River—is a grove of cotton-wood trees known as Double Dives.

Viewed from the surrounding dry hills, it looks like an oasis amid sagebrush and grasses and sedges that have been munched down by livestock. Where the rivers knot, towering cottonwoods form a cool refuge with a grassy floor and songbirds in the treetops. In the early days of the reservation, the freighters who brought rations by wagon from the rail terminus in Casper, 120 miles to the east, would stop here. They would set the horses loose to graze, bathe in the river, build fires, and tell stories over dinner. The depth of the glade, with twisty paths through the shrubs and draws, offered space for several camps.

To get there today, you have to follow one of the many two-track roads that crisscross the hills around the river. Some might have been cut by wagon wheels in the early days. The desert West has seen a lot less traffic than most of the world, but every heavy vehicle that compacts the soil leaves a signature good for a century. On the parched hills, nothing grows tall enough to offer shade; and when weeks pass without moisture, the air tastes like dust. But when I visited, it had rained the day before, and in the ruts of the road my tires caked with bentonite. It was a September afternoon and the sun was going down. I parked on a knoll rather than risk miring the car and leaving it overnight. From the broken glass and empty beer cans, I figured the hill would get busy later on. An informal survey indicated that if large bottles of malt liquor were fashionable, Budweiser was still the runaway favorite.

That was what Michael Marlowe, a teenager who lived mostly in a blue trailer between the highway and the Little Wind, was drinking when he joined some friends parked on the knoll on a Friday night in August. The dog days were hot and long and boring, time-killing days with neither job nor school. The nights were better. Sometimes in the dark on the knoll, with a breeze in his face and music pounding from the car stereo, he could taste the scent of elk in the mountains, a heavy odor of wet fur with a hint of biley entrails that carried all the way from the high meadows down to him here, among his friends, drinking and taunting one another. He wore a gray sweatshirt from the Riverton High School cross-country team—not his, but his cousin Ray's—with the arms cut off. He'd been smoking weed and drinking since noon, when Ray came by to shoot baskets on a bent hoop outside the trailer.

Now Ray joked and talked with some other guys who'd driven up—a couple of young men from Arapahoe, a small reservation town to the east. One of them was a marine home on leave. Michael had dropped out of school the year before and was thinking about going into the service himself. He'd worked in the summer for an elite Indian firefighting team that traveled to fires around the West, and he wished it hadn't ended; certainly being in the infantry had to be a little like that.

Michael Marlowe was quieter than his cousin, and he didn't have so many words. But he was stronger, and Ray needed him for protection. They had had some trouble with another family down the road, and one of their enemies had said he was going to "get" Ray. The cousins stayed close after the threat was passed; no one would shoot at Ray then, because Michael Marlowe would get after them. He wasn't afraid of anyone. He had broad shoulders, and his short hair crowded around his forehead. There was a mustache of sorts, black accents near the corners of his mouth. His face rarely showed what he was feeling—even Ray sometimes didn't know what he was about to do. His girlfriend had stolen a handgun from her father, and he kept it under his bed.

His cousin LeeAnn handed him a joint, and he took a deep drag. The sweet perfume had trailed him most of his life, since he was nine and an uncle who was a few years older gave him his first toke. He liked the smell of fire generally, especially the big smell of a burning forest; it gave him a peculiar surge, an adrenaline rush he'd felt in Idaho on his first fire. The marines were always training for wars that almost never happened, but the forest crews went right at the real thing, digging and cutting and dodging a terrifying force. Fire was strong enough to frighten him, yet it was indifferent to him, and he respected that. When he went out on a big one, he would work until he had no strength left even to eat, working steady and hard without any of the anger he felt at other times, secretly imagining that he could win the respect of the fire itself. He wished he could trigger that kind of force among his friends, who seemed lifeless to him. In the woods, even in a wet year like this, it was there in the trees: an urge to burn, to transform from stillness into consuming force.

He saw now an orange flame through the cottonwoods below at Double Dives. A couple of friends they'd expected to meet at the knoll might have gone down there instead. But it was more likely to be white kids from Riverton, since the trucks parked at the end of the road looked big and new.

"Let's go down and check it out," Ray said. But Michael had his fourteen-year-old cousin with him, LeeAnn, the daughter of his uncle, Sumner Marlowe.

"Come on, man, they got a keg down there."

"Ray, you know, we got our own beer."

"Shit, you pussy," said Ray. But he meant himself, really. Michael was always ready for trouble, that's what got him in trouble; Ray had to get stoned before he could stir himself for a fight, but he was a lot bolder when he walked into a situation with Michael.

LeeAnn said, "Hey, I'm up for it." The marine and his friends were getting into their car and Ray Brush was following them.

Michael looked at LeeAnn and shook his head no. The old Pontiac fishtailed away, with Ray shouting from the cramped backseat, "We'll go party, you pussy! We'll go fuck with them!" He was laughing.

Michael put a beer bottle to his lips and drank, then leaned against the truck and stared hard at the broken taillights going down the hill. He was tired and about to lose his temper.

He handed LeeAnn the bottle and wiped his mouth. A couple of other vehicles were parked farther out on the knoll, and one had a loud rap tape playing. A skinny fellow with long hair reeled into the shrubs and peed loudly. LeeAnn looked bored.

"Hey, it's not my fault," said Michael.

Now something was going on down in the trees by the river. LeeAnn walked away from him toward Double Dives, to get a better view.

To the fellow stumbling around trying to zip his pants, Michael said, "Go turn the noise down, man." When he did, they heard shouts down by the river and the sound of breaking glass. Car doors slammed. From the brush emerged a pickup that Michael recognized as belonging to the family in Arapahoe that had threatened Ray. The Pontiac, parked by the edge of the cottonwoods, wheeled around and started back toward the knoll in a hurry. There was a loud cracking noise, then another, bouncing around the empty hills, fading into the big sky.

"Get in the car," he said to LeeAnn. "Home."

She gave him a look but got in.

His girlfriend's gun was under the couch in the second trailer, unless Ray or someone had found it.

Gunshots had been fired near Double Dives almost a century earlier, as homesteaders readied themselves to rush in and claim lots marked with stakes in a mirage of a town just north and east of the juncture of rivers. A local newspaper reported with frontier aplomb that on April 14, 1906, there occurred a "little disorder and on that night bullets were scattered about rather promiscuously, but not with malicious intent." Around midnight some squatters sneaked across the reservation border to beat the official opening and grab the lots in what they figured would constitute the business district of the new town.

It was an excellent place for a trade center, the merging not of just two rivers but four—just upstream from Double Dives the Popo Agie and Little Popo Agie Rivers joined the Little Wind from the south and, just below, the Little Wind joined the Big. During the late nineteenth century, when fast-moving entrepreneurs cased the West for the next railroad spur or new mining town, this place had possibilities now that White Hair had convinced the tribes to sell. It could be the locus of a farming empire spreading from the soon-to-be-irrigated fields on the northern half of the reservation.

More than ten thousand would-be farmers had filed for a drawing of 160-acre homesteads. If things went as the federal government planned, half the 3 million acres of Indian land north of the river would soon be watered and productive, the Union Pacific would arrive with passenger and freight cars, and the boom would be on. Splashy advertisements around the country touted one of the last chances for venturesome Americans to grab a piece of open space in the West for virtually nothing. The Indian agent tried to delay settlement for sixty days by sending a contingent of black army troops stationed on the reservation to drive the settlers off. Many refused to go. That stubbornness, and entrepreneurial ardor, was etched in the future town's character like a dominant gene.

But the engine that was supposed to drive the local economy— the great irrigation system—was shaky from the start. "There's no sign of irrigation and there won't be for the next fifteen years, and by then most of us will be dead," one visitor told a local paper as he boarded a train back to Nebraska. A few years later, only short stretches of ditch had been completed. Such failures were not uncommon in the West, where grandiose development schemes were the biggest cash crop. But there was no cynicism in Riverton's boosterism. Flagging spirits were spurred by headlines in the *Riverton Republican* that shouted "OH, IT'S COMING! IT'S COMING!" Destiny was a matter not of geography or resources but of character—a community's determination to exist and, further, to embody the turn-of-the-century dream of hatching robust little frontier empires. "Adventurers and optimists, that type of people came because of the land being opened," said Robert Peck, the town's newspaper publisher today, and a lifelong resident. "People who could see the possibilities—and the possibilities are all river-related."

By comparison, the town of Lander, on the west side of the basin, had been growing slowly, since immigrants passed to the south of it on the Oregon Trail. Located in the foothills of the Wind River Mountains on the Popo Agie River, it began as a military outpost, first intended to protect the wagon trains from Indians, then to protect the Shoshone from other Indians when Washakie allied himself with whites against traditional Shoshone enemies like the Sioux and Arapaho. Lander nestles prettily near the forks of the Popo Agie River, the gentle upslope of the mountains rising westward behind it, crowned by white-capped peaks. Sheltered from the harsh winds of the plains and the colder temperatures on the western slope of the Rockies, with fish in its streams and elk in the forests above, Lander grew steadily through a combination of reservation trade, apple orchards, and small ranches, as well as the beginnings of a mountain recreation industry that is the town's mainstay today. Lander was linked economically to the reservation but not—after tribal lands south of the Popo Agie River were sold to the government in 1872—surrounded by it. Like any Western town, it had its hyperbolic promoters, but compared to its new rival on the eastern side of Fremont County, Lander was complacently modest.

Riverton, the younger and homelier town, campaigned from its inception for new enterprises, especially after the trumpeted irrigation project on the ceded reservation lands failed to appear. The town had the personality of a gate crasher who, noticing there's no extra table setting, stays on so long that either he's invited or no one else will eat. The Riverton movers and shakers were eager to take on anything, and schemes of greater and lesser probability abounded—whether a tie factory for the railroad, a hog-processing operation, a sugar beet factory, oil drilling, or uranium mining. Some settlers gave it their best shot and moved on, but those who stayed were unflagging. When the local banks failed in the 1930s, the Lions Club issued its own scrip, including fifty-cent pieces made of buckskin. Today, the appetite for enterprise is unsated: In the 1990s, wheeler-dealers entertained the idea of attracting a nuclear-waste storage dump to the area.

Reservation residents claim that another aspect of Riverton persists to this day: indifference or hostility to Indians. Early on, it could've been the insecurity of newcomers settling on Indian ground, and the sense that Indians might be a hindrance to their outlandish dreams. Sited on the east side of the reservation, the town was far removed from the Shoshone settlements, so this insult was inflicted primarily on the Arapaho, whose status at Wind River remained tenuous and second-class. Anthony Sitting Eagle, an Arapaho elder, remembered going into town as a little boy and seeing signs reading: "No dogs or Indians allowed." Yet the town had fought its way to prominence in western Wyoming; and as the largest community within the reservation, it would provide many Indians with shopping and services.

Riverton also had the best medical facilities in the area, and so Bob Harris, a Shoshone leader who some called King Harris for his long tenure on the tribe's ruling council, spent his last years in a retirement home there. I visited him when he was in his eighties, pale, thin and bent as a blade of grass, tethered to an oxygen tank and no longer the powerful figure he had once been. Harris told me the old men of the tribe had selected him for leadership back in the 1930s because he was articulate and a "breed." He laughed when he told me what one elder had said to him half a century ago: "You're not good for nothing, so you've got to work for us. You're half-white, half-Indian. You're just like that bat. He flies like a bird, but he's not a bird."

Harris was old enough to be a member of the Poke Noses, one of the ancient Shoshone clans, but his political talents fit the modern world, as the elders had suspected they would. Under him, the tribes protected the first wilderness area in the United States, negotiated lucrative settlements for treaty violations, wrote a tough tribal game code that rebuilt enviable herds of elk and filled the lakes with fish, then went to court to fight for control of the water in the Wind River. These last efforts allied Harris with Wold Mesghinna and a young Shoshone biologist named Dick Baldes.

Baldes had grown up not far from the retirement home where Harris spent his last days. Like Harris, he was a "breed"—his mother was of Latino descent—and his home was in a section of southern Riverton that some called the barrio. Baldes had a kind of dual ethnic citizenship: when his friends stopped by after school, they were treated to his mother's homemade tortillas and beans, but he is an enrolled Shoshone because of his father's Indian blood. His mother, Juanita Baldes, jokes that she was Indian "for a while"—eligible for benefits as a lawful spouse—but not since her husband passed away.

Baldes's father was a tie driver in the 1940s, one of the men who rode rafts of timber down the river from the forests in the northwest corner of the Wind River Valley. Huge jams of logs came to rest where the river widened just below the town, and were removed to be cut and treated to make railroad ties. The plant was across the river from the small barrio.

Baldes earned a biology degree, an uncommon choice of major for tribal members. (The handful of college-educated reservation residents today are more likely to have degrees in education or sociology.) For that matter, it was an uncommon level of education. Baldes didn't know what a biologist was when he left high school, but a lifetime of fishing and camping with his father had instilled a desire to work in the natural world. Norman Baldes took his sons camping for weeks at a time up the South Fork of the Little Wind River, where the water was so soft Juanita could wash their clothes on the rocks. Norman was strictly a bamboo-rod fly fisherman— unusual among Wind River folk of the time, who had no qualms about a hook and a worm.

After college, Dick went to work for the Montana Fish and Game Department, then for the U.S. Fish and Wildlife Service in Arizona. He was offered a position in Wyoming with the FWS, working with the Wind River tribes. When he arrived back in Wyoming for the job interview, Bob Harris gruffly told him that he should get back on the plane, before he was plunged into the complex intrigues of reservation politics. But before deciding, Baldes went to see his mother and walked along the river. "I came back here and I smelled the same old smells," he said. "Especially the damp river smell . . . and then I remembered." He took the job.

The black railroad bridge that crossed the river behind his house is gone, but we could still walk along the track bed to a promontory. From there we could see a boxy cement structure where hoboes used to sleep. (They called it the Jungle Hotel, and when the bums were drinking, Juanita Baldes would tell her kids, "You see them, you get the hell home.") Actually, the cement pillbox was the pumphouse that supplied drinking water straight from the river to the town of Riverton. When Dick was as young as five years old, his mother would take him with his brother and sisters to play by the river and fish. The family didn't have much money, but they enjoyed a great backyard. With willow poles they would catch trout, ling cod, sauger, and flathead chub, a smallish minnow that

Juanita pan-fried. In the summertime they swam in the river almost
every day.

So did other Indian kids along the river, from Riverton all the
way up to Crowheart. But when Baldes came back with his biology
degree, he was told the river near his home was no good for anything but suckers and carp, and not healthy to swim in. By now a
cement plant had been built just upstream from the pilings of the
old bridge; and farther up, within the reservation, uranium mill tailings had been dumped on the banks. The river was too slow, too
warm, too trashed. He had to agree. In early August, the sluggish
flow of water was foamy in places, the bottom silted brown.

What Baldes couldn't agree with was the contention of farmers
that this stretch of river had *always* been like this—that the silt problems were natural, and that cold-water fish like trout had never
thrived there. Certainly the river had always run high and muddy in
the spring, but it flushed itself, too, and it had good fish habitat in its
holes and rocky bottoms. He could point to an island in one of the
meandering curves below the cement plant and remember its soft
sand from when he ran barefoot there with his friends. "That eddy
right behind the island"—he pointed—"I caught the biggest ling
you ever saw." (A ling, sometimes called burbot, can give a trout
fisherman quite a shock when it splashes out of the water looking
like a prehistoric eel. The long body is decorated with a yellow
wormy pattern, and under the chin is a single, hairlike barbel. But
don't throw one back just because it's ugly—ling are good eating.)

Part of the U.S. Fish and Wildlife Service mission is to assist
reservations in husbanding their wildlife resources, "trust" responsibilities the American government assumed under Indian treaties.
Many tribes don't trust the FWS biologists, and keep them at arm's
length. But at Wind River, Baldes was in an opportune position: He
had access to tribal government as an enrolled member; he knew
the river and the mountains intimately; and he had the education to
develop programs that would revive wildlife in the abundant habitat of the sparsely populated reservation.

The wilderness that stretched up toward the Divide from the
Wind River Basin made this a dream assignment for any wildlife
biologist. There were elk in the forests and bighorn sheep on the

crags, antelope roaming the plains, black bears in the mountain meadows, and rainbow, golden, brown, and brook trout in the streams and lakes. Harris discouraged Baldes, because he wanted him to get the most out of his science and not get tangled in social and economic problems that had plagued the tribes for over a century. The old councilman sensed the young biologist's impatience with politics. Indeed, Baldes thought his work to protect and improve the natural resources of the tribes would supersede politics, and the matchless wilderness would salve some of the social ills on the reservation.

Baldes saw, too, that reservation management differed significantly from that of the United States generally. On most public lands, you have to let everyone in. Not on a reservation. "The only places in the country you can get those big-rack elk are next to a national park or on a reservation. Part of me would like it to be open to everybody. But then those lakes would be fished out. The beauty of this place is you can keep it like it is, or better."

With the help of other scientists, Baldes studied the Wind River and its tributaries. He tried to enforce professionalism in himself and his staff, bringing in outside biologists to conduct stream-flow or habitat studies, and to do a fish census year after year. But it became personal, too. This was his home. His insistence that farm practices had made the river unhealthy, and continued to damage it, rubbed some people the wrong way. In one respect he was a greater threat than Kate Vandemoer; while she was an outsider, easier for the tribes' adversaries to denigrate because she brought her ideas in from elsewhere, Baldes had gone to high school with some of the Midvale farmers.

Just the thought of his critics makes the veins bulge in Baldes's neck. He's compact and stocky, a common physique among Shoshone, with short, graying hair and a wide mouth. His temper and righteousness are never far from the surface, and there's not much gray in his spectrum of loyalty. He forms intense friendships, and enemies are indelibly branded. Though he didn't spare Indian farmers his wrath, his strongest words were for non-Indian farmers and state water officials. Conflicts with Baldes had a way of becoming personal. One of his frequent targets was Craig Cooper, the state water engineer in Fremont County.

The State of Wyoming is divided into five water districts, one of which—Cooper's bailiwick—encompassed the Wind River and Bighorn Basin. At the top of the state's water hierarchy was the state engineer. Since 1987, that had been Jeff Fassett, the engineer who got his feet wet in Wind River Canyon in 1978. In the 1980s, the controversy surrounding the Wind River was Fassett's biggest headache. For Craig Cooper, it was a migraine of disabling proportions. Cooper came from a local farming family: His grandparents had danced at firemen's balls in Pavillion, and like his father before him, he still farmed land along one of the ditches that draws water from the Wind River. While that gave him an intimate knowledge of the river and the people, it also looked rather distinctly like a conflict of interest. A bespectacled, gentle-voiced man, Cooper was dismayed when Baldes accused him in public meetings of damaging the river by bowing to the irrigators' influence. He seethed quietly, then vented his anger in a series of letters to Baldes's superiors, arguing that Baldes was impossible to work with because of his "propensity for flying off the handle," his "short fuse," his "prejudice against the irrigators," and his "misinformation."

As the struggle over Wind River water intensified in the early 1990s, Baldes's fury matched Cooper's, but Baldes's was more confrontational and less selective. He seemed to trust nobody. He even found reasons to be critical of Kate Vandemoer, who had relied on the FWS research to determine instream flows, and of Wold Mesghinna, who had provided the ammunition that courts used to affirm the tribes' water rights. Tribal leaders who didn't, in his judgment, stand tall enough on the water issue he thought should be run out of office. Every dispute became a matter of principle, and respect. Soon it wasn't just Cooper who was criticizing Baldes, but BIA officials, tribal members, and even some officials at the FWS. He suffered from stomach pains and a nervous twitch in his eyelid. Another biologist, a longtime friend who thought Baldes was working up to a heart attack or stroke, took him aside and told him to back off.

But Baldes couldn't turn down his thermostat, and he insisted on casting his position as a matter of integrity and honor. "Change the way I act with these people after near twenty years?" Baldes asked me rhetorically, his voice rising. "I can't do that. We'll fight the sons-of-bitches on every stream and creek, until we get the system cleaned up. There's no other way." To get some advice from his old mentor, Bob Harris, would have been a good idea. But Baldes couldn't bring himself to visit the old man, who was unhappy in the nursing home and would beg for help to return to his ranch or the mountains.

Cooper and Fassett had their own principles. Chief among them was a belief that Baldes and Vandemoer and tribal leaders had neither the knowledge nor the sensitivity to balance the competing interests thirsting for the Wind River. The state engineer's office had promised irrigators "certainty"—a history of consistent water administration dating back over a century—in contrast to the instability of a newly arrived hydrologist and a hotheaded Shoshone biologist. Jeff Fassett tried to project a mixture of authority and understanding. He asked the tribes to work with him, to talk privately and keep the water dispute out of the newspapers and the lawyers' hands. But Baldes and Vandemoer had aroused the normally reticent tribal leadership, particularly young leaders like Wes Martel and Gary Collins and John Washakie.

The main target of reservation wrath was the non-Indian Riverton Unit—now better known as Midvale, after the irrigation district that runs it—which pulled its water out of the heart of the reservation, the Wind River. But there were also non-Indian farmers upstream in Crowheart, and in two smaller and older irrigation projects near the town of Riverton, LeClair and Riverton Valley. While Midvale had to answer to the U.S. Bureau of Reclamation—which as a federal agency acknowledged at least some duty to listen to tribal concerns—these smaller ditches were regulated solely by the state. And in a dry year, they took the last drops out of the river. LeClair farmers rammed old car bodies nose-down into the riverbanks to shape the streambed. They were the ones who claimed trout never had lived in the Wind River where it flowed through

Riverton and the barrio. They were the ones who were trying to invalidate Baldes's memories.

Attorney Norman Young represented the farmers on LeClair, an irrigation ditch west of Riverton that was originally dug by Shoshone hands in the nineteenth century. A laconic native of rainy southeast Oklahoma—"where the problem with water was how to get it off, not how to get it on"—Young drove around the LeClair Project to talk with farmers and educate himself about the irrigating business. "I was amazed at the amount of work involved, from the very beginning, when they cleared that sagebrush by hand," Young said. "I mean, what they had to go through to make it productive! That's what makes them real resistant to threats. 'We've busted our ass out here and we're not going to give it up.' They're truly invested in it."

The threats came from the reservation—and from Baldes, who went to the U.S. Army Corps of Engineers to complain about LeClair's bulldozer work along the river. (Because the river is classified as "navigable," under federal law the Corps has jurisdiction over the streambed.) The ditch now served a handful of mostly non-Indian irrigators and was run by a fellow named Johnnie Hubenka with aggressive indifference to both the tribes and the state water engineer. Craig Cooper, nominally in charge of seeing that the state's water was distributed fairly in the basin, hadn't been given a gate key with which to monitor the LeClair headgates, even though he watered his own fields with LeClair ditch water.

Young had been involved in the legal battle over Wind River water from its beginning in the 1970s, a portion of his life long enough to evoke traces of both nostalgia and weariness. "We lawyers who were on that case spent so much time together," he said. "We watched our children grow up and we went to their weddings." But it had begun to seem, twenty years later, that the fundamental conflict—divvying up water when the river got low—would go on forever. Litigation had been fought all the way to the U.S. Supreme Court, and endless negotiations seemed to recycle the same script over and over.

In the 1990s, looking for a change, Young ran for county attorney and won.

On New Year's Day, his first on the job, Norm Young was roused early in the morning by a call from a sheriff's deputy asking him to drive to a crime scene out beyond the eastern edge of Riverton, where the river curls north and run-down trailer parks house an ever-changing population of impoverished people—drifters who arrived during the last oil boom and never moved on, poorly edu- cated youngsters with babies on their hips and poor job prospects or Indians with little to live on besides a small monthly share of tribal oil and gas revenues. When Young drove his truck out of town on the lonely, unlit Route 136, it was still dark. He turned off the highway through a break in the fence on the rutted dirt road to Double Dives and aimed at the red lights flashing on the hill above the river: an ambulance, a sheriff's department truck, and two BIA police cars. The deputy didn't say anything, just nodded and pointed his flashlight at the backseat of an old sedan with two flat tires. Leaning into the stale air of the car, he saw the body of an Indian teenager. His head was thrown back, his eyes and mouth were open, and a halo of cracks radiated in the rear windshield. There was a smell of beer on the seat, muddy newspapers on the floor, and a balled up, bloody sweatshirt lying on the seat next to the body.

"There he was, with trash and broken glass all around and his head in a pool of blood," said Young, years later. "I thought: 'Wel- come to your new job.' "

Sumner Marlowe heard the radio news report of a shooting death at Double Dives as he drove in the dim morning light toward the trailer where his daughter lived with his sister-in-law and her cousins. He had been awakened that morning by a phone call from his sister-in-law, who insisted, hysterically, that he come to the trailer by the river. He was surprised, having thought they'd been living in Riverton since last spring, when the Big Wind River had flooded the trailers and houses near the highway. He didn't know from night to night where his daughter was sleeping, because she wasn't speaking to him. He asked his sister-in-law over and over about LeeAnn, but all she would say was, "Something bad has hap- pened, Sumner, something *bad*."

He passed a cluster of BIA police standing by patrol cars with their lights flashing, ignoring their attempts to wave him down. He turned northwest on a county road that runs between the Little Wind and the Big, toward the former Catholic mission school of St. Stephens and the small town of Arapahoe. Tucked in the angle between the highway and the county road, on the outside of a curve where the river turns briefly north, is an alluvial terrace with a few run-down houses and trailers. They're not well situated. During years like this, when the snow melts suddenly and unseasonably, the Big Wind River jumps its banks. When the water started rising that spring, tribal officials rushed around warning the residents to evacuate, but several were out playing bingo and no one sandbagged those trailers. Some had never been cleaned up; they sat askew on their cinderblocks, surrounded by disgorged trash and furniture. Sumner's sister-in-law and several family members lived behind her father's old house in two trailers, one blue and one gray. There was a small wading pool in the back, and the river just beyond. Rusted farm equipment sat in the unmowed field beside the house, and a couple of abandoned late-model cars, one with some river snags in the driver's side window that showed where the river had crested.

Sumner Marlowe skidded on the ice-filmed potholes and stopped by the first trailer. The paint was peeling in places, a broken television antenna lay on the roof, and several windows were boarded up. He entered the second trailer, where they slept and cooked meals, and found his sister-in-law crying on a couch in the living room. He asked her about LeeAnn.

"She's all right. She was there with Ray, but she's all right. They got her." She sobbed and waved him back toward the first trailer.

There he found Michael Marlowe, his nephew, lying with his head on his arms at the kitchen table. In Arapaho families, it was common to adopt the children of siblings and other close relatives. Michael's father had died when the boy was two, and Sumner, who had no boys of his own, had helped raise Michael.

The older man had not seen tear streaks on Michael's face since he was a small child. But they rarely saw each other these days. Only a few weeks earlier Michael—now taller than his uncle—had stepped toward Sumner as if to hit him. His daughter LeeAnn and her cousins had stopped speaking to Sumner the year before, when he'd left to finish his graduate degree on the West Coast. They accused him of abandoning them, though he'd asked LeeAnn to come along. When he returned in June, he came by the place to check on her. A party was under way in the gray trailer, and Sumner went in. "They'd been partying night after night, a bunch of them. I went in to kick them out, sometime after midnight. They said to me, 'This isn't your place. Why did you come back?' That was when Michael and Ray Brush stepped threateningly toward Sumner as he stood in the doorway. Sumner Marlowe is a big man, long-muscled with big hands, but there is sometimes a wounded glint in his eye, signaling either tenderness or a well-known temper. "I told them I didn't want to fight them. So I left. As I was going, the boy said, 'You can't save us.' But I didn't stop."

Now his broad-shouldered, stone-faced nephew was crying like a baby at the kitchen table with a .38 semi-automatic pistol lying in front of him. He didn't look up. Sumner took the gun and checked the chamber. It was loaded, and he put it in his pocket. He stood for a moment in the doorway, looking at Michael's large hands pressed against his eyes. His nephew wouldn't even acknowledge that he was there.

He went back in the other trailer. His sister-in-law, frightened and bleary-eyed and confused, told him Michael was threatening to kill himself. Something had happened to his cousin, Ray Brush. Nobody would tell her more than that, and she didn't want to know.

With the gun still in his pocket, Sumner Marlowe went back outside, got in his car, and drove toward town. The BIA officers made no attempt to stop him. He drove to the Maverik Store, where he called his ex-wife, who told him LeeAnn was with her. He filled his gas tank. Then he circled back to the law-enforcement barricade, which now included reservation police, Riverton cops, and sheriff's department vehicles. They looked as though they were checking their weapons, perhaps planning to storm the house, so he stopped to talk to them. They assured him they weren't planning an assault, so he made a map of where he thought guns were kept in the house. He told them to wait, that he'd go back inside and talk to Michael.

Sometime in the dark hours before dawn, on the chilly knoll above Double Dives east of Riverton, Michael had shot his cousin Ray Brush in the head. Police would find snapshots and videos, taken that night, showing Michael and Ray and LeeAnn posing with Michael's girlfriend's gun, making gang symbols with their hands, pointing the weapon at one another, smiling or looking tough.

To hear the kids tell it, this kind of horseplay was common. Michael and Ray had grown up as brothers—wrestling, watching videos, playing basketball together. "Sometimes it got rough," said a relative, "but that was just the way they played around." Guns were commonly flashed, too—"never loaded," Ray had told his stepmother—and liquor and drugs were part of the diet. Reservation leaders deplore the gang-style posturing of the young people, as well as the conditions, particularly in some of the housing projects, in which murder and suicide and other violent explosions incubate. They also bristle at the media's focus on these unhappy scenes and events, which they insist are not typical. Not typical, perhaps, but they occur enough to harden the FBI and Bureau of Indian Affairs law-enforcement officers who police the reservation. BIA police have it particularly bad, working for low pay without nearly enough manpower to cover the huge span of scattered communities.

"You go out in the middle of the night on a gun call," remembered a BIA agent from another tribe who worked at Wind River. "Someone comes running out of the trailer with a gun, you don't know what he's going to do. You have no backup. You think you have him talked out of it, and then he turns the gun and puts it in his mouth and shoots himself, all over the wall, with the officer watching." There are feuds that start with beatings and escalate to shootings. Wrongs between families are rarely forgotten. When violence occurs, drugs and alcohol are almost always involved, according to law enforcement, and the violence is usually Indian against Indian.

Since the August night when shots were fired on the knoll at Double Dives, trouble had been festering between Ray Brush and the men in Arapahoe who had made threats against him. On New Year's Eve, Michael and Ray and LeeAnn were out driving around and had a car-to-car encounter with the Arapahoe bunch, one of whom waved a gun out the window as they drove away. They were drinking, back at the trailer, when Michael Marlowe urged his friends to drive with him back to Arapahoe for some serious mischief. The plan was to have LeeAnn knock on the enemy's door; when he answered, she would step aside and Michael would fire. There were elements of posturing and make-believe in the tough talk of these teens, much of it copped from the movies—but drive-by shootings were not just a fantasy, they had happened here before.

Michael grew more restless as the evening of videos and drinking wore on. They took a drive out toward Double Dives, and when they stopped on the knoll for a swig, Michael said it was time to go to Arapahoe. LeeAnn and Ray Brush said they didn't want to go— they wanted to go back to the trailer and watch movies. The edgy boredom in the car began to twitch. Michael called them "pussies" and held the black automatic .38 to LeeAnn's head. She'd seen him messing with the gun earlier, pulling the trigger and nothing happening. Fearless at fourteen, she challenged him, "If you're going to shoot me, do it." In a split second, Sumner Marlowe could have lost his daughter. Michael pulled the trigger; it didn't fire, and he laughed like it was a joke. Moments later, sitting in the backseat with Ray Brush, he tried the same stunt. "Never loaded," Ray had told his stepmother. This time, the gun worked. Ray's eyes were extinguished before he fell backward.

"I shot him, I shot him," Michael said, panicking. To LeeAnn, he said, "You were there. I don't want to get in trouble. Let's leave, let's leave."

LeeAnn Marlowe ran, hysterical, to another car parked farther out on the knoll. A couple of teenagers had already gotten out; they'd heard the firecracker sound of the gun going off. She said, "He's been shot."

The teenagers wanted to get out fast, but they loaded up Michael and LeeAnn, dropping him off at the house where his uncle found him and taking LeeAnn to her mother's place. Michael could still hear the roar of the gun in the car; he felt as if the skin on the back of his head were burning. He was ready to kill himself so he would stop remembering.

But when the investigators talked to him he was dry-eyed and expressionless. He told them, "I was just messing around. That's just the way we are." When Michael filled out the forms at the jail, he listed no job, no income, and assets of $60. Over 70 percent of the working-age men on the reservation are unemployed, and for many families the only income is a "per capita" share of royalties from tribal oil and gas leases, which has dwindled, in 1997, to $90 per month.

Sumner Marlowe's résumé might once have read the same. A lot of Indian men, even respected elders, lose a good number of years to drink and bad behavior. Sumner was that way when he started his family, and he made a botch of it, as his daughter often reminded him when she was speaking to him at all. But he had sobered up a decade ago, gotten himself a job, and gone back to school. He moved to Utah, a five-hour drive from the reservation, and worked on an education degree at Utah State. He was lonely that far from home; his wife and daughter felt even more estranged in a university town, and after a few months they returned to the reservation. "After that," he said, "my family just don't understand what I'm doing."

Sumner eventually came back to Wind River to work in a drug-and-alcohol rehabilitation program. Tall and lanky, with his long hair in a ponytail, he played basketball in a reservation league, where he met a young attorney from Portland who was temporarily in Wyoming on the Wind River water case. When his friend moved back to the Northwest, he invited Sumner to visit, convinced him to enroll in graduate school, and introduced him around. Marlowe became a minor celebrity, invited to speak to church and business groups about the culture and spiritual beliefs of his people. But feeling more and more removed from his home and family, he decided to take a break from school and return home to be with his daughter and relatives.

A psychologist who testified at Michael's sentencing hearing for involuntary manslaughter argued that the young man felt a great deal of remorse and depression, but it was concealed behind a "flat affect," the masklike face that Indians commonly show the white world. Sumner Marlowe, when he uncoiled his long body in the witness chair and looked fiercely at the handcuffs on Michael's wrists, showed no "flat affect." His gaze was direct and his words were defiant. "It's our protection not to show remorse to white people," he told the judge. "It ain't going to do him no good. We've been cheated, we've been deceived, we've been lied to and exploited all our lives." Yet he did not seem entirely given over to his anger; there was something soft in Marlowe's eyes, a glint of tenderness even for the accusers. His lifelong effort to armor his heart had been only somewhat successful. That was what attracted people like the Portland lawyer to him, and as we crossed paths repeatedly in the valley, it was what drew me.

Norm Young was pushing the court to give Michael Marlowe a tough prison sentence. The only hope he saw for young men in trouble on the reservation—and there was little hope once it had gone this far—was to get them far away, even if that meant prison. In Young's ears, Marlowe's combative words could only hurt his nephew's case. It was the kind of broad-brush finger pointing that sounded like an excuse, a flight from personal responsibility.

As for Sumner Marlowe, he didn't want anyone telling him what his words meant, and he didn't really know himself. Gone was the easy smile and teasing way that ingratiated him to so many. Who was he speaking for? For his people, his family, or himself? He'd abandoned his place in the white academic world, and he hardly had the heart left to work at his job; the young people of his nephew's generation, the people he cared most about, wanted nothing to do with him. That night he drove past the trailers, perched precariously near the river, unlit and almost invisible in the swirl of falling snow. Snow gathered on the old farm equipment and transformed it into fantastic creatures; it landed on the river-banks, it covered the gouges left by the floods and it floated for a moment on the open water before losing all color and shape, disappearing, as Michael Marlowe soon would, to some faraway place.

You can't save us. And on the witness stand, he hadn't.

CHAPTER 4

Lower Arapahoe

The journey upstream involves more choices now, as the two main stems of the valley—the Little Wind and the Big—branch apart like a thumb and an index finger. The Popo Agie and Little Popo Agie, branching off the Little Wind a little farther west, could be the middle and ring digits. (Let's say the fifth finger was lost in a roping accident.)

I took the route that Michael Marlowe and his friends would have taken if they'd gone out that night to harass their enemy in a housing project in Lower Arapahoe. It was a two-lane blacktop that runs east-west across the heart of the reservation, between the Little and Big Wind. West of Riverton, the landscape opens upward. The gentle slope that separates the two rivers near their junction lifts into a hogback, a barrier that rises and widens as it extends west thirty miles to the forested flanks of the mountains to the west.

In the creases along the Little Wind, you find small Indian settlements: St. Stephens, Lower Arapahoe, Ethete. These are not towns platted and paved and centered on a grocery store or post office. Homes are scattered along the roads the way tepees once were strung along a creek, and the boundaries of each family are not demarked by sharp-edged lawns and picket fences. In some of the shabbier yards you'll see old car bodies, tall weeds, and a mangy dog or two (the Shoshone accuse the Arapaho of being dog eaters, a tease with some historical vinegar). There are few signs of luxury or comfort, except perhaps a satellite dish and a basketball hoop

erected over bumpy dirt, which may explain the extraordinary drib-
bling talents that come off the reservation. You can see squalor if
you wish, but there's a kind of good-humored freedom, too, as
if many of the residents simply didn't take this boxy habitation—
government issue, much of it—all that seriously.

Perhaps if the teenagers had left the stale smoke of the Riverton
trailer and gone somewhere other than Double Dives that New
Year's Eve, the threats would have lost their density in the open air.
The enemy might not have been at home. They could've just driven
on, to visit friends in Ethete. Nothing would have happened.

This eastern portion of the reservation is considered the
province of the Arapaho people, and when the tribes quarrel, which
they often do, the Arapaho sometimes suggest quite seriously that
they split the place, dividing the reservation along a north-to-south
meridian. For some Shoshone, even the suggestion is presump-
tuous; for them it's still a sore point that the Arapaho are there
at all.

The Arapaho tribe arrived in 1878, wraiths in rags who hardly
resembled the proud bison-hunting band of a generation before.
They were one of the last surviving tribes without a home, their
numbers diminished to a few hundred by starvation and disease.
For more than ten years they had wandered from one unsafe place
to another, awaiting direction to the homeland promised them at
Fort Laramie in 1868. Now, battle-weary and winter-worn, they
straggled, under military escort, into Wind River—the end of a journey that had begun centuries earlier and covered thousands of
miles.

Before the arrival of Europeans, the Arapaho were believed to
have farmed in the Red River Valley of what is now Minnesota; the
tribe's language relates it to such plains tribes as the Cheyenne and
the Gros Ventre. Bands of Algonquin-speaking people migrated
west and south as population pressures—first from other tribes and
then from whites—increased in the Northeast and Great Lakes
regions. Their roots and language were so different from the Sho-

shone, who came east from the Great Basin, that they might as well have arrived from Greenland. But with the arrival of the horse, both tribes joined the chase after the huge bison herds of the prairies and enjoyed the brief prosperity of the Great Plains warrior culture in the early nineteenth century.

The name *Arapaho* was first heard, somewhat inaccurately, by the explorers Meriwether Lewis and William Clark when they asked the Pawnee for the name of this tribe, whom the Pawnee called *laripihu*. This meant "he who buys and sells," an acknowledgment that the Arapaho dwelt at a crossroads of Great Plains commerce, bartering among widely dispersed tribes that included the Taos Pueblo, the Sioux, and the Blackfeet.

By the 1870s, in any case, the vast bison herds were gone and the plains were cross-hatched by the fences of immigrant farmers. The Arapaho, without much fight left in them after the battle along Nowood Creek, needed a haven if they were to survive at all. A southern band had settled in Colorado, the southernmost portion of the tribe's territory during its plains period, when Arapaho ranged along the eastern slope of the Rockies from the Arkansas River to the Musselshell River in Montana. The northern band had resisted attempts by the U.S. military to locate them with their southern relatives or with tribal allies like the Sioux or Cheyenne. When offers of reservations along either the Sweetwater or North Platte River came to naught, the Arapaho leaders expressed keen interest in the lands of the Shoshone, despite past hostilities. Chief Washakie was a tough old warrior with a reasonable heart and a history of cooperating with the whites to get what he wanted, and he agreed to give a "temporary" home at Wind River to the remnant of his traditional enemy, rather than have them perish out on the plains. The Arapaho settled far east of the Shoshone communities and the agency buildings in the western foothills. Followers of Black Coal erected their tepees a short ways upstream from Double Dives and Riverton, where the Popo Agie joined the Little Wind, and his band was known as the Forks People. Sharp Nose and another group would settle farther west near the Little Wind.

Such settlements of exhausted Indians were a magnet for missionaries, and in the 1880s Catholics prevailed over Episcopalians for proselytizing rights near the Arapaho camps. At St. Stephens Mission, the Jesuits started a boarding school, though it was only a short hike from the Indians' cabins and tents and tepees. At the time, the federal government encouraged missionary schools with gifts of reservation land and money, sometimes taken from the Indians' own funds, which the government held in trust (a practice that continued through the 1940s). Black Coal, whose band was closest to the school, encouraged his followers to send their children to St. Stephens, and those who went learned to grow vegetables and tend cows and sheep and pigs. Since government rations were sparse, there was no one around to instruct the Arapaho in large-scale farming, and the beginnings of a tribal cattle herd had been bought or stolen by whites. Game was dwindling. But the Arapaho adapted, planting gardens in the style of the priests, digging root cellars and using their traditional skills to forage wild foods. Well into the twentieth century, the old people would still go down along the riverbanks in the summer and knock bullberries from the bushes with sticks; in the fall they'd follow the water upstream into the canyons to collect chokecherries, which they would mash into a paste and dry in patties. Sickness and starvation had taken a toll, and no one had seen any of the white man's money, but as one old-timer put it, "You could make a pretty good living."

The missionaries were cultivating souls, too, and they did that strictly in English. Pius Moss was taken to St. Stephens after his mother's death, when he was five years old. He was an old man when I met him. "They took my language away from me thinking they'd make me a white man overnight," he said. "I got whipped twice with my pants down and that cured me of talking Arapaho." It's hard to picture Moss as a frightened little boy, because today he's a big man whose barking voice brings an immediate hush to a classroom of children. He is back at St. Stephens school, this time as a grandfather telling stories, resting his wrists atop his cane and waving large, blunt hands at the children. Like many of his generation, Moss once discouraged his own children from speaking the tribe's language, thinking it would only handicap them in the modern world. Telling me this, he chokes up. He has been hired by the school to teach the little ones Arapaho.

Sumner Marlowe has both Shoshone and Arapaho blood, but he follows Arapaho traditions. The tribal elder who guided him through the Sun Dance, Anthony Sitting Eagle, lived in a small housing development at Lower Arapahoe, just west of St. Stephens. The twenty or so houses in the subdivision are cookie-cutter jobs, and though the colors differ, they all share the pale nullity of cheap paint. Few of the people living here show respect for the government's lame attempt to create a neighborhood. Though Dumpsters are spaced less than a hundred yards apart, windblown garbage tumbles down the street until it catches on fences. Some of the windows are boarded up or covered with plastic. In a flat-tired car next to one of the peeling homes, several teenage girls sat listening to music.

The door to Sitting Eagle's house opened and shut frequently during my visits—mostly young men, like the stenchy fellow in a yellow sweatshirt who came out the door one day as I was entering, clearing his head of catarrh and swearing at the sun. The head of the household sat on a sagging couch that smelled of cigarettes and didn't introduce me to the people moving in and out of the room. Sitting Eagle was a small, gray-headed man who wore thick glasses and sometimes leaned forward, coughing heavily. There was a lull before we even started talking, and he looked wanly around the room. By then I knew not to "interview" old people, so we just sat. I told him I had visited St. Stephens, and he said, "The nuns called me a heathen and a devil." Then he laughed. Like many Indians, he had served in the military, which got him off the reservation and away from the NO DOGS OR INDIANS ALLOWED signs in Riverton. There were also barriers in the larger world. In the army, he'd once entered a diner in Texas that was divided into black and white sections. "Didn't say nothing about a red section, so I wasn't sure where to sit," he said, chuckling. The waiter had a third option and told Sitting Eagle there was no room at any of the tables, black or white. So Sitting Eagle went in and sat with two black men, and when the waiter came over, "I said, 'As long as I wear this uniform, you're going to serve me breakfast.' "

Sitting Eagle was one of the Four Old Men, tribal elders who guide the Arapaho and, in ways that are beyond my understanding, link the tribe's temporal and spiritual worlds. Sitting Eagle never mentioned this during our visits—these elders work largely behind the scenes, and there's nothing "official" about their title. In both tribes, men with spiritual power usually stay out of politics and designate surrogates like Bob Harris to deal with the outside world. I once asked Sitting Eagle about references I'd found in various anthropologists' studies to the Water-Pouring Old Men, or the Water-Sprinkling Old Men, a group of elders who, before the reservation days, directed tribal ceremonies. I was intrigued by their titles' connection to water, and by descriptions of how their wisdom and power were expressed in stillness and silence rather than warfare and speech. In the old days there were as many as seven levels or "lodges" that Arapaho adult males passed through as they gained age and prestige. The Water-Sprinkling Old Men could cure the sick, foretell the future, help hunters and warriors succeed, and even assist in matters of love. Sitting Eagle looked mildly surprised when I mentioned the Water-Sprinkling Old Men, the last of whom died in 1894, before he was born. Then he shook his head and looked away. "Can't tell you much. That was a long time ago."

The Four Old Men are in some ways descended from the seven Water-Sprinkling Old Men. Their power, too, reverberates back through time, to the four directions in the sky, to the four keepers of the tribe's Sacred Pipe and the overseers of the Sun Dance. *Four* turns up everywhere in the Arapaho world.

On another visit, when Sitting Eagle talked about his own youth, he was boyishly happy. It had not been an easy life—taking care of cattle and horses, piling ties at the age of thirteen—but he was outdoors most of the time, and he felt himself growing strong. His parents spoke Arapaho, and "I knew the land, my father's farm," he remembered. "That was powerful."

I suggested it ought to help that young people on the reservation can be outdoors in a vast wilderness that belongs to them, but he wasn't listening. "Our biggest problem here is our loss of culture, and our language." He glanced toward the door, then lowered his eyes. "They don't care about life." Was he suggesting, I asked, that he was a better person because his family lived in a tent and he drank water from the river, clean and pure? He laughed. "I just didn't have any time to get in trouble." Then he put a tired hand on the side of his head. "Now everything is torn up. Some kind of evil goes around. The beauty of the earth is gone now, even the beauty of life."

The sleepy young men—it was midday—came and went, gathering on the porch to smoke, shouting slurred commands in the kitchen without acknowledging him or me. "We're home all the time," Sitting Eagle said of himself and his wife, "but they do these things we don't want them to do. There's nothing for kids. They start wandering off, and they get into alcohol." He admitted that he, too, had been a drinker as a young man. "It never did any good."

Outside, a group of four young men was gathered around a disabled truck, having a smoke. The door to Sitting Eagle's house would not close cleanly, thanks to a hinge being loose. Stepping out, I looked back and he remained on the couch, where I had found him on each of my visits, looking at his hands, waiting. Across the street, someone had pulled a horse trailer up to the back of a house, and the trailer was filling up with garbage.

On another day, Kate Vandemoer came to the Arapaho community to convince the people of their wealth as owners of the water that flowed through their reservation. Her office was on the west side of the reservation, and she didn't know many people from the east. To visitors, the community where Anthony Sitting Eagle lived appeared to have no center, neither street nor landscape to direct you toward its commercial or political heart. Nearby, St. Stephens was no longer a Catholic boarding school, and the Sunday services were uncrowded; the store and gas pumps installed by the Arapaho had been closed down; and the Arapahoe school, up along the Little Wind, was struggling to survive as its funding and enrollment shrank.

On a December evening, Vandemoer brought her message to a

gathering of about thirty people in St. Stephens. "What's the economic future of this reservation?" she asked. "That's the ultimate question to tribal members. You know oil and gas revenues are going to go. What do you use to substitute? This water is one of the keys to economic development in your future."

That was just the opening salvo of a series of seminars Vandemoer was holding around the reservation—a revivalist crusade of sorts, three different topics, four different stops, twelve meetings in all. The tribes and the state were locked in a fierce court battle over water rights, and the complex maze of hydrology, law, and politics was increasingly hard to follow. At the St. Stephens meeting, she handed out fifty-page packets loaded with charts and lists of hydrology vocabulary to Arapaho grandmothers with scarves on their heads and to squinty old ranchers with missing fingers. Members of the tribal business councils were invited to each of these meetings, but it was Vandemoer's show. An ambitious plan for using tribal water rights was taking shape, but in reservation politics nothing is more dangerous than getting too far out in front of the people you lead. She understood the risk. She could survive the enmity of Midvale farmers, but not without support within the tribes. The old folks looked curiously at the blue covers of the booklets and set them aside.

Though the map Kate Vandemoer projected on the screen didn't even show Arapahoe, that wasn't a comment on the decline of the town. Rather, she wanted to show the outline of the entire reservation and the pattern of the major streams passing through it—the veins and arteries, minus the major organs. After several reductions in its borders over the years, the reservation today has a boxy shape, about fifty miles square, like the rectangular states that were carved from the Northwest and Dakota Territories a century ago. But the reservation boundaries aren't so arbitrary; they're tailored to encompass most of the Wind River basin, from the mountains that rim the bowl in the west to the mouth of the canyon that releases that water into the Bighorn River and, ultimately, the Missouri. The reservation is one of the few principalities that follows, somewhat inadvertently, the organizational principles of John Wesley Powell, who suggested that the only sensible political division of the arid

West was along watersheds, letting the communities within the drainages make decisions about its most productive uses. Unlike those of the states surrounding it, the historic boundaries of the Wind River reservation largely encompass the watershed, precisely the sort of jurisdiction Powell had envisioned. This distinction wasn't lost on Vandemoer; indeed, it was an element in her large ambitions.

The map she projected isolated the reservation as if it were an island, though that isn't in any way true. Wind River sits in the center of the Wyoming rectangle, a huge chunk carved right from the state's heart—a fact that's given Wyoming developers and politicians palpitations for over a century. In 1869—only a year after the treaty was signed creating the reservation, and reducing a much larger Shoshone homeland described in an 1863 treaty—the Wyoming territorial legislature passed a resolution telling President Ulysses S. Grant that Wind River was "utterly valueless to the Shoshones . . . being for them, in fact, neither home nor hunting ground; its acknowledged existence as an Indian reservation but imperils the lives of honest and industrious miners and settlers." The lawmakers suggested the Shoshone be removed and the reservation be reopened to "bona-fide citizens of the United States."

It's still a large reservation (2.3 million acres), though not the largest. What makes it extraordinary among reservations is its resources, from the forest and wildlife in the mountains to the oil and gas underground. From the time Washakie signed the Fort Bridger treaty in 1868, other tribes griped about how "rich" the Shoshone were. What Vandemoer hoped to convey to the people who owned it was that their true wealth was in something they had been taking for granted for generations: the reservation was the collecting point for a huge hydrological system that began with the glaciers on the flanks of the Wind River Mountains and eventually funneled out through Wind River Canyon. Understanding the plumbing of the basin was the first step, she figured, toward putting the water to work for the tribes. At a second meeting, she would talk about what it meant historically to have rights to water in the West, the system for regulating the water—which over the years had begun to resemble a Rube Goldberg contraption—and the peculiar status of tribal water rights arising from treaties. All this was merely prefatory, building an understanding among a people who considered water a sacred gift from nature, not a commodity to be bought and sold. Her third seminar would address some innovative alternatives to managing the wealth of water that flowed through the Wind River Basin. Whether she was fully aware of it or not, that session would be about power and revolution.

But she had to begin with the basics. First, there is a special vocabulary for talking about water. I would look sideways at the crowd attending the St. Stephens meeting when "alluvial aquifer" and "evapotranspiration" were invoked, and see a few educated heads nodding reflexively while the old people stared with fixed expressions. These words have a familiar sound that makes you think you understand them when in fact you haven't a clue. Later, back in my office thumbing through hydrology textbooks, I made a game of responding to the sound of the word before I checked its definition. *Hydrology* had the right heavy-pipe sound and the Greek authority to suggest the mythology of the plumbing trade (dictionary version: "a multidisciplinary subject dealing with the occurrence, circulation, properties, and distribution of the waters of the Earth"). *Turbidity* carries onomatopoeic silt along the tongue ("the blockage of light passing through water, caused by suspended matter such as clay, silt, organic material, and microscopic organisms"). *Evapotranspiration* sounds a religious note ("the combined loss of water to the atmosphere by evaporation or through the pores of plants' leaves"). *Weir* sounds vaguely Welsh and druidical ("an overflow structure across an open channel to divert or measure the rate of flow and volume of water"). And few words in the language flow as sweetly over the sands as *alluvial* ("deposited by a stream or running water").

Some other water terms Vandemoer thought the Arapaho people should know, and which many of us only think we know, include:

aquifer A geological formation sufficiently permeable to store and yield significant quantities of water to wells and springs.

artesian   Pertaining to groundwater under greater than atmospheric pressure by overlying impermeable material, so that it may rise above the aquifer containing it.

consumptive use   a use of water that removes it from the hydrological cycle, either surface or underground, resulting in a reduction of available water.

Discharge   The volume of water and sediment that passes a given point within a given period of time (often measured in cubic feet per second), either in streamflow or groundwater.

percolation   Slow laminar movement of water through soil or geologic formations.

piezometer   An instrument mounted in a pipe inserted vertically in the ground to measure the pressure or compressibility of the water table.

recharge   The process of replenishing water in an aquifer, through the downward movement of water either naturally or artificially.

safe yield   The amount of water that can be removed from a well without reducing water available, lowering the water table, or allowing low-quality water into the aquifer.

water table   The surface of an aquifer, where the unconfined water is exposed to atmospheric pressure.

Geology and hydrology are closely linked, and water makes the science of rocks less dry and dusty. The link is easy and constant. Water is forever evaporating, falling, percolating, cascading over rock. It sits on the shoulders of mountains in snowy epaulets, it trickles downslope with a little heart-tickling gurgle, it carries the mountain to the sea in bits and pieces.

To illustrate the hydrologic cycle, Vandemoer showed a slide familiar from ecology textbooks: a drawing that compresses into a small frame the images of clouds, mountains, slopes, snowfields, trees, lakes, streams, and oceans, with arrows to indicate a circle of precipitation, runoff, evaporation, percolation, and discharge. Except for the ocean, all the elements of the process are contained in the Wind River Basin. But her lesson grew more complicated when she showed the dense topographical lines of the basin and threw out numbers to explain the seasonal variations in runoff and domestic use.

The cycle becomes less simple, too, when you add in some of the variables of this particular basin. For instance, the glaciers—the largest number in any mountain range south of the Canadian border—that feed ice melt into the system. Or the basin's underground recharge system, complicated by the Rockies' unpredictable folding and faulting of geological strata. Then come the manmade variables, such as landfills and oil wells, and the radioactive residue at the nearby uranium mill. Finally, the rejuvenating circle of water leaks into the squiggly tangents of numerous ditch diversions.

With repetition, though, the general outline sinks in, and my comprehension went from simple ignorance to complexity and back to simplicity again. While rock stands inert and anchored, water is always on the move, carrying both sand and mayfly downstream. If rock is the stoic straight man, water is all chuckles and action. We know how it works on the surface—feeding bugs and people, scouring the stark face of stone. Vandemoer emphasized instead what couldn't be seen—the water moving underneath the ground, slipping through the fractures in the granite of the Rockies, then pushing back up to the surface at a lower elevation.

"It's all jumbled up, but I'm convinced that even those lakes up in the mountains are recharging, much more than you find in, say, Colorado," she said later. "It's really complex, particularly right at the center of the basin, under the Wind River. Figuring out the relationship between surface water and groundwater, that would be absolutely fascinating."

Were the Indians fascinated? Hard to tell. They helped themselves to doughnuts and coffee, a staple at meetings on the reservation, and sat quietly. When Vandemoer opened the meeting to questions, they didn't ask about water rights or hydrology. Who hired you? they asked. What are we going to get from this? How much are you being paid?

"I was there to do this nice thing," Vandemoer remembered, years later, "and it was, you know, 'Who the hell are you?' "

At the end, many of the blue-covered packets were left lying on the chairs.

But word got around, and soon even people who didn't attend the meeting were interested. She had touched on some pressing local concerns. When she talked about groundwater—another huge resource the tribes were claiming—she worried aloud about a pile of uranium tailings that had been sitting on reservation land just east of Arapahoe for twenty-five years. The uranium mill built by Riverton businessmen had shut down in 1963, but Vandemoer suspected that radioactive residue was still flushing through the groundwater—and perhaps invading drinking-water wells.

That was the kind of bold talk that got Vandemoer in trouble, but not with Mark Soldierwolf, whose family once owned the land where the uranium mill was built. Soldierwolf is a long-legged man with a big, mobile face who lives with his family in a roomy house he built himself west of the mill. He and his wife were newlyweds when they were forced off the land, and then they lived upstream of the mill, in a house he built with a big open living room and kitchen. When I visited Soldierwolf, he sat at the table drinking coffee and did some bold talking of his own. His long gray hair hung loose over his shoulders, and he had one of those big voices that stand out in drum groups at powwows. When he first met Vandemoer, he told her that she had to stop fighting over water. "Every time you fight," he would say, "it freezes up there, and we get less water." She wasn't sure whether he was serious. I had the same uncertainty when he informed me that the Ancient Ones, Arapaho ancestors, have been in the high plains forever, and had their own horses before the Spaniards arrived. Paleontologists would differ, I think.

But I got used to Soldierwolf's style, a mixture of bombast and teasing and serious argument. He was actually modest about his own knowledge, and a Vandemoer supporter: "She was the only one among those agencies with the gumption to go further. Things have been deteriorating fast. The river around here, the ditches—they're bad. Have you seen?"

Soldierwolf had seen. He knew the Wind River from trickle to torrent as well as anyone. Every year he canoed a different stretch of the big river, from the narrow whitewater riffles in the Wind River foothills to the placid waters of Boysen Reservoir. He invited me to join him the next time. Just recently, he had floated from Diversion Dam—where Midvale took its irrigation water out of the Wind—to the Riverton Country Club.

CHAPTER 5

LeClair and the Lower River

West and north of Arapahoe, I crisscrossed a big hogback between the Little and the Big Wind Rivers. The Big Wind has been a line of demarcation since 1906. If an Indian wants to compare his situation with the whites', he'll talk about how much better they have it "on the other side of the river." If a non-Indian tires of such complaints, he'll say that reservation farms could be just as productive as his if they worked as hard "on the other side of the river."

I sat in a pickup on the other side—the north side—with Johnnie Hubenka, a sixtyish farmer with receding, disorderly hair and a neat late-model truck. Hubenka works in the fields and the ditch of the LeClair Irrigation District with a pair of arthritic shoulders that his doctors say have been ripped apart by decades of lifting and pushing and pulling on the farm. If Hubenka works as violently as he talks, it's no surprise. Now and then, though, as he talks about hurling someone into the river, a smile creeps into his pink face, and you wonder how much of his bluster is bluff.

The notion of anybody like Soldierwolf canoeing or rafting this stretch of river *for fun* evoked a mirthless chuckle from Hubenka. I had to agree that the river didn't look very inviting in August—a sluggish meander through rock and brush and sand, overhung with bewildered cottonwoods. He'd heard the Indian claims that this poky stretch of brown-bottom river could attract recreationists, and it irritated him that know-it-alls at the U.S. Army Corps of Engineers no longer let him dump old concrete chunks to stabilize the riverbanks because a rafter might snag on the rebar. A *rafter?*

Another absurd example of government regulation based on sheer fantasy. The only floaters he'd seen on the river were "that bunch of arrogant SOBs" known to the rest of us as the U.S. Fish and Wildlife Service, and some old cuss who snuck down the river every year to poach game.

Later I asked Mark Soldierwolf if that description fit him, and he laughed. "I'm not a poacher, I'm a *spy.*"

Riverview Road follows the north side of the river west from Riverton, past the country club, about a mile north and roughly parallel to the road through Arapahoe. The floodplain here is wide enough to fit a subdivision and eighteen holes of golf between the road and the river itself. Once there were farms right up to the edge of Riverton, but increasingly these spreads have been carved up into "ranchettes": split-level, dormered, burglar-alarmed estates whose owners cultivate only a few acres of hay for their horses. For Hubenka, the manager of the LeClair Irrigation District, it's a headache. Instead of a few farmers turning out water for big fields of pinto beans and sugar beets, he's got dozens more neighbors who use the ditch to water their lawns.

Riverview Road twists west through a series of knobby hills that separate these suburbs of Riverton—if a town of ten thousand souls can be said to have suburbs—from the big swaths of fields that fill the valley bowl west toward the mountains. Get high enough and you can see the valley of the Little Wind running parallel to the south, edging toward its union with the Big Wind at Double Dives. From the steep wall of the Rockies in the west, the various strands of the drainage cascade into the bowl of the valley, and then slow. In the mountains and foothills, the cuts are steep-walled and fast, but down here they meander, and in the spring the river drops off a payload of mountain mud. The ridges between the rivers are the light-gray and brown colors of sagebrush and soil, but as they slope up toward the Continental Divide, squat cedars add a mosaic of dark green to the ridgetops and flanks.

I trespassed on some private land near Riverton that belonged to an old Indian who no longer lived there. Cultivated fields sloped gently away to the south, draining toward the river—fields watered by the LeClair ditch. The Indian's land was mostly hills, just above a small lateral ditch marked by tall grass and scrub trees that edged along the north side of the river's floodplain. In the middle of the field to the south, at the end of a road with the beginnings of a hedge and a crayon-green lawn, stood a new house of many gables—not an Indian's home, not the sort of place a farmer could afford to build. The two-room cabin above the ditch where the Indian landowner sometimes stayed appeared to be empty.

The river has moved back and forth across the valley over time, and it often modifies its channel during flood season. Farmers can lose valuable acres to a channel change, and they've done what they can to stabilize its banks. Some used the trick of planting old car bodies nose-down on the outside of the river's curves. From my vantage on the hill, the river was more than a mile away across the valley, shrouded by green tangles of cottonwoods, with breaks here and there where the river surface shone in the sun. To the west, the valley curved slightly north and narrowed, hemmed by the widening ridges that sloped down off the Wind River peaks. The Continental Divide here runs southeast-by-northwest, its mountains banded by a thick horizontal stripe of pine forest, and then, above the tree line, the glacier-capped backbone of the continent, much of it over 13,000 feet above sea level. The peaks of the Wind River Range—with names like Knife Point and Lizardhead—are so densely packed that they look from below like a thicket of candles on a centenarian's birthday cake. While the seasons and settlers change the shape and color of the valley below, the distant mountains remain white and unchanging year-round—a daily reminder for a worker in these fields of the promise of perpetual water first heard by homesteaders a century ago.

The hill that afforded me this view is also the site of an arrangement of stones that forms a wheel about fifteen feet in diameter, with twenty-seven spokes. In the middle of the wheel is a cairn, made of smooth-polished river rock, with a cap of curved sandstone on top. A hand-rolled cigarette, stained yellow by moisture and heat, lay beneath the cairn. A number of Indians in the Wind River area speak of this wheel, but few visit it, and no one can vouch for its origin or age. Across a dry gully lie more circular arrangements of stones, possibly tepee rings.

Along the exposed curve of the distant river where it breaks from the cottonwoods, a rubber raft came around the bend in the summer of 1994. This time it was the SOBs: the Wind River office of the U.S. Fish and Wildlife Service. Three agents, including Dick Baldes, had floated forty-five miles of the river on a twelve-foot rubber raft. This one was similar to the rafts you see running the whitewater of bigger rivers, with oars and a platform of tubular steel mounted at the center, but off its front end sprouted two antenna-like wands with metal hoops dangling like earrings from the ends. In front of the oarsman, a panel of dials and a generator were anchored to the rowing platform. Baldes and Jeff Kimber stood on either side of the raft, near the front, holding twelve-foot poles with plastic gloves, alertly watching the surface of the water, while Dave Skates handled the oars.

Now and then, when the bright streaked belly of a rainbow trout floated up, or the sickly yellow of a carp, Baldes and Kimber would dip their nets in and scoop the stunned fish into the boat. They were electrofishing, one method of taking a fish census in a river. The wands at the front of the boat—actually vaulting poles bought from a sports-equipment dealer—suspended an anode in the water, and tubes running alongside the raft were the cathodes. The positive and negative poles set up a high-voltage electrical field in the water, which would first attract the fish and then stun them into temporary paralysis, or taxis. The knocked-out fish would roll to the surface, where they would be captured and put in a "live car" of aerated water. At various times the raft would pull over, and the biologists would measure and weigh the catch before returning the fish to the river. The carp sometimes ended up in the woods with their bladders cut, because carp are unwelcome invaders.

Tell an electrician how you went electrofishing, and he'll tell you you're out of your mind. It's dangerous work. Biologists who have slipped into the charged water have taken debilitating, and even fatal, jolts. (Because of their size, fish form a smaller electrical field and take less of a charge.) But Jeff Kimber, whose father was an electrical engineer, had designed this raft with numerous safety features, including a footswitch that shut down the system when a netter, falling overboard, lifts his foot.

At this point on the river, everyone was tired: the raft was heavy with equipment, the dentist-office hum of the generator was irritating, a day of sun had drained them, rowing was a real chore—and Baldes, right then, was not great company. Upstream they'd been pulling in whitefish, trout, an occasional ling, in good numbers and varied sizes. Down here, the water was turbid and shallow, and the trout scarce. It didn't have to be, insisted Baldes. "This river could be good for trout, but they suck it dry. We're lucky we can get the raft down it."

During the dry years of the late 1980s, there were times you couldn't have gotten a child's bathtub toy down this stretch of river. Several small irrigation ditches along the river serve the reservation to the south, and three larger ones carry water north of the river, mainly to non-Indian farmers. The biggest one is the Midvale/ Riverton Unit, which takes by far the largest amount of water from the river, but still must let some go by for downstream users with a senior state water right. LeClair lies downstream, and when water is low it gets the last drop, even bulldozing the streambed to divert the last trickle of the Wind River into its canal. Some water seeps back from the fields, but in dry years there's not much flowing under the bridge by Riverton.

Baldes and tribal leaders claim this stretch of river could be a blue-ribbon fishery if managed properly. To give this thesis more scientific heft, Baldes brought in an FWS biologist affiliated with Colorado State University, Eric Bergersen, to study the river, and his study blamed the non-Indian diversions and ditches—particularly Midvale's—for changing a cobble-bottom stream into a muddy mess. "There's so much excess sediment in the system," reported Bergersen, whose funding for Wind River research has been discontinued. "We certainly can show what happens above and below Diversion Dam in terms of fish population and fish health. It's not good."

Diversion Dam is part of the Riverton Unit, often called Midvale for the irrigation district that uses it. Though LeClair and another downstream diversion, the Riverton Valley Irrigation District, may take the last trickle from the streambed, the Midvale irrigators take a lot more water. LeClair and Midvale are often at odds over the river they share. But they agree on one thing: It's no trout stream, and leaving more water in it during August isn't going to change that. "There's no fish in there," Hubenka snorted, walking the banks near the LeClair ditch with me in the fall. Cottonwoods canopy the dirt road that runs along the river to the LeClair intake, where the water swirls against a cement face on the river's north bank, entering the dirt-banked canal through a metal door raised and lowered by hand. "It gets too warm for trout in the summer—that's when it's good for swimming. Maybe in the spring of the year you can catch a pretty good trout, but that's it."

There are no fish, certainly, when the riverbed is dry, as it was in 1990, but quite a few car bodies. There's a line of them, rammed into the banks as if they dropped out of the sky, just below the LeClair pullout, along Hubenka's property. "I'll admit, there's some old cars there," he told me. "But they been there a long time, since the 1970s. Truth is, car bodies are about as good rip-rap as you can get. If you fly from Riverton to Dubois, there's probably three to four thousand car bodies."

Wyoming streambed reclamation: In the old days, struggling to hold on to marginal farms, landowners used whatever was at hand to save cropland from erosion. Hubenka learned to farm during the Depression years with his father—"As a boy, I'd go along with him so I could drive the pickup through the gates"—but he and many other local farmers have little hope their kids will follow them now. At an age when most farmers are turning the place over to the next generation, Hubenka is on his own. Of course, he wouldn't be an easy man to work with.

"The trouble with agriculture today?" he asks rhetorically. Like most farmers, he has the answers, and he recites them mechanically as he drives past fields that look as though they haven't been planted in years. "Diesel fuel was seventeen cents a gallon in the 1950s, now it's ninety cents. Five dollars for a bag of beans in the fifties, now they're fifteen dollars. Lots of paperwork. Livestock does pretty well, until the doctors and the lawyers get into the cattle business, and then they dump livestock, driving the price down." Hubenka could sell his thousand acres for a good return to one of those cowboy-doctors or -lawyers, but despite the four surgeries on his damaged shoulders, he stays with the land out of what he calls "sheer stupidity and stubbornness."

More than that, Hubenka feels in his own abrasive way responsible for this land along the Wind River; he can't accept that anyone with a fancy degree or title could learn half as much as he knows from simply being on the land as long as he has. Anyone poking around without his permission can expect to be confronted, as Shoshone Business Council chairman John Washakie discovered a few years ago, when he brought some representatives from an agribusiness corporation to look over tribal lands on the tablelands south of the river across from LeClair. Washakie, a great-grandson of the famed Shoshone chief, was then the tribal water engineer, and he was exploring ways to tap outside investment to use the tribes' water. Hubenka crossed the river and confronted them, angrily asking them what they thought they were doing. "It took me a moment to realize that *he* was the trespasser," Washakie said later. "So we cleared that up. Then he said he was out looking for a missing bull."

The FWS crew shut the generator off and pulled the raft over near the LeClair headgate, and Baldes's heart sank. Downstream, dikes of junk had been built along the streambank to keep the river from eroding Hubenka's land. "The mighty Wind River," said Baldes. "Aw, shit. This is more disgusting than I could ever imagine."

They made an inventory of the riprap along the bank. Among the items:

> *Tractor wheels*
> *Old manure spreader*
> *2 engine blocks*
> *240 feet of culvert*
> *15 car bodies*

dishwasher
lawnmower bag

Hubenka had claimed no car bodies had been pushed in the river since the 1970s, but there was a Chevy Citation with a 1989 license plate. Baldes moped around, pacing on the bank while pictures were taken. He half expected Hubenka to show up, and he half wanted him to. Later, driving home, he said, "This is one of the worst days of my life. You know, if you were a biologist new on this job and I brought you here, you'd say, 'What happened? What has the FWS been *doing* all these years?' "

The U.S. Army Corps of Engineers, which issues permits for streambed alterations, shows little stomach for tangling with Hubenka, despite pestering complaints from Baldes. Nor does the state. In 1990, when Wyoming lawyers were insisting in court that only the state had the authority to decide who gets how much water from the river, Craig Cooper, the state official in charge of water rights in the Wind River Valley—and a LeClair water user himself!—had no key to LeClair's padlocked gate and couldn't get one. Said Hubenka, "The state can tell you what to do, but they can't come out and do it for you. Anybody wants to go up there anytime, let me know, I'll take you up." The tribes suggested installing a satellite-monitored gauge on the headgate to track how much water was being diverted, but LeClair said no. At that point, Vandemoer went out and bought a set of boltcutters that came up to her armpits when stood on end. Though she is gone from Wind River, the boltcutters still stand ready in a corner of the tribal water engineer's office.

Hubenka claims vandalism is the reason he won't let anyone visit the LeClair damworks without him along. At the locked gate on the narrow LeClair road, Hubenka dug out trenches on either side of the gateposts, "to keep the Indians from going around." In fact, he blames reservation residents for much of the trash in the river around his place. "Indian kids go to Kinnear and get liquor, then they go party at this dump just up there." He gestured up the river. "The kids would roll that stuff into the river."

Tribal and state officials don't seem much interested in Hubenka's offer to escort them to the headgates—he's just not fun to be around—but Baldes has taken him up on it. Baldes had accused LeClair of damaging the fishery by bulldozing the river channel. Hubenka sometimes wonders why he didn't knock the biologist off the riverbank when he had that chance a few years ago. "He's an ignorant SOB," he said. "Anytime you got a little guy like that, he's got a big mouth." Hubenka extends the height-mouth correlation to Wyoming State Engineer Jeff Fassett, who's also short. Fassett, said Hubenka, "wouldn't look me in the eye. He's got that 'little-man syndrome.' Short men and fat women got the same problem."

Hubenka is of average size, gray-haired and snub-nosed, with the genial face of a rodeo clown who's been knocked around some. He's affectionate with his young grandson, and when he lets his guard down he'll make fun of himself. Driving along the LeClair ditches he shows an intimate knowledge of both the engineering and the history of the system. But he thinks no better of his Indian neighbors than he does of short people.

"Indians are their own worst enemy," he told me on one visit. "You put a white person in that office [the tribal water engineer] and he could do all that they do by himself. They just don't want to work. They done that to themselves." On another occasion, pointing to the plateau above us on the south side of the river, he derided a proposal to irrigate some tribal land there (a project that would incidentally reduce the water available to LeClair): "As far as using the water, they have no interest in it. They just want money. Work isn't in their vocabulary."

Hubenka makes his living on a ditch that was originally dug by hand. Indian hands.

Of course some would say Edmo LeClair was no Indian, or at least not a Shoshone. He was a "breed," the son of a French surgeon who joined a trapping expedition to the Rockies in 1833. Mischelle LeClair, Edmo's French father, married a woman who, according to different accounts, was Iroquois, Bannock, or Shoshone. Edmo grew up among fur trappers in the wild country of the Northwest Territories, fluent in several Indian and European tongues. In 1875, he married a woman of French and Flathead descent at the Wind River Indian Reservation, which made him, in a roundabout way, a relative of Chief Washakie, who also had Flathead blood.

LeClair fought with the Shoshone alongside the U.S. military as it subdued hostile tribes in the late nineteenth century—he was with Washakie at the 1874 ambush of Arapaho on Nowood Creek—and he carried a last message from George Armstrong Custer to General Crook shortly before the Battle of the Little Bighorn. He and his wife settled along the Wind River on lands that were eventually "allotted" to them as tribal members.

Lands were allotted to Indians under an 1887 law that if allowed to run its course would have done away with reservations completely. The General Allotment Act turned Indians into private landowners by giving families 160-acre plots that had once been communal, reservation holdings. After a period of adjusting to the "civilizing" influence of private property, Indians would receive fee patent deeds to their allotments. This was part of the government's effort, on several fronts, to assimilate Indians into the dominant society. For many non-Indians in the West, the key consequence of the 1887 act was this: Once every reservation Indian who wanted an allotment had been assigned one, the "surplus" could be purchased by the government and opened to white settlement.

Initially, Indians were to be protected from real estate predators by a twenty-five-year period during which their land would be held by the government in "trust" and couldn't be sold. But Congress changed the law in 1906, so that an Indian declared "competent" to care for his property could get a deed right away. This revised allotment process got under way at Wind River in 1907, just as whites were homesteading the ceded lands north of the river. In short order, non-Indians were buying up Indian allotted lands within the diminished reservation from "competent" Indian landowners who couldn't, for one reason or another, make a go of it.

For Indians making a genuine effort to become yeoman homesteaders, things often didn't go well. This was the arid West, and the 160-acre allotments were generally too small to ranch. Irrigation projects made some plots feasible, but many Indians couldn't afford the construction and maintenance fees they were charged for irrigation water. If an allottee died, usually without a will, lands were often sold or leased to get around "heirship" uncertainty. Indians who didn't put their allotments up for sale sometimes lost them in other ways. If a landowner couldn't pay property taxes, the Indian agency could put the land up for sale. And Indian women sometimes found themselves suddenly irresistible to white bachelors with an eye on choice reservation land.

Early in the century, a map of the reservation—even the area not opened to homesteading in 1906—was dotted with private inholdings. This happened on Indian reservations across the country. By 1934, when Congress ended the allotment era, Indian-owned land nationwide had shrunk from 150 million acres to 52 million acres. Some reservations, including the Southern Arapaho's home in Oklahoma, had been eliminated altogether.

Allotments worked for some Indians, though. Pius Moss, for example, learned to farm and raise livestock at St. Stephens. Edmo LeClair and his family smartly clustered their various allotments along the Wind River and dug their own ditch—nine feet wide and a foot deep—to distribute water. Edmo and his wife, Phyllisete, built a large home by the river, and their granddaughter remembered the log house as a social center where travelers always stopped and locals gathered to dance in a ballroom with a hardwood floor. Where Edmo and Phyllisete once entertained—"dancing was indulged in until a late hour when delicious refreshments of sandwiches, pickles, cake and coffee were served"—the big house is gone, and Johnnie Hubenka's mother lives in a cottage among a collection of musical wind chimes.

Edmo LeClair wore wire-rimmed glasses in his old age, suspenders, and a white Vandyke beard. He enjoyed telling stories about his days as a soldier, scout, and frontiersman, like the time at a rendezvous when he saw the legendary trapper Jim Bridger shoot a tin cup balanced on the head of a Swede named Jackson. Bridger didn't just hit the target, LeClair said; he shot a hole so perfectly centered that the whiskey trickled down the Swede's face into his mouth. Like Bridger, LeClair wasn't going to let facts get in the way of a good story. He also claimed to have once captured Billy the Kid and Sagebrush Sam near Meeteetse, Wyoming, by lying on the trail with camouflage grass in his hat while the outlaws approached. A good story is in the details: Billy, said Edmo, was singing "Oh what a gal she was, dressed in blue."

In 1914, after the lands north of the river were opened to non-Indian homesteaders, the U.S. government took over the LeClair ditch. The idea was to save the cost of building a new ditch by simply extending LeClair's water to the nearby non-Indian homesteaders. An elderly Edmo LeClair told a water-rights hearing that he had "paid for his ditch with work, and that he was looking out for the Indians and the Indian homesteaders." The white homesteaders were looked out for once again by Wyoming Republican representative Frank Mondell, who inserted an amendment in an Indian appropriations bill to spend $100,000 on enlarging and extending the LeClair ditch, to benefit "certain Indian lands" as well as "considerable lands owned by white settlers." Like the Indian appropriations invested in the Riverton Unit, this project benefited primarily white farmers. The canal extension, completed in May 1916, served 1,200 acres of tribal land and approximately 11,500 acres of homesteaded land.

Records are sketchy, but Indians like Edmo LeClair and his family, and some non-Indians too, paid their share of construction costs with labor. As for the rest, lawyers have wrangled for years over how much repayment is owed by the farmers on the LeClair ditch. Negotiations have lowered the price tag considerably, but as of 1994 the LeClair District was still about eighty years late paying back the Indian appropriations that extended the ditch.

You can see the irrigated LeClair lands from the hill where I hiked on the old Indian's land. You can also see the course of empire: suburbia creeping west into the farms and ranches, displacing them with chalet homes and split-level houses with hot tubs and gazebos.

A medicine wheel is an oddity in such surroundings, but not long ago the Wind River Valley had a wealth of such sites—man-made arrangements of rock, often gapped toward the east, as if to open an entranceway to the rising sun. Many early peoples of the West paid homage to the sun, and the Sun Dance is still an important religious ceremony on the Wind River Reservation. But neither the Shoshone nor the Arapaho can explain the specific purpose of wheels like this one, though both tribes have a general interest and often identify them as sacred sites. In the watershed there are also numerous petroglyphs—etchings in sandstone that depict animal and human forms. In 1873, an army reconnaissance journalist was awed by the volume of messages in the rock: "It seems a little remarkable that all of these carvings should occur in the Wind River Valley, and, especially, that all should have been recorded upon light-buff sandstones, which are all so soft that the designs are even now greatly obliterated." Erosion continues to do its work on the large number of petroglyphs that survive today, and there has been vandalism, too.

But the wheel outside Riverton, whatever its vintage, remains relatively undisturbed. A Shoshone suggested to me that in earlier times it had been a place where Indians went on vision quests.

They still do. Several years ago, Sumner Marlowe went into the hills between the Little Wind and the Big Wind to fast alone for three nights and days. He had been drinking and feuding with relatives. His daughter, not yet a teenager, was afraid of him. A friend drove him up and left him there. He had a bedroll and nothing else. From brush he built a small sheltering lodge. When the sun rose he prayed, and when it fell he prayed. He had no water and no food, the same deprivation undergone by Sun Dance participants. At the Sun Dance, though, there are not only spectators but also "grand-fathers" like Anthony Sitting Eagle, who advise and look after the young dancers. Sumner's friend came up once or twice to check on him, and they sang and prayed together. Then he was alone again, utterly alone. "How that feels—it's really much harder than Sun Dance," he told me. "You see things, and you're all alone with your thoughts."

Dreams experienced during a fast sometimes bequeath new powers to the dreamer. There's an old story about an Arapaho medicine man who traveled into the ground on the third night of his fast and visited a tent where a pipe lay between two rows of men. The men on one side were painted black with yellow streaks, those on the other yellow with red streaks. They poured incense on the fire, sang, and smoked the pipe. The head man, who was painted red, then leaned forward, and two rattlesnakes emerged from his mouth. They coiled on the ground, but the man blew on them and they disappeared. When the dreamer returned from his fast, he could feel the snakes inside himself. After that, he could doctor rattlesnake bites—and during the cure, patients would see two snakes dangling from his mouth.

Sumner sometimes spoke about magical things that happened to him in the mountains. I asked him what was magical about the vision quest: what he prayed for, and what revelations he had, during his fast in the hills above the Little Wind. "You do it for a reason," he said. "I had mine." We had been sitting in a Mexican restaurant for over an hour, and he had to get back to work. He smiled. "Hey, I'm just going to say, 'None of your business.' Thanks for lunch."

CHAPTER 6

On the Riverbanks

Traveling west, upstream, from the lonely ridge where Sumner Marlowe retreated to his brush lodge, the country becomes more copious and peaceful. Horses graze in tawny fields, neat little homes sit on section corners, alfalfa has been harvested, and the roads take sharp 90-degree turns along property lines. The ditches that run next to these two-lane blacktop roads are part of reservation irrigation systems, with names like Subagency, Coolidge, and Lefthand. I couldn't fail to notice how much smaller and more atrophied they are than at LeClair. Nevertheless, the cultivated fields and pastures have a look of modest good health.

When the reservation was whittled down by McLaughlin and others at the turn of the nineteenth century, major rivers like the Popo Agie and the Big Wind became the margins—Indians on one side, whites on the other. The Little Wind, though, is cushioned all around by reservation land, and it has an unhurried beauty as it wanders east. Bank swallows swoop from the soft cliffs cut by its steeper turns, and the edges are firmly held by thick bushes, so the water runs clear and blue and cool. The farms and pasture irrigated from these primitive ditches are mostly well kept (some are Indian; others are leased or owned by whites), and the uncultivated lands in between are a kindness to the river, allowing it to rest for long stretches. Driving in a sleepy summer sun through the Little Wind's bottomland, I turned north on a dirt road just before the town of Ethete and drove toward a cluster of tepee poles visible above the cottonwoods along the river. As I approached the Arapaho Language Camp, I could hear high-pitched yelps and the splash of bodies hitting the water.

It was Sumner Marlowe's job, when the kids went swimming, to wade into the current downstream and catch any who floated away. He was an assistant instructor at the camp, which brought hundreds of kids to the banks of the Little Wind River to learn the language and swim in the *niicii* (river). As a boy growing up near here, Sumner had often ridden horses to the river with his friends, and there they dove off the backs of their mounts into the pools. They had plenty of freedom; until they were in their teens, little work was asked of them, and they made adventure of whatever was at hand. In the spring, when the big cottonwoods were torn from the banks during high water, they would board one and ride it downstream. But the camp kids charging through the alders, splashing and yelping into the river—hundreds of them, from five-year-olds up to high-schoolers—had grown up differently. They didn't understand the current, and many of them hardly knew how to swim.

In most cases, they didn't understand the language, either. It has taken generations, but the combined efforts of boarding school disciplinarians and missionaries and government overseers early in the twentieth century to silence Indian languages has finally come to fruition—ironically, because in recent years the federal government has become a booster of native languages. Today's Indian kids are more familiar with rap and video games than they are with river currents, horses, or *Woohoox*, the Arapaho word for "horse."

In the early afternoon, with the kids splashing in the *nec*, Merle Haas had a chance to lean against the trunk of a cottonwood. The fortyish Haas is no bigger than some of the children in the camp, but she has an electric head of black hair that flares on either side like a juniper bush. In her face—with its wide full-lipped mouth and high cheekbones—there is a semblance to photographs of Yellow Calf, an ancestor who succeeded Sharp Nose as an Arapaho leader. Growing up in a household where Arapaho was spoken, Haas spent evenings listening to stories passed down from Yellow Calf and others, about eagles who saved a man trapped on a cliff, or the white man who sharpened his leg and got it stuck in a buffalo. "But I don't consider myself fluent," she said. "I had lots of brothers, and if you were to tease or say something bad in Arapaho, it would have been disrespectful to speak, so I didn't talk much. The language is holy, and you have to be careful how you use it."

As I puzzled over that riddle, a small child ran by us with braids flying, shouting *"Woohoox! Woohoox!"* Or at least that was what I heard—the only Arapaho word I knew at the time, having just learned it in a language class in a tent pitched across the meadow north of the river. Was the little girl being disrespectful? "With children," Haas said, "it's different."

Behind the tree where Haas rested, in a shady grove of cottonwoods, sat several old people on folding chairs: Helen Cedartree, Joe Oldman, Francis Brown, and Pius Moss. The little girl was charging pell-mell toward them when she suddenly reined in, lowered her head, and slowed to a walk. Pius Moss leaned forward on his cane, squinting, and smiled at her. The old people who sat here every day during the camp didn't talk to the children much, and when they did it was often a command in Arapaho—*"Niitoni* you!"

They were simply there, and in their vicinity voices quieted, eyes lowered, and the pace slowed a little. This show of respect was reinforced every morning after breakfast and prayer, when an adult spoke, in Arapaho, about some aspect of respect: for teachers, for the gifts of nature, for elders, for yourself. Language lessons followed immediately, and often began with a discussion of the talk they'd just heard.

After swimming, Sumner Marlowe wandered off with a group of older boys carrying axes and knives; they were going to cut green willows for making bows and arrows. In the tents, children were learning to work with leather, to bead, to sew dance regalia, and to make cradleboards for dolls. Late in the day there would be dancing and sometimes a shinny game—a rustic form of field hockey into which Sumner dragged me, and which, as my bruised legs later affirmed, is appropriately named. On another afternoon there was an informal peewee rodeo when some children discovered a group of terrified sheep huddling in the alders.

This busy but carefree life for the campers fits with accounts of the way children were raised in earlier times—not much discipline, lots of affection. For the teachers, though, camp lessons are colored with a sense of urgency. The tribe is losing its language. "It's the same with many tribes," according to Denny Salzmann, an anthropologist who studied the Arapaho language in the 1950s. "They're very interested in preserving it, and I don't want to discourage them. But when parents can't speak the language to their children . . ." We were talking on the phone, and there was a long silence. "Well, I don't want to say it's a lost cause. But it's hard."

Loss of indigenous language is occurring everywhere, propelled by the hegemony of international media, which brings English and a few other languages into the most remote corners of the world. There are about six thousand separate languages in use worldwide today, where linguists estimate there were twice as many ten thousand years ago. Most of the languages used only by smaller societies are on the way out. Experts know of more than 500 distinct indigenous languages that existed in North America, and many more dialects, but only 187 Native American languages survive in the United States today, and only about 40 are formally taught.

Salzmann, an animated Czech who is now retired from the University of Massachusetts faculty, would much prefer that children learn at language camps rather than from the Arapaho dictionary he compiled. "They're a talking people. We're the ones who write everything down," he said. "The English spelling is so idiotic. And languages change so fast. The dictionary is for teachers, but I wouldn't bother teaching the children to write it. They should speak it."

They do speak at the camp, but not in many homes. The old people passed on to their children the harsh lesson they learned in school: Forget your old tongue and learn English or you'll be frozen out of the modern world. "It breaks me up to think about it," said Pius Moss. "We were punished. Ten loads of coal, carried up the stairs. We were spanked. We were whipped." So Pius tried to protect his children by speaking only English to them; now, he and a diminishing number of fluent speakers try to reseed his first language in the minds of grandchildren.

Between the very old and very young is a "lost generation" of Shoshone and Arapaho—about Merle Haas's age—that can't speak its native tongue. When parents come to pick up the campers, many are unable to understand what their children are saying. Few expressions of culture are as important as language, which provides profound clues, in its variety of words—and their declensions, and inflection, and conjugation, and genders—to the things that have mattered to a people through centuries of change. A clue to the immense value of horses to nomadic plains tribes is found in the Arapaho language, which has different words for the horses that hunt, pack, or carry warriors into battle.

The name *Arapaho* doesn't exist in the Arapaho language. They called themselves *Inunaina*, "our people," and were called "Blue Sky Men" by the Sioux. The Northern Arapaho called themselves *Nakhaaseinena*, "Sagebrush Men."

For many tribes, including the Arapaho, there is a large gulf between their earliest stories—what the anthropologists call myths—and the histories written by non-Indian scholars who caught up with them in the eighteenth century. The ancient stories that survive include the creation of the earth: curds of dirt were retrieved by a turtle off the bottom of an endless sea and given to Sacred Pipe, who then blew the dirt around, and "that's where the earth started." The elder who told me this story explained that in the old times it could only be told during the Sacred Pipe ceremony, but the story had recently been recounted in books, so now he could tell it. The Sacred Pipe of the story is the great animating spirit, and the tribe remains connected to that spirit through a medicine bundle brought to ceremonies like the Sun Dance—though the actual Sacred Pipe is never uncovered before people outside the tribe. Other old stories describe the journeys and travails of the tribe as it crossed ice sheets and oceans and fought with enemies. Historians who like things written down and verified by multiple sources have little to show for the period between creation and the tribe's arrival on the Great Plains. By the nineteenth century, when ethnologists arrived to study American Indians, the tribe's elders had few stories to link the Arapaho to woodlands or cultivated fields. They had become part of the flamboyant Plains Indian culture, which featured fine costumery, skilled horsemanship, and warmaking heroics. Many of the "traditions" of this era recorded by scholars had in fact developed fairly recently, and would not be long-lived. Indian peoples across the continent already had been hugely displaced. Disease wiped out large settled populations as early as the sixteenth century—the population of North America numbered in the millions before the first European arrived—and the arrival of the horse instigated an era of such hunter-warrior profligacy that much before it was obscured and forgotten.

On horseback, the Arapaho roamed the Great Plains from Colorado to Montana and from the Black Hills to the Wind River peaks. They allied themselves with the Cheyenne and Sioux and their relatives the Gros Ventre; they fought with the Crow in the north, and with the Shoshone and Ute in the west and south. Though they journeyed as far as Comanche country in Texas, they centered themselves in what is now southeastern Wyoming and northeastern Colorado.

In the 1840s, while the Shoshone under Washakie tried to accommodate white settlers, the Arapaho were viewed as less friendly, less clean, and less trustworthy. They were lawless, "troublesome people," wrote frontiersman Finn Burnett, who would later supervise farming on the reservation, "eager to destroy the Shoshoni (sic) and whites alike." Perhaps so, but their enemies seemed bent on exterminating them. In 1864, the southern band of Arapaho and Cheyenne were massacred at Sand Creek by army troops, and over a hundred men, women, and children were killed; then, in 1874, came the ambush of the northern band in the Owl Creeks.

The southern band was given a small reservation in Colorado in 1869—later lost through the allotment process—and the northern band continued to wander until, in 1878, in poverty and despair, they arrived on the doorstep of their traditional enemy, the Shoshone.

There are sixteen letters in the Arapaho alphabet, including four vowels and a few consonants that don't match Roman letters. When you first try to learn the language, which is very inflected, the fricatives sound out, as if you're having trouble clearing your throat. But in the mouth of a fluent speaker, the words have a rounder sound, punctuated now and then by the click of an ending consonant. The language imparts gender and animation to things English treats neutrally: rocks and tepee poles, for instance. Like the Germans, the Arapaho build onto words as one makes additions to a house, lengthening them as the speaker modifies the term with more description and relationships—particularly when it's a complex concept, as an elephant *(honookowuubeeet)* would certainly be to a Plains Indian.

FAVORITE ARAPAHO WORDS I MAY NEVER USE AGAIN

here	*hiit*
now	*wow*
hello, friend (men)	*heebe*
devil	*hoocoo*
glove	*zooxe*
fire (hearth)	*sitee*
Saturday (when they gave rations out)	*hooxobeti*
ice cream	*siisoowoo*
spirit (untrue person)	*ceyotowunenitee*
water monster	*hiincebiit*
white man (spider, trickster)	*nih oozoo*
he sees himself	*nonoohobetit*
monkey (hairy white man)	*biisnih'oossoo*
heart (personal medicine)	*betee*
elder (big person)	*beesnenitee*
water	*nec*

I scored 94 on a test I took in Dickie Moss's class, correctly translating *"Hinen no'oteiH Nee'eesih' it neisonoo"* as "My father's name is Powerful Man." These words are so foreign to me now, only a few years later, that I can only assume it was an open-book test. I passed the class, and my guess is I'm the only graduate of my high school or college with a first-year Arapaho credit on my transcript.

If you listen to Salzmann, though, assembling lists of words won't save the language. Fluent Arapaho speakers agree. Nor are they very comfortable with written versions of prayers or stories or songs. "The white man puts the song on a musical scale, so they won't forget the song," said Alonzo Moss, Dickie's brother and Merle's brother-in-law, who senses time is running out for his language. "My dad told me, 'Arapaho's not supposed to be written.' Maybe it's the only way we're going to save it. But the ancient prayer was never the same every time—every time an old man prayed, it was different."

Anthropologists and folklorists who transcribe Native American stories often transform them into orderly Aesop-like fables. But more direct translations produce stories that wander, repeat phrases over and over, and at least in English, rarely come to an aphoristic zinger.

"When you tell these stories to Indians, and to children, you don't have to explain," Merle Haas said. "Non-Indians, especially adults, they question you and analyze. I'm more and more uncomfortable telling these stories to white adults."

Alonzo said, "You have to get away from that written story, and just tell it. The stories don't translate into English."

When they do, sometimes it can be a little embarrassing.

I once interviewed Alonzo's uncle, Pius Moss, on a public television show. He told some wonderful stories in English, including one from his childhood, when his mother cooked him a meadowlark and told him, "Eat this, it will give you the gift of words." Near the end of the show, I asked Pius to tell a story in Arapaho, figuring that viewers would be fascinated by the sounds alone, and the expressive hand gestures that often accompany stories. Moss knitted his brow and put his cane beneath his chair, and the soft guttural sounds of Arapaho flowed. When he was done, he sat back and smiled—it must have pleased him to speak his first language. Then I surprised him by asking him to tell us the same story in English.

His eyes went a little wide—the show was live, and we hadn't discussed this before going on the air.

Gamely, he started into it. The story was about Nihooooo, who got into a boasting contest with a bunch of elk. Nihooooo, he was fast, and he offered to race the elk. But when they reached some bushes up ahead, he told the elk they should all close their eyes as they ran by. "So they started, nip and tuck, until they got to the point where he was supposed to close his eyes, and then . . . then the white man stopped a little bit. All the elk went over the cliff. So he had a lot of meat then."

While the largely white public television audience had heard the pleasant lilt of Arapaho without any idea of what it meant, and the name of the trickster (Nihooooo) bounded by in the stream of words, Arapaho listeners watching the show would have recognized and laughed at the familiar deviltry of white man. He is as common as a coyote in Arapaho stories, though not quite as smart. "All the stories refer to the white man, because he's completely different from the Arapaho," admitted Moss. "He respected nothing. All he wanted was material wealth."

The old man picked up his cane, leaned his chin on it, and smiled.

Another time, Pius Moss told me, "Always at night, the stories were told. That's the way you control the sleeping end of the day."

At the end of a day at the language camp, Merle Haas and Stella Addison shared a tepee with a dozen youngsters who were spending the night. There was no heat or electric light in the tepee, just sleeping bags and lanterns. The comforting sound of rain beat on the tepee skin, but no one felt like sleeping. They wanted stories.

Merle told short animal stories. Most of the ones she knew came from the late Ralph Hopper, an uncle, who in turn had learned his stories from his grandfather, Yellow Calf. Though Alonzo had said prayers change with every telling, they are nevertheless a gift passed down through generations. Whenever I've heard a story or song told by an Arapaho or Shoshone elder, or even words of advice, they have been prefaced with a phrase such as "That's what the old people told me" or "My grandfather say to me." It sounds like a blessing, and when a ninety-two-year-old woman tells you "The old people say," you might reel for a moment with the weight of years in those words. Encrypted in these old stories are instructions on how to live, and so, as Merle said, "this is something you can't play around with. My ancestors lived in a world of adventure and magic." Making up a story from scratch, as we commonly do, would not be art but sacrilege.

The rain on the tepee got heavier, and the kids gathered in. They wanted a ghost story.

"I don't have those," said Merle. They kept asking, so she told the closest thing she could think of, a story about twins. Even as she began, she had some doubts. The children were as young as five, and the story had some gore in it. In her presentations about Arapaho culture around the region, its violence had already raised a few eyebrows. Feeling defensive, she'd said, "Well, look at 'Little Red Riding Hood.' "

Now distant lightning put a brief glow in the tepee's canvas skin. The story she told went something like this:

In the old days, when people got married, it was sometimes to someone they didn't know well. Marriages were arranged by families, and the young couple would often start their lives away from the band so they could get over the awkward beginnings of life together without the scrutiny of other people.

This young couple had set their tepee up apart from the others. The woman was pregnant, and was close to having her baby when her husband told her he had to leave the tepee and hunt for meat. He told her that if anyone came around, she was not to look out, and she said she wouldn't. She sat in the tepee and made moccasins for the baby, sewing with sinew and bone needle.

One night she was sitting by the fire in the tepee, doing her work, and she heard footsteps outside the tent. Whoever it was circled the tepee four times, and cried out, "Aaaaaa-woooooooh! Aaaaaa-wooooooh!" [*A distant roll of thunder drummed against the hills. The children ducked their heads, looked at each other, and moved closer to Merle.*]

The woman didn't respond, and after the stranger had circled the tent four times, he went away. Her husband came home later, without any game. She told him what had happened, and he told her again: If anyone should come, don't respond, don't look out.

It happened again. She heard the footsteps outside: Crunch, crunch, crunch. Again the visitor circled the tent, and cried out. Again, she didn't respond.

When her husband came home this time, he had found only small game. He had to go out again if they were to eat. He gave her the same warning.

For a third time, the visitor came. Around the tent he went. He cried out, "Aaaaaa-wooooooh!" She didn't respond. She sat by the fire and worked with her bone needle and sinew, sewing moccasins for the baby inside her.

Once again, her husband came back, and still there was not enough meat. She told him what had happened. He warned her again, and went away to hunt.

The fourth time, the stranger came and circled the tent. Crunch, crunch, crunch. She had to see who was out there. She took her needle and she stuck a hole through the wall of the tepee. There, right before her, was his fierce face. He hollered: "Waaaaay-heeeeey!" [At the very moment, lightning flashed above the river and thunder crashed, shaking the tepee poles. The children screamed and cried, and Merle was buried beneath them. When she and Stella Addison recovered themselves, they had the little ones under their arms. She asked the children if they wanted to hear the end. They did.]

The stranger came into the tepee and sat down. In an Arapaho home, you always offer a visitor food. The young woman took out a rawhide plate and put food upon it, and she set it before him. He looked at it, and said, "I won't eat food like that." She removed it.

Next, she laid the food on a buffalo robe. Still, he said, "No, I won't eat on that." She took the food away.

Next, she opened her buckskin suitcase and took out a quill dress, the kind of dress the people used to wear. She put the quill dress down, and she laid the food upon it. The visitor said, "Almost." She took the food away.

Now she knew what she had to do. She knew what

this meant. The fourth time, she lay down on her back, and she put the food on her stomach for him to eat. He said, "This is the kind of plate I use."

The visitor pulled out a knife, and he cut the woman open. There were twins inside her. He removed the twins from inside her and took them outside. One he hurled in the direction where the stream comes out of the mountain. The other he threw where the timber grows tall. Then he went away. [*It was raining hard now, a steady tattoo on the tepee. The children were packed solid around Merle and Stella Addison, watching Merle's face.*]

The man came home, found her body, and let out a wail. He wrapped her body in a buffalo robe in the tepee. Indian people mourn for a year. They cut their hair; sometimes they cut their bodies. Early every morning the man would wrap himself in a buffalo robe and go up on a hill and cry.

The boys, meanwhile, were growing very fast. Nature was raising those children, and a day was a year. When the man was up on the hill, the children would come from their places and visit the tepee, and they would play around the fire. One would go outside the tent now and then to see that the father was still on the hill, crying. When the man came back, he would see their small footprints.

So he set a trap. He talked to his buffalo robe, and he told the robe to sit on a rock on the hill and cry. The robe did it—in those days, they had that kind of power. Then the father hid close to the tepee. The boys came to play, and after a while, one said to the other, "Go and see if father's still crying." When the boy comes out, the man catches him. He tells him he is his father. The boy says, "No, you're not." The father says, "Because you're my son, I'll make you a bow and arrow, and paint them both black."

Later, the second boy comes out, and again the father captures him. He struggles, and says the man is not his father. This time the father makes a bow and arrow, and paints it red.

The sons have special power from growing up with nature. They tell their father, "Go build a sweat lodge. Then put our mother's body in it." The father knows that power is something you have to be careful with— even the word. He does as they've told him.

Then the son with the black arrow shoots an arrow through the lodge. As the arrow flies, he cries, "Get back! Get back! Get back!" and the arrow turns after passing through the sweat lodge, and comes back through the same hole. The arrow stands in the ground before them. The son with the red arrow does the same. "Get back! Get back! Get back!" he cries, and the arrow comes back through the lodge and stands in the ground.

And after that, their mother was alive again.

The old people say: It says in the Bible they can bring people back. We can, too.

Later that night, after the storm had passed and the children were sprawled around the tepee in a damp and dreamy torpor, the few who were awake listened for the crunch, crunch, crunch of a stranger outside. What Sumner Marlowe heard in his tepee was the sound of the river rising, like a quickening of breath, as the day's runoff completed its journey from the foothills through Bighorn Draw and Norkok Creek, through the north and south forks of the Little Wind River. Still later, at that hour when spirits do indeed close in on us all, anyone who was still awake heard the river surge still higher, as the snowmelt from the day before arrived.

It was a twelve-hour journey from the mountaintops to the camp by the river.

CHAPTER 7

Ethete

When Kate Vandemoer described to Wind River residents how the river rose and fell in the early morning hours, like the chest of a sleeper rising and falling beneath a blue sheet, they already knew about it. While they'd never read the streamflow data that was picked up by river gauges and broadcast to satellites and then bounced back to Vandemoer, many of them had slept by foothill streams on hunting trips, or awakened in their homes to the heightened pitch of accelerating water. On sleepless nights, they had wandered outside in the moonlight and looked at the current's seamless undulations, mindful of the pale glow of snowfields on the peaks in the west.

Vandemoer was holding another of her informational meetings, this time in Ethete, just a few miles upstream from the camp where Arapaho children learned their language. The name Ethete was coined by Episcopal missionaries, who Anglicized the Arapaho word for "good" or "good place," hethadee. West of where Black Coal and Sharp Nose settled their bands, but not so far west as to crowd the Shoshone settlements nearer to the mountains, Ethete lies in an indentation amid soft hills, with a hot spring just up the road. It feels like a town more than Arapahoe does and has a small store, schools, and the Arapaho tribe's government headquarters.

Vandemoer brought her seminar to Ethete in the same year the Arapaho moved their government there from Fort Washakie—a move of less than ten miles but symbolically a much bigger upheaval, like a spouse leaving an unhappy marriage. For years the

Arapaho had bridled at sharing offices with the other tribe, particularly in the Shoshone enclave at Fort Washakie. It was inconvenient for the many tribal members who lived to the east, and seemed to assign the Arapaho a lesser status. That sore point dates back to 1878; even the least-educated Arapaho knows the Shoshone have been pulling seniority for over a century. And while Americans are famous for putting their pasts behind them, erasing their ethnicity, starting over anew, Native Americans have survived culturally by doing just the opposite: living every day with their history and applying its lessons over and over. Even now, when many on the reservation have relatives in both tribes, old differences remain unreconciled.

The new Arapaho headquarters was located in a nondescript building next to the older, equally nondescript Wyoming Indian High School. The year the government moved, the high school was moving, too, up the hill to an imposing new building. That was one of many giddy developments for the tribe in the late 1980s, when a young business council was pushing costly new projects despite a chronic shortage of funds. Also on the table were new articles of government, a controversial proposal that would give the tribe a kind of constitution and stabilize its sometimes tumultuous rule. For a people whose elders were always concerned by how "fast" the modern world moved, the Arapaho tribe was moving at light speed in all directions.

In that regard, Kate Vandemoer's timing could not have been worse. That the reservation was in the news almost daily—a dispute over income from the tribe-owned Arapaho Ranch, a lawsuit over what degree of Shoshone blood qualified for enrollment, county commissioners refusing to maintain roads on the reservation, four Indians on trial for the bludgeoning death of the son of a BIA policeman in the Holiday Inn parking lot—caused huge discomfort among a people who assiduously avoided scrutiny by outsiders. The water controversy grabbed more headlines than any other subject, and Vandemoer was almost always quoted. Now she was proposing a radical tribal water code and holding public meetings about it, *press invited*. Just the *newness* of the code raised suspicions among people who had been fleeced before by outsiders with fancy ideas. Somewhere between her first seminar on the proposed water code at St. Stephens and her mid-December meeting in Ethete, Vandemoer began worrying less about the hostile farmers at Midvale and more about opponents within the tribes. She continued to talk to the reporters, whom she felt needed coaching in the complexities of hydrology and water law. Though encouraged to speak out by some of the younger tribal leaders, she was experienced enough to know that a consultant in any field survived the longest by remaining as invisible as possible, and this was especially true on a reservation. Even tribal members risk ruin if they pose a high profile: leaders survive by appearing to follow.

But Vandemoer didn't feel she had much choice. Events beyond her control, including court decisions, were forcing the tribes to take a more active role in protecting the water. This was the moment, and the only place it all fit together was in her head, so who else could sell it? If it was done right, the water code would support other good things that were beginning to blossom on the reservation, like government reform and economic development. She wanted to work as a team with the tribal leaders and lawyers, but she wanted them to follow her script. As the pressure increased, she began to demonize anyone who criticized her; she ridiculed Jeff Fassett's engineering science, spoke darkly of an office clerk who was talking behind her back, faulted an attorney on the case for cowardice. Her critics whispered about her insecurity, her megalomania the same sort of thing they said about Dick Baldes. And Baldes and Vandemoer, not surprisingly, didn't have much good to say about each other.

Before a small workshop crowd in a classroom at the old high school, Vandemoer described how on mornings when the valley was cloaked in fog, at 13,000 feet above sea level sunlight was knifing through the thin atmosphere and striking glacier ice on the granite peaks of the Wind River Mountains with blinding force. She wanted to give them a picture of an enormously diverse system that was also minutely interconnected, from the slabs of ice near the summits to the deep underground pools beneath the dry hardpack of the plains. She described the relationship amongst aquifers, sandwiched between layers of sand and rock, and surface water in the streambeds. Water percolated through the moraines from the snowfields and recharged the aquifers, which were also in motion, pulled down by gravity and flowing laterally through openings in the strata. Sometimes these underground flows encountered pressures that squeezed the water back up in artesian springs. There was also pressure from deeper down, through mysterious faulting that vented heat from beneath the earth's crust, cooking the water until it boiled over in hot springs.

Monroe Marlowe, Sumner's father, sat in the audience at the workshop. He moved slowly these days, his shaggy black head bent by arthritis and a variety of maladies. He was wary of the messianic undercurrent he heard in Vandemoer's talk. He irrigated some pasture for his horses, and he wanted a secure water supply, but he was tired of hearing about water to the exclusion of everything else. He had poured years of his life into promoting education, and now, with the beautiful new school opening on the hillside above Ethete, all anybody was talking about was water water water. While he supported the programs she was pushing, he worried about the details, the inevitable problems on the ground that could be fixed only by more staff and money.

The problem in Ethete was *too* much water: The water table was high and there were pollutants in the river; a new water-treatment plant was needed. Tribal members kept building houses anyway. Canals and pipes that supplied irrigators and homes were a mess. The winter before, rancher Willie Trosper had found a gush of water flooding his pasture and figured he'd been blessed with an artesian well. Not so: the pipe carrying drinking water to Ethete had split and was pouring into the ditch. "Oh well," Trosper said, laughing. "We had 'spring' water for the bulls all winter. Pretty good deal."

Residents were warned not to drink from the tap, but some did anyway, and the recurrent outbreaks of hepatitis, dysentery, and other stomach ailments seemed plausibly related to the water supply. "My family buys the big blue bottles," said Alonzo Moss, a lifelong Ethete resident. "When I was growing up, I could drink from ditches and creeks. The ditch by our house was pure water."

"It's funny," said Gary Collins, who was also in the audience at Vandemoer's workshop. "We're just about at the Continental Divide, and we've got poorer water quality than they do downstream in central Nebraska."

Collins sat with a pad of paper in his lap, drawing cross-sections of groundwater and surface water. He was one of the young leaders who had dominated the tribal councils when Vandemoer was hired two years before. He was also one of the few tribal members who easily followed her hydrology sermons. He had a college degree in geology and had worked in Texas for oil companies doing in situ gas production, pumping solutions into the ground to force out more natural gas (a process similar to that used in some older Wind River oil fields). It seemed nonsensical to him—as it did to Vandemoer—that when the courts tried to determine the tribes' water rights in the basin, they left out groundwater and awarded only surface rights.

The intricate interplay of groundwater and surface water in the Wind River Basin was another thing Vandemoer found unique in this place. The moisture raked from eastward-moving storms by the teeth of the Continental Divide didn't all flow down the streams or evaporate. Some of it found cracks in the tilted strata of the alpine country and slipped underground, where sheets of porous limestone tucked up against the slumbering granite of the mountains. The water filled enormous aquifers. Pressure developed, and water was forced back up in springs, as when water is poured down a hose into a balloon. Vandemoer figured some of those springs rose invisibly into lake bottoms and streambeds, complicating the equations that a hydrologist used to calculate how much water there was and where it came from.

Collins was a rapt pupil—as a geologist, as a farmer, as a tribal leader. He had lost his seat on the Arapaho Business Council the year before, in a close election, but he would run again in two years, and in the meantime his head was filling with ideas. He agreed with much of what Vandemoer said but thought he might be better suited to explain to these people the immense value of water in the arid West. His mind effortlessly converted resources into dollars. For years, chronic unemployment on the reservation had been alleviated by revenues from oil and gas, much of it distributed to tribal members in per capita payments that ran as high as $500 a month. When oil prices were high and production was going full-bore, you saw new trucks and new enterprises all around the reservation. But jobs were still few, and when the oil prices dropped, so did the per capita payments. Think of water as the successor to oil and gas, Collins would tell his people, with even greater promise for the tribe's future because it can last forever.

And, Vandemoer was saying, if the tribes controlled water rights in the basin, they could forge a new path in resource management, incorporating traditional beliefs about water as a sacred element and applying more rigorous science. They could develop a complete model of the basin's hydrology that integrated the groundwater, surface streams, and glacial storage "banks." With that information, they could tweak the system at one end and predict the results downstream. Water management on the reservation could "provide a lesson to other states"—and why not think big? The tribes could cut the wastefulness inherent in the "use it or lose it" doctrine of Western water law, and keep water in the streams during dry periods by pumping groundwater into the irrigation ditches. They could attract new industry and tourism. Wes Martel, who lived just down the road from Ethete, was with her this time, assuring the audience that water quality would improve, too, under the proposed code—they could clean up the pollutants that made Ethete children sick. The vehicle for this revolution, they told the audience, would be a tribal water code.

Monroe Marlowe raised his hand. "It seems to me," he said, "that this water code is just going to hit me in the pocketbook, like everything else. The water was all paid for, a long time ago. Now they got me paying O and M, when my ditch don't run and my headgate don't work?" He might have added: When my family can't drink the water without getting sick.

"O and M" is operation and maintenance fees, paid by farmers to cover the cost of maintaining and managing irrigation ditches. For over a century, tribal members had been told that tribal revenues managed by the federal government were being invested in irrigation systems and water rights. Why, then, did they have to pay "maintenance" fees for leaky ditches? Their skepticism was great.

Were they being fleeced by the lawyers handling water-rights litigation, who had been paid millions, or by this young hydrologist?

Collins had been thinking, as he doodled, how few people understood the true value of water. Vandemoer was trying to change that, but he wondered if she understood the risks: Showing off your formal education on the reservation could set you apart, and political survival depended on blending in, subjugating yourself to the tribal consensus . . . or at least appearing to. When Vandemoer described in the workshop how a water code would manage their rights, a few heads shook. They had survived by subverting government attempts to "manage." Would this mean new rules and, more important, new fees to keep water running to the pasture? A discussion that was really about the future of the reservation—perhaps even of the West—was turning small and wary, much like the Arapaho General Council meetings, which often deteriorated into arguments over who would get the money, and how much. Sharing tribal assets was an ancient tradition, but the tone was now suspicious, even a little greedy.

The money issue had cost Collins votes in the last election. Rumors flew about millions of dollars in tribal funds that couldn't be accounted for, and the FBI was supposedly investigating. Collins sighed inwardly. He had lost his seat by sixteen votes. Money seemed to be the first thing anyone thought about. He looked at his diagram of groundwater and surface water intersecting. Down the hall, he could hear the faint thump of a basketball on hardwood.

That was the other thing people thought about.

They looked like shaggy-headed spiders in the weak yellow light of the gym. Scrawny little boys in red tanktops and shorts crouched and skittered backward across the basketball court, touching the floor with one hand, clapping between their legs, then slapping the hardwood with the other hand, back and forth in a long row across the court. All ages and sizes of kids warmed up together—lanky varsity stars alongside little freshmen, darting sprites with squeaky voices and toothpick arms lost in their baggy uniforms. The thump of the bouncing balls and the shriek of pivoting high-tops shrank into the shadows above the gym's rafters. At the far end were bigger boys, who an hour ago were napping in art class, boys whose muscular aloofness suggested they weren't using all their strength, an air of experience that kept the little ones at a distance. The little spiders strained to keep up with the varsity players and mirror their agility, back and forth across the court, sweat spraying from their foreheads.

"Don't walk! Hustle! Let's go!"

Alfred Redman is the athletic director at Wyoming Indian Schools. He is short himself, thick around the middle in a sturdy sort of way, with lidded eyes, graying hair, and a dimpled smile rarely displayed when he's exhorting his young troops. His air force background contributes to his disciplined routines. When a spindly kid weighing no more than sixty pounds lost his grip on a heavy medicine ball in a passing drill, it was time for push-ups.

Across the court they went, forty dark-eyed boys, each rolling a basketball over his head, between his legs, down his back, forward then backward, legs always moving. A ball rolled away, a whistle blew, the kid dropped for ten. There were no complaints. Redman had their respect before he even said a word. He'd played with their grandfathers at St. Michael's School, and coached their fathers; he had won the state championship just a year before, and another two years earlier.

There is a 1940s picture of Redman as a boy of about thirteen, sitting on a bench with eleven other boys wearing high-top sneakers and black socks, smiling a big smile. The faces—all the boys are smiling—are what you notice. Old pictures of Indian children do not feature many smiles.

"Well, that was basketball," Redman said half a century later. "We had a pretty good coach. I was a day student; I'd walk down to the mission. But it only went to eighth grade." Most of the students boarded. The smiling coach standing next to the team was an Episcopal priest.

In the early days, schooling for the children of Wind River came down to the three choices: They could be shipped off to faraway

Bureau of Indian Affairs boarding schools, or they could go to the missionary and boarding schools right on the reservation, or they could disappear into the sagebrush.

The notion of removing Indian children nationwide from the reservations to boarding schools came from Captain Richard Henry Pratt, who started the Carlisle Industrial Indian School in an abandoned Pennsylvania military barracks in 1879. Pratt expressed great admiration for Indians and felt their segregation on reservations was an injustice, not a recognition of sovereignty. He wanted to take the "tabula rasa" of young Indian children and write something civilizing on it. "Kill the Indian in him and save the man," he wrote. Funded by the federal government, similar schools cropped up in Kansas, Oregon, Oklahoma, and Nebraska.

It was like taking a child from a tropical island and putting her on an ice floe. Cut off from their families—who wouldn't have been able to read their letters home—the children were taught in English and surrounded by diversions that mimicked white institutions: baseball teams, orchestras, even Greek fraternities. The boarding schools were trade schools, where girls were taught to type and cook and make dresses while boys raised livestock, made shoes, and worked at a blacksmith's forge. The immersion in white culture was complete; when the school year ended, students were given summer jobs far away from the reservation, where it was feared they would revert to their old, squalid ways. The late Ben Friday, Sr., a revered Arapaho leader, was removed from his family for five uninterrupted years.

Friday described this experience to his grandson, Pat Goggles, who told me about it. "It took three or four days by train to get to Genoa," said Goggles of the boarding school in Nebraska. "When they got there, the first thing they did to the children was they stripped them of all their clothing. They were made to bathe and use various kinds of cleansers, to cleanse themselves and their body and their hair of lice and whatever else it was thought they had. Their hair was all cut. And they were immediately put into barracks, where they were still treated somewhat like prisoners of war.

"I remember him telling me, the first word in English that he knew was *broom*. I said, 'Why was that?' And he said, 'Well, if you got talking "Indian," they made you kneel on that broom for three or four hours, until you wouldn't talk your language anymore.' You were forbidden to talk your language, you were forbidden to talk about your tribe, you were forbidden to sing your music, you were forbidden even to do crafts of your own culture."

The old chiefs, surprisingly, exhorted young people to go, and even sent their own sons to the boarding schools; it was partly a negotiating ploy (a show of good faith in exchange for government aid) and partly a genuine belief that for the tribe to survive they had to master the knowledge of the society that had conquered them. They were thinking, as always, of the future. Sharp Nose sent his son Dickens and Black Coal his son Sumner, each fourteen years old, to Carlisle in 1881 with a dozen children from both Wind River tribes. It's hard to imagine how difficult this must have been for traditional people, accustomed to close extended families, and unschooled themselves. Fewer than half of this first batch of children would live to return to the reservation. At boarding school many Indian children were exposed to new diseases, none perhaps more debilitating than homesickness, when being taught, as one school administrator put it, "to despise every custom of their forefathers, including religion, language, songs, dress, ideas, and methods of living."

Even when schools were built on the reservation, children seemed to wilt in the shoes and coats and dresses they were made to wear. The Reverend John Roberts came to Wind River in 1883 as an Episcopal missionary and soon was being paid by the government to run a boarding school on the west side of the reservation for both Shoshone and Arapaho children. Putting missionaries in charge of reservation schools was government policy in the late nineteenth century, despite constitutional prohibitions against mixing church and state. President Ulysses Grant's administration saw it as a way to clean up corruption among Indian agents, but it also gave the missionaries a large trap for capturing young heathen souls. Like so many other policies, it forced Indians either to adopt the culture of the conqueror or live in secret, in the wilds or in one's mind. There were bars on the windows of the Government Industrial School at Fort Washakie, and a frightening death rate among Indian students.

Roberts, who would devote his life to his Wind River ministry, wrote to the Indian Service in 1901: "In school they have good care, wholesome food well cooked. They have plenty of fresh air, out-door exercise, and play. Yet under these conditions, in school, they droop and die, while their brothers and sisters, in camp, live and thrive."

Roberts would later run his own missionary school in a more lib-eral style, allowing the children to sing their native songs and dance during certain periods of the day. Conversions were few in the early years, but he learned both Shoshone and Arapaho languages and befriended Chief Washakie, who subsequently donated 160 acres for Roberts's school.

In addition to government funding, missionaries cultivated wealthy patrons back East who wanted to do something progressive about the "Indian problem." Promotional literature from St. Michael's Mission in Ethete, founded in 1912, described the failure of both government and churches to stem "the disgraceful uncleanliness" and "excessive" birth rate among Wind River Indians. "Vice has also made appalling inroads upon them, and all this in spite of fifty years of constant supervision and help by the government, and on most reservations of long and continuous efforts on the part of the Churches." The St. Michael's plan was to build a winter village as well as a school, so that there would be jobs and a community to prevent students from "reverting to type." A wealthy Eastern bene-factress helped pay for construction, and the Indians, perhaps with-out knowing it, paid for the church school out of tribal income collected by the federal government.

The missionaries at St. Michael's tried to incorporate some of the trappings of Arapaho culture. One of the ministers erected a tepee in front of his office, where he would meet with Indian lead-ers. But what former students remember sounds like most other boarding schools. Some ran off, figuring they could elude the BIA police—Indians themselves—who would be sent looking for them.

"One day, I just walked away," Monroe Marlowe told me. "I went to my great-grandfather, one of the old medicine men. I told him I wanted to be like him—just hunt and work around the place. He didn't say anything then, just went and saddled the horses. We went back in along the Big Wind River to hunt. He says, 'Well, you gather some wood and get a fire burning, and I'll take care of the horses.' We both went off.

"I got the wood, and I got the fire going, but he never showed up. I wanted to look for him, but I didn't want to leave the fire. I stayed overnight. The next day, I tracked the horses, walked all the way back. He was at home. He didn't say anything about leaving me. That night, he said, 'Well, tomorrow we'll go fishing.' I said, 'No, I think I'll go back to school.' He said, 'I thought you weren't going.' I said, 'I will as soon as somebody takes me.' He said, 'Well, you walked home from there, didn't you?' "

Others remember their boarding school experience with grudging appreciation for the discipline, which, like old people in most cultures, they find lacking in today's youth. The clergy who ran the St. Michael's school thought of themselves as progressives, but they didn't trust Indians to run the store that was built to teach them thrift. "Jesus people" got special favors. Verna Thunder recalled wearing uniforms at St. Michael's, "praying all the time," and being punished for speaking Arapaho, though the punishment was milder than in the past. "Demerits," remembered Thunder. "We could whisper our language at night, as long as no matrons were near. And we'd go home on weekends and catch up. I think I cried when I first got there; to go there and not go home, it was so strange. I must have been six. It was like the military: You'd stand in front of a cottage and salute the flag, then march to the mess hall."

How things have changed. Thunder told that story sitting in a gleaming office on the lower floor of the new Wyoming Indian High School—a big, modern public school with an all-Indian board of trustees. (The student body, mostly Arapaho, is open to Shoshone and whites as well.) Thunder spends several days a week here in a cubbyhole office with two older men, Chris Goggles and Abraham Spotted Elk, and any kids who drop by. Between classes, before basketball, during lunch, these "grandparents" are available. They can tell stories, offer comfort, recount the tribes' unwritten history, or talk to a young man about auto mechanics, as they did when I was there.

For a while, I was visiting the school late in the evening for Arapaho language lessons. Often, an old janitor was hanging around the halls, smoking a cigarette, with a dust mop or a vacuum cleaner near at hand, as if he were about to spring into action. He was a big man, with the waddling, toes-apart gait of an old cowhand, and he wore the right hat for it, though he was in a broom closet rather than a corral. His name was Francis Brown, and we chatted sometimes. He would put his feet up on a classroom desk and laugh loudly while discoursing on the weather, the Middle East, and the perfidy of man. I asked him, on one of our visits, about the Water-Sprinkling Old Men, the ancient circle of elders. "I don't know nothing about them," he said. "They were gone before any of us was born. They had supernatural powers, but that's all I know."

Brown has a powerful voice with which to deliver his many opinions, but he began pulling out the cord of the vacuum when I asked about this. I wanted to know if, as others suggested, the Water-Sprinkling Old Men had taken their medicine with them because it was too dangerous in the white man's world. Hadn't many of the ancient songs and rituals been discontinued on purpose? "Well, there are a few with supernatural powers still, just one or two. I don't think they'll go away." His back was turned and he was heading down the hall, apparently this time seriously intent on doing vacuuming. "There's lots of changes coming up. You ask me, it may just come back."

The presence of "grandparents" is one of the innovations that comes with an Indian-run school. There are also language classes in Arapaho and Shoshone, and a crafts workshop where Leo Her Many Horses teaches students how to make dance bustles—part of the colorful outfits worn at powwows—and hunting bows and other traditional objects.

Education on the reservation, once the indoctrinal tool of the government and churches, is now a preoccupation of the tribes. Along with government agencies, both tribal and federal, schools are a primary source of jobs. They are also a source of hope for the future, though there are problems: The schools are underfunded, and fragmented in several elementary school districts; they are Indian-controlled, but the boards and the staffs can become battlegrounds for families vying for jobs and political power. Student attendance has been a problem since before the bars were removed from the government-school windows, and when students traveled to Wyoming public schools off the reservation—as many had to before Wyoming Indian was built—they often failed to graduate. It was not unusual for reservation kids to try on schools like tennis shoes—a year at Fort Washakie, a year in Lander, an Indian boarding school in Oregon, then back again. Few Wind River students go on to college, and those who do are often back on the reservation within a year.

When the school at St. Michael's burned down in the 1950s, it turned out the insurance had lapsed; and locals began campaigning for a high school that would belong to the reservation, not to a church or one of the public school districts based in Riverton or Lander. Wyoming Indian began as a Bureau of Indian Affairs "contract" school and now is a public state school with a board of trustees based in Ethete. Today there are brightly lit classrooms with wall-to-wall computers, Indian teachers whose example might motivate kids to pursue a college degree they can use on the reservation, and in the big gym a basketball team that . . . well, that beats the pants off white teams.

At one state tournament, a coach who had lost a championship game the year before to the Wyoming Indian Chiefs said to me, out of earshot of Al Redman, "They play like all Indian teams—they run like crazy. But look, some of my kids are four-sport types, and they still have to hit the books. For Indians, basketball is everything, they play it all the time. I mean, for many of them, this is the pinnacle of their existence."

Not all Indian teams run like crazy, but a lot do. All through the West, stories are told of legendary teams and players—Larry Pretty Weasel of the Crow, Gary Cross Guns of the Blackfeet, Shannon Brown from St. Stephens on Wind River—who came quietly out of the sagebrush and blew away everyone in the gym. Indian kids feel a special affinity for basketball that they don't seem to feel for football or baseball. Reservation kids grow up bouncing a scuffed ball on packed dirt, making their moves around flinching dogs and rusted car bodies, shooting at a bent rim with a wisp of net waving in the desert breeze. They're good at it, a sport as hip and modern and street-smart as the reservation is not. In another respect the game makes sense: Basketball fits almost too easily into the ancient warrior mold. It favors agility, speed, and guile rather than brute, murderous strength. When the Arapaho and Shoshone roamed the plains, wealthy with horses and bison, warfare had evolved from mere conquest to a stylized show of courage and character. What better sport than basketball for a people who had once revered counting coup—risking one's life to touch an enemy during a battle—as a more profound act than killing?

Mission priests at St. Stephens and St. Michael's in the 1940s saw the way Indian children took to the game and used it as a lure to stem the chronic truancy at their schools. They set up leagues for younger and younger children. Pretty soon, tots at Wind River were bouncing a ball as early as they put on their tiny bustles and feathers and began to dance at powwows with their grandfathers. In 1961, St. Stephens reeled off a state record winning streak of forty-six games, an astonishing feat for a school that had graduated only two students two years earlier. The year of the championship, fourteen seniors received diplomas.

But after teenage glory, what next? Rarely did the Indian kids go on to play college ball. Instead, it was dimly lit rec-league games, and often booze and despair and early death. "He gets into a college, he stumbles once, then he quits altogether," said Redman of the atypical Indian student who gets even that far. "It happens all over. They want to be home on the reservation with their families, and"—he shrugged helplessly—"in many ways we want them back." Back home, they face what most young adults face on the reservation: boredom, unemployment, few mature role models, and a terrible insecurity about the unwelcoming world outside the reservation.

But there are small success stories. Alfred Redman himself dropped out the first time he tried college, bounced around, went into the service, and finally went back to school and got his degree. He returned to the reservation not to escape the outside world but to teach the youngsters what it feels like to win, in your own style, against people who otherwise have all the advantages. Sumner Marlowe played for Wyoming Indian in the 1970s. He got a college degree and then came back to an elementary school on the reservation, where he was a physical education instructor and coached fifth- and sixth-graders. His teams went undefeated for two seasons—he was prepping the players for Al Redman. But there were times when he sensed a kid holding back, watching him. The reservation, big as it is, has the ears of a small town. His life off the court was not going well, he was drinking. "What about when they saw a coach coming out of a bar, kissing a woman, drinking?" he asked himself. He had prayed about it during Sun Dance; he had made vows to priests. He had tried halfheartedly to stop before. "But this was when I finally thought about it," he said. "Maybe I could do it for them. Working with those kids, how they responded!"

In 1985, Redman's Wyoming Indian team was closing in on the state record for consecutive wins, a record that some of the boys' relatives had set twenty years earlier at St. Stephen's. The 1985 Chiefs ran tirelessly, but their most effective weapon was a full-court press—scrambling, trapping, diving for steals. When teams from small Wyoming towns with mascot names like Buffaloes and Cowboys came to play the Chiefs, they found themselves for once not competing against kids who looked like themselves in front of rooters who looked like their parents. A visiting team would go into shock when ponytailed Jerome Bell pounced in front of its point guard and big Alfred Spoonhunter closed in on the trap, while a crowd of Indian fans shouted the roof off. You could see the stunned surrender in the point guard's eyes as Dale Wallowingbull dove in front of his pass, and then Myron Chavez, the star of the team, would bring the ball up, driving, juking, passing behind his head to young Michael Redman for a snaky layup.

Michael Redman's father (and Alfred's brother) was Vincent Redman, chief of the Arapaho Sun Dance. Every year before the Chiefs left for the state tournament in Casper, 130 miles away, the team crossed the field behind Redman's house to a mound of tarps lying across bent willow branches. I joined them on a cold January afternoon, when the gray underbelly of the sky snagged darkly on the mountains just to the west and a billowy paunch slopped over the belt of peaks. Boulders that had been dropped in a bonfire were lifted by shovel and carried across the snow to the mouth of the sweat lodge, where a canvas flap had been thrown back. The boy with the shovel leaned into the opening, his arm trembling, and dropped the rocks in the pit at the center of the lodge.

With towels and blankets around their shoulders, the basketball players filed in, crouching and then crab-walking around the hot rocks. The lodge was about five feet high at the center, tapering down to the outer edges, and the players and coaches were packed shoulder to shoulder and calf to calf, their heads bent forward by the low ceiling. Once the flap on the doorway was pulled down, the only light was the sanguine glow of the rocks. Vincent Redman, sitting to the left of the entrance, threw some cedar into the heat of the pit and prayed in Arapaho. Water was sprinkled on the rocks—I thought immediately of the Water-Sprinkling Old Men—and a wave of sweet fragrance and hot air rolled out around us and rebounded off the walls against our bare backs. The boys were quiet. The medicine man fanned the rocks with eagle feathers. An herb was passed around three times, each person first touching the dirt floor, then putting some in his mouth. There were more prayers, then quiet sighs and bowed heads. The air was thick and oppressive, and in the dark I lowered my head between my knees to breathe easier. As I did, the rocks were doused with more water, and the wave of humid heat hit my face so hard I jerked involuntarily. My leg cramped and trembled, and the boy next to me pulled his leg away slightly, to spare me embarrassment.

Between rounds of praying, singing, and sweating, we would step out of the lodge into the cool air. On the fourth round, the glowing bowl of a pipe circled the lodge and we inhaled what I later learned was a mixture of fine tobacco and willow shavings—to my jaded senses, it smelled like grass. ("For once it's legal," Redman said to me, and there were a few chuckles.) Vincent threw more cedar on the hot rocks, and red sparkles reflected in the averted eyes of the boys; then a wave of singed cedar filled our lungs. I heard myself say, "Bless my friends and relations," as others had, and then Vincent said, "Think of the sick," and I was lost in a dream.

Later, as we stood shirtless and bare-legged outside on the snow,

Al Redman said, "They used to sweat before going into battle a long time ago. They would have a smudge ceremony, too." To tie the Indians' way of playing basketball to their warrior heritage seems too easy, but there it is.

"So do you think that helps you win?"

He looked surprised. "It isn't to win. It's to assure that no one gets hurt."

The following year, the Chiefs had two consecutive state-championship banners on the wall and were three games short of the longest winning streak in Wyoming history. There were additional pressures. A campaign called "fast break for excellence" had linked the team's success to the bond issue for a new high school. Monroe Marlowe had been lobbying tirelessly in Cheyenne for state money, and now the proponents were asking property owners to ante up. Word of the winning streak had reached the national media, and blow-dried people with cameras were standing at the locker-room door; college scouts from New Mexico and Syracuse were rumored to be watching Myron Chavez from the stands.

The reporters wanted more than just a basketball story. They wanted to write a story that has been written a hundred times: the reservation as ghetto, where a flashy basketball dynasty rises from the grinding poverty and emptiness, carrying the Indian community to . . . what? The earlier versions of this story, in newspapers and magazines like *Sports Illustrated,* were cautionary tales, about Indian hoop stars who reverted after the glorious championship to drugs and the broken hoop in the dusty backyard. At Wind River in 1985, the reporters had the perfect hook: While Redman's team glided on the court, Indian teenagers on the east side of the reservation were hanging themselves.

A contagion of suicide had struck the reservation in the fall of 1985. In the space of a few months, more than a dozen boys and young men, some of them members of the St. Stephens basketball team, took their lives. Alcohol was a factor in several cases, and some of the kids hanged themselves after attending the funerals of friends who had committed suicide in the same way. The most troubling aspect of the deaths was that the young men left no explanatory notes, as if their despair were beyond expression. When the U.S. Bureau of Indian Affairs briefed the media on the copycat suicides, bewildered officials noted without irony that despite 78 percent unemployment, "relative to other reservations, Wind River is well off."

Though most of the suicides took place a distance from Ethete, Redman didn't have to ask his players if they had friends among the deceased. "Of course everybody is related and knows everybody else on the reservation," he said. But he avoided reporters' questions about the suicides, as most reservation residents would: bad things happen when you talk about such things, one elder told me. The BIA flew in health experts to consult with social workers and doctors on the reservation. A television crew from Salt Lake City was attacked while trying to videotape a boy's funeral. Health officials did not know what to do. Bingo was canceled. The media were banned from the reservation. A dozen youths were dead, and eighty-eight suicide attempts were verified. Then an Arapaho woman whose son was the third to take his life spent months drinking herself into oblivion, and once she had righted herself, she tried to tell me what had gone wrong for him. But she broke down crying and could only say, over and over, "Nobody spoke badly of him." In the picture she showed me, her son wore his basketball uniform; he had long hair and big eyes and looked very young. Tribal elders revived an ancient paint ceremony to armor the young people against this danger.

Al Redman's basketball team kept winning.

I don't know how to make connections among all these things. Boys like Michael Marlowe can't tell me or you what hurts so inside them. But I know that shopkeepers continue to eye Indian teenagers suspiciously as they walk the aisles in stores off the reservation; educators whisper derogatory comments about the academic rigor at Wyoming Indian; fifth-graders look at their coach and see in his face the wear of a night of liquor, the same face some see at home; psychologists talk about the blank face that Indian youths erect against the world, a wall against intervention.

Well, if life seems sorrowful on a Friday night, one thing you can do is drive to Elk Redman Memorial Gym and see the boys running like antelope up and down the floor, and see the smiles on the faces of the old people, and hear full-throated cries fill the big gym. It seems not a bad place to start.

Even before the team set a new state record, the bond issue passed, and Monroe Marlowe tried to put it in perspective for me. "Basketball," he said, "is a very small part of what we're doing. If those kids can think as fast as they move on the court, then let's challenge them."

Kate Vandemoer, a former Ivy League basketball player herself, had a challenge for the kids playing hoops down the hall from her workshop at the high school. She wanted the tribes to take firm control of their water rights and to put their young people to work managing that water. The U.S. Geological Survey and the new tribal Wind River Environmental Quality Commission had found indications of serious underground pollution—heavy metals, radioactivity, oil, and grease. In an area of little industry, low population, and no upstream neighbors but shining mountains, this was surprising.

Vandemoer insisted she wasn't trying to make headlines with the workshops; originally she planned to exclude the press until they raised a fuss. Her mission was to make tribal members aware not only of their rights but also of some of the problems they would have to fix—and fix their own way, instead of relying on someone else to do it for them, or do it wrong or not at all. Tribal water-management agencies would require skilled technical people—college-educated people with degrees in chemistry, engineering, hydrology, environmental science. Why keep farming these jobs out to consulting firms? Send Indian youths to college with a compelling reason: a course of study that could bring them back to do a job for their people. If Wind River instituted forward-looking, challenging programs that overturned outmoded concepts of resource management, she figured, Wind River technicians could then be hired out to other reservations, other governments, to train and teach. Yet more jobs.

Her ambitions to put young Indians to work were coincident with the ever-widening scope of responsibilities she saw for her department. The tribes would need to conduct years of studies to develop baseline data on water quality, stream flows, and groundwater; water use would have to be gauged and regulated, then managed in a more significant way than the states did; lawyers would have to write innovative codes and regulations; cleanup programs would have to be instituted for abandoned tailings, polluted streams, the leftovers of oil and gas operations.

She worried particularly about oil and gas, an industry whose financial windfalls to Western states and reservations made it seem untouchable. Oil companies were drilling, pumping, shipping, and dumping their wastes on the reservations virtually unregulated, while big royalty checks kept the impoverished tribes from complaining.

On a spring day in 1989, Vandemoer got a call from the bathhouse at Washakie Plunge: a film of crude oil was spreading on the surface of the brilliant blue pool. The oil appeared to be coming right out of the spring itself.

One more task for a busy office. She was adding staff as fast as she could train them, and now looked around for someone to go with her to the hot spring. There was Ruth Thayer, beginning her computer training to create maps using the Geographic Information System. There were Gary Holt and Baptiste Weed, just back from wading into Bull Lake Creek to check and adjust stream-measuring gauges. And there was Michael Redman, once a member of the record-setting basketball team, now an environmental-quality technician.

CHAPTER 8

Washakie Plunge

A busy stretch of road climbs gently west from Ethete to Fort Washakie, following the Little Wind River, an axis connecting the nerve center of Arapaho government to the umbilicus of Shoshone culture. Along these eight miles the Little Wind is joined by Trout Creek from the south and Sage Creek from the north, and roads connect outlying communities from all four points of the compass. It's the very heart of the Wind River Basin, with protective hills to the north and south and generous streams arriving from all sides. A colt sleeps on its side while bay and dapple-gray mares graze in the soggy pasture by the river; smoke rises from the fire at a sweat lodge in a grove of cottonwoods; pickup trucks and old wide-body sedans pass busily back and forth, giving wide berth to a kid riding bareback by the gurgling ditch. The mountains, which heretofore have seemed distant and unattainable, are almost upon you here, rising from behind grass-covered foothills like the gates to another kingdom.

Then comes a place where once a weary rider would stop and set the horse loose and pull off his boots and shirt for a muscle-softening bath in a steaming pool. Or where, a few generations later, a carful of kids would pull the Model-T over into the sage-brush and run ripping at their clothes to climb the old wood fence for a skinny-dip. This is the hot spring that Chief Washakie figured would suffice to soothe the aches of his tribe, back in 1892, when he gave away the big Thermopolis Spring for a few dollars and steers.

Just south of the Little Wind River, the hot spring rises in a bed of white clay covered with thick mats of algae, which darkens the turquoise water to a deep green. The road west from Ethete to Fort Washakie runs close by, and across hayfields to the north a twisting line of cottonwoods marks the path of the river. The spring's plume of steam drifts west over a softball field, where the base paths are overgrown with brittle weeds. The smell is mildly sulfurous. A collecting pond feeds water into a smallish concrete pool with a slide and a diving board.

Even before the oil spill, some travelers would take a look at the sudsy scum that gathered sometimes along the edge of the pond, or at the cracked and muddy bottom, and decide they were in too much of a hurry to stop. Bathers were few, and it wasn't always clear whether or not the Washakie Plunge was open for business.

The spring pumps about four hundred gallons an hour at a temperature over 90 degrees Fahrenheit. The water emerges from the red sandstones of the Chugwater Formation, but it issues from a deeper, hotter source; faults along the Sage Creek anticline allow water to rise from hot Precambrian rocks, billions of years old and thousands of feet deep. The schematic detail of this underground plumbing is a mystery, but in the West such springs often change after seismic activity hundreds of miles away, suggesting a pressurized labyrinth of enormous size.

Vandemoer could smell the oil once she arrived. It formed a light film, thin along the side of the pool closest to the river, and had come up in some of the bathhouse soaking tubs, too. The attendant told her that in the past some darker oil had shown up in the spring, and pointed out that there was an oil seep—where oil emerges spontaneously from the ground—just across the river to the north.

The softball recreation complex adjacent to the bathhouse was weatherworn and unkempt, and the bathhouse looked out of place, with a brightly colored zigzagging roof that would have been more at home as a California drive-in, circa 1950. This run-down look is not unusual in the West, where facilities at many hot springs tend to be rustic and informal; chemicals and minerals in the water cake on the surfaces, and the sulfurous odor soaks into the walls.

In the earliest days of the reservation, this was a more popular spot than it is today. In fact, it was coveted. The soldiers stationed at Camp Brown—renamed Fort Washakie in 1898—enjoyed a good soak, and whites from nearby communities visited as well. Around the century's turn, there were three bathhouses: one for the soldiers, one for the general public, and one for Fort Washakie boarding school students who came here for their weekly bath.

The military liked the spring so much they tried in the 1880s to fence it off, along with valuable hay lands, for their exclusive use. A guard was posted in 1890, ostensibly to scare off white squatters and "fancy women" who were transacting unfancy business with soldiers. Though when the guard turned an Indian away, Chief Washakie was furious, and repeated to the commanding officer his insistence at the Thermopolis negotiations that the spring would "remain, as it always has been, for the free use of Indians and whites."

The federal agents actually might have wanted the tar pit even more than the hot spring. They were anticipating that the reservation might soon be thrown open to settlement—after each Indian was given title to his or her own piece of land under a federal allotment act—and wanted to reserve a supply of timber, hay, and tar for the military post. Washakie claimed he'd discovered the oil seep back in 1852, but whites were generally unimpressed with Indian claims of ownership. When the South Pass area was still part of the reservation (it was ceded in 1872), they didn't hesitate to move into the gold fields there; and when word got around about the tar pit by the Little Wind, a couple of enterprising fellows staked a claim to that, too.

The proud new owners probably didn't know they were invading a Shoshone burial area, but they surely knew they were on reservation land. Nevertheless, they went ahead and built a cabin over the seep, hoping to continue working through the winter. They built bunks, stored their tools, and put up a fireplace to keep warm.

David Love told me this story. A geologist now in his eighties, he grew up in the Gas Hills south of the reservation, and it's generally assumed that he knows more about the unknowable geology of the region than anyone else living or dead. Somewhat famous, thanks to John McPhee's *Rising from the Plains,* he's a light-footed, cheerful man who has spent much of his life sleeping outdoors and is still moved by an abiding curiosity to turn over whatever rock he finds at his feet. Vandemoer had corresponded with him since she began her work at Wind River, and the year after the oil appeared in the pond, they went together to have a look.

For the geologist, it was a homecoming of sorts. As a boy, Love rode horses on the reservation with Indian friends and skinny-dipped in the hot spring. His mother was a schoolteacher, and his Scottish father, a rancher, was a friend of Chief Washakie's.

The squatters at the oil seep didn't last long, according to Love, but evidence of their presence is found in globs of hard, fudge-like tar in the sagebrush hundreds of feet away from the seep. The underground deposits leaking up through these cracks also hold pockets of methane, an odorless, flammable hydrocarbon gas. When the would-be oil barons of the Washakie oil spring lit their first winter fire, the gas ignited. Their enterprise entered a phase of explosive growth, and wood and tar were scattered all around.

Whether the story is true or not—I can't find anyone else who knows of it—Love has scientific data for some of his other notions. He rendezvoused with Vandemoer at the spring in his usual gear: worn hiking boots, a red bandanna around his neck, a flop-brimmed hat, a magnifying glass on a string around his neck, a notepad in his breast pocket, and a jagged half-smile that fits his soft, chortling voice. On this visit, he also brought a scintillator— what used to be called a Geiger counter—to measure background radiation.

Colliding continents, uplifting mountains, and soft spots in the earth's crust have created beneath the Rockies an underground goulash of minerals, aquifers, and gases. Geological time zones are topsy-turvy. Oil drilling is a bettor's game. An expert like Love, who has eyeballed and walked and slept on so much of the Northern Rockies terrain, can make an educated guess about where you'll find oil or uranium or gold, but you never really know until you unpack a rig and drill some deep-down core samples. To figure out why oil was rising in the hot spring, Love and Vandemoer would rely on what she called "just good old plain bushwhacking geology."

Over several hours, they marched back and forth between the hot spring and the Little Wind River, looking at the soils and rocks, reading the scintillator dial, and mapping a grid, talking all the time. The readings confirmed what Love had noted during an aerial reconnaissance of the area in the 1950s, when uranium prospecting was in vogue: high radiation readings around the hot spring. "It's quite radioactive," said Love. "There's an area just north of the hot springs where the counts per second were about two thousand, whereas background radiation in that area is normally about sixty. When we went swimming there in high school, I guess we should've kept our knees together."

The oil in the hot spring might have come from a massive underground reservoir tapped by oil wells several miles to the north, at what's called Winkleman Dome. The field there has been producing since 1917, and in recent years oil companies have been injecting liquids back into the drill holes to increase the pressure underground and squeeze the last drops out of the deposit. Vandemoer theorized that the pressurized oil and brine had found its way through the faults running through Sage Creek anticline, the path of least resistance, and into the hot spring.

If she's right, bathers will want to look before they leap, especially if they've ever visited an oil field. Housekeeping at these sites isn't very pretty; the strangely colored water in retaining ponds around the rocking-horse rigs doesn't make for attractive wading pools. And Love, concerned by the radiation, cautioned the Indian Health Service about serious health problems among residents living near the hot spring. Nevertheless, it's an attraction. When the bath house was fixed up the following year, efforts were made to reduce the radon levels in the soaking tubs.

No one wants to speak ill of oil, either. This "black gold" makes the Shoshone and Arapaho rich by comparison with other tribes. Luckily, the value of oil wasn't as high in the nineteenth century as it is today, or McLaughlin might have been back in town for another negotiating session. Pioneers used the oil seeps in the Wind River Valley to lubricate their wagon wheels, but true fortune hunters were more interested in gold.

It was oil and gas revenue that gave the tribes enough wherewithal to hire their own lawyers in their fight for Wind River water, rather than relying completely on the federal government to look after them. And it was an incident involving oil and gas that shaped a generation of younger leaders at Wind River and taught them, as every generation of Indians has had to learn, that the government's treaty obligation to look after the tribes is no substitute for looking after themselves.

The patronizing idea that Indians a century ago were so befuddled and demoralized that smart white men robbed them blind doesn't quite gibe with what I've read in transcripts of meetings from that time. There were always outsiders ready to graze their cattle on Indian land or prospect for gold, especially during the years when disease and poverty at Wind River had reduced the Indian population to mere hundreds. And while a few Indian agents tried to clear out the thieves, others were running their own herds on reservation land and passing along sweetheart contracts to their non-Indian friends. Tribal leaders developed an early, and justified, distrust of rosy revenue promises. The problem of the Arapaho and Shoshone was that they lacked the legal authority, and the money, to shove aside the agents and do their own work.

Imagine this scene from around 1911, when they were asked to approve a plan for extensive leasing of reservation lands for grazing and coal mining. I picture a smooth pine plank table at tribal headquarters, and double-hung windows opened to clear some of the smoke from the air. Two government men sit on one side of the table in suits and ties and mustaches, with a stenographer on one side and a translator on the other. Opposite them are several empty chairs, because the Shoshone have said their piece and left the room. The Arapaho have deferred to them, because the leases in question are in the upper country, on the western, Shoshone side of the reservation, and because there is still tension over the Shoshone's claim to own the reservation exclusively. The agents sit upright, their expressions firm. One of them, the superintendent, talks fast, trying to make a quick sell; the other, from Washington, D.C., wipes his brow and smiles when he encounters resistance from Yellow Calf, an older Arapaho leader. The Washington man, a Mr. Cronin, hushes his blustery cohort and then tries to tell an instructive fable, Indian-style, to convince Yellow Calf to accept the leases: "Suppose an Indian has two saddle horses, and a white man comes to the Indian and says that he wants to hire one of the horses for a week and that he will give the Indian five dollars for the use of the horse for a week. The Indian says that it is all right, and the white man rides the horse for a week, but when he comes back with the horse at the end of the week, he tells the Indian that he hasn't got the five dollars now but will give it to him next week. After this white man has gone, another white man comes to the Indian with five dollars in his hand and says that he wants to hire the other horse for a week and that he will give the Indian the five dollars now, but the Indian says, 'No,' that he does not want the five dollars as the other white man has not paid him yet."

If his listeners were still awake, the moral of the story was: Sign this paper. Don't insist on meeting the people we're going to lease your land to. Trust us. Sign.

Yellow Calf is in his later years, a broad-faced man with soft, full lips. He hair is parted in the middle and pulled into braids that fall on the lapels of his jacket. He wears a white buttoned shirt, and holds a knotty cane. He is both a political and a spiritual leader, which is uncommon: As a young man, during the Arapaho's darkest times, he fell into a deathlike coma and returned with a vision of a renewing ritual he called the Crow Dance, which is still performed by his descendants today. He listens without expression to the horse story. When he speaks, I imagine that while his words are sarcastic, his expression is stoic and his voice monotone—a style of put-on you'll see among Arapaho today. He is deadly serious, too. He says:

"It was all good what was said and we would vote on it at any time, but I would like to think it over some more; this is not the only day, there are more days coming, and we can think this matter over. When we do anything good, we do not do it quick. You people are in a hurry for your meals. Although you have three meals a day, you are in a hurry for your supper.

"You have told us something interesting; how the government has arranged to have things in the best way that would be a benefit to the Indians, and we all appreciate that, but we ought to see the man who is going to lease this country, then we could say something to him.

"Not long ago we had a big council and Mr. McLaughlin was there"—it seems he was *always* there—"and since then we have woke up. We have never realized anything from these things that he promised us. He was so cunning that he had three coyotes following him.

"What Mr. Conin said about us having the best land is true; we have gold, silver, iron, oil, and many other things, and we have given leases for many of these and have not got anything from them, and if we got money from these we would be willing to lease others. I think we ought to talk with the man that is going to lease this land, and then we could lease whatever we wanted to."

Now it's 1981. Oil rigs are pumping on leases throughout the reservation, and though unemployment is high, there are sizable per capita checks—a tribal member's share of oil revenues—coming monthly. Wes Martel, a member of the Shoshone Business Council, and Pat Goggles, a member of the Arapaho Business Council, are flying with me back to Riverton from Arizona on a Frontier Airlines jet. They are young men, and though it's late at night after a long afternoon on airplanes, they're drinking and talking freely. In Arizona, the Council for Energy Research Tribes—an organization some critics call the Indian OPEC—gathered together leaders from about thirty reservations to discuss environmental protection, new leasing arrangements, and the price of oil and coal. We have rows and rows of seats to ourselves—the plane's virtually empty. So is the pale landscape below; on a clear, windless night, the Wyoming plains are a stirring sight. Goggles is telling me the tribes caught the oil companies with their hand in the cookie jar, and that big changes are afoot. He has a round face and curly hair, and he looks at me sideways with lidded eyes and a half-smile. "We're going to bring in new industry, do a lot of things. You better watch out. I don't know, maybe I ought to run for governor." Martel, his big head of hair bobbing in the seat behind, has a laugh so loud it nearly drowns out the engine noise of a Boeing 727.

Only when we get up to leave the plane do I realize several other tribal council members were sitting toward the rear: the old men, hunkered down in their seats, wearing dark glasses and cowboy hats. They smile at me as they shuffle silently by.

Since the beginning of the reservation era, traditional leaders in both Wind River tribes have often stayed in the background, choosing intermediaries (often "breeds") to speak for them and run the government according to their wishes. But in the 1970s, younger tribal members who had lived off the reservation and attended college returned with a stir of ideas, and something close to hope in their hearts. They had seen armed young Lakotas seize the world's attention by occupying Wounded Knee in 1973; they'd also learned from Third World oil producers, who successfully organized a cartel to push up prices. They came home energized by an odd mixture of youthful idealism, nostalgic hankering for tradition, and worldly realpolitik.

Still in his twenties, Wes Martel started a weekly reservation newspaper. "I just thought we needed one of our own," he said later. "I asked a lot of questions, and that was new, sort of semi-investigative reporting. The business council would call me in and say, 'What are you trying to do to us?' So I got elected. I became 'us.' "

Old tribal government hands like Bob Harris were still in charge, but young college-educated friends of Martel's like Orville St. Clair and John Washakie were finding their way into tribal posts. Washakie was the Shoshone finance officer. His wife worked for the Bureau of Indian Affairs, and one day she overheard a U.S. Geological Survey oil field inspector named Chuck Thomas talking to BIA officials about oil companies allegedly stealing from the reservation.

Oil prices were skyrocketing in the 1970s, but the tribes' royalties were not. In 1980, Thomas pulled over an oil truck driving across the Wind River Indian Reservation and asked to see the driver's "run ticket," which is required to remove minerals from a federal lease. He didn't have one. Suspecting such piracy might be widespread, Thomas began collecting evidence of underreporting of the quantity of oil the companies were shipping. Most of it was removed by pipeline, so he looked for breaks in the protective seals and for pipes that bypassed the measuring gauges. Neither the USGS or the BIA—both woefully understaffed—seemed very interested, but the younger tribal leaders certainly were. Late at night, Martel's van would sometimes be parked just off the highway north of Fort Washakie, counting and photographing the tankers that passed in the darkness, streaks of spilled oil on their gleaming sides. He and his friends had to set up shifts: "Those trucks just kept roaring by, twenty-four hours a day." When the van drove one day up to the old field at Winkleman Dome to see what Amoco was up to, a roughneck told them, "Don't you Indians come out here and get yourselves hurt."

"We knew how dirty it can get," Martel recalled. "Hey, it can get deadly. From then on, there were rifles in the back of the van."

Orville St. Clair consulted John King, a friend in the oil business from Denver, and he volunteered to help the tribes find the culprits. The business council refused the offer; older tribal leaders said they were skeptical of outsiders' advice, and noted that King had once been convicted of stock fraud.

Meanwhile, Chuck Thomas had been transferred to Alaska. With King's help, the young "oil scouts" (as a Shoshone attorney would later call them) brought Thomas back, and in the dark of night they toured the fields so Thomas could show them how it was done—bypasses on the pipes, oil in the wastewater ponds, no locks or seals. They took photographs, and then went public, brashly sharing the story with newspapers. They bypassed the Shoshone Business Council and took their evidence to the General Council, a gathering of the entire tribe, where they convinced the participants to discard the regular agenda and elect John Washakie as chairman. Thomas was the ambivalent, edgy star of the show—slicked hair and black clothes, necklaces dangling in his open shirt, imagining himself in a movie, one minute as a swaggering undercover man and the next a trembling assassination target. He was so nervous about his moment in the spotlight that John Washakie and an older tribal leader, Rupert Weeks, had to stand on either side of him as he addressed the people to keep him from running away.

Stories appeared in the Denver newspapers, and then in *The New York Times.* "Right about then," said Martel, "all those trucks disappeared."

For Washakie and several other young "oil scouts," it was the beginning of a career in tribal politics. Washakie soon sat beside Martel on the Shoshone Business Council, later joined by Orville St. Clair, and a group of young college-educated Arapaho, including Gary Collins, were elected to the Arapaho Business Council. "It was the beginning of a big shift," Washakie said. "From then on there was much more management by the tribes. Instead of working three half days a week, the Business Council would work six days a week." Though there are still sudden political shifts on the councils, a younger, more worldly cast has settled in. "Very soon, you'll almost have to have a degree—it's moving more and more toward an executive department. We used to sit in there and make decisions on whether we were going to buy a toilet. Now it's contracts, waivers of sovereign immunity, oil and gas, accounting, water litigation."

The tribes found it wasn't easy to cancel the oil leases, which were signed by officials from the U.S. Department of the Interior rather than the tribes, but they did recover millions of dollars in lost royalties.

The Washakie Hot Spring lies in the middle of the reservation, a midpoint between the largely Arapaho community on the east side and the Shoshone on the west. In the springtime, when the cottonwoods along the Little Wind are budding and the hayfields have begun to green up, you can lie on your back in the pool and look at the big blue palette of the sky. The Wyoming sky is always bright and unsoiled, but never the same: brush strokes of cirrus like the eyebrows of an old man, or flat-bottomed stratus burned red by the falling sun, or muscular thunderheads jousting with one another. When a wave of steam from the hot spring blows over you, it wipes the slate clean for a new design.

The pool was empty on an April twilight in 1988 when two pickups arrived at the spring from opposite directions. The two men wore jeans and boots, and one of them smoked.

"What are we going to do?" asked John Washakie, stubbing out the cigarette. He was now cochairman with Martel of the Shoshone Business Council, and Collins was chairman of the Arapaho side. In the council chambers, they worked with older leaders like Starr Weed and Burton Hutchinson, but what was bothering them now seemed too urgent for the slow-moving meetings of the joint council. Collins had been on the phone for hours before he called Washakie and asked to meet him halfway, at the hot springs.

Gary Collins squinted toward the west. He had been talking to Dick Baldes at the U.S. Fish and Wildlife Service. "They've completely cut it off," he said. "There's not a drop of water in Bull Lake Creek. Every chance they get, Midvale's going to sacrifice the fishery for their dam. There's fish stranded in pools."

"No more of this bullshit," said Washakie. "We have to just block the road." He stubbed out his cigarette and climbed back in his truck, and drove west.

CHAPTER 9

Fort Washakie (Part 1)

John Washakie drove west, upstream, where the river gets smaller and it also gets livelier, because the ground is getting steeper. We are beginning to climb the flanks of the mountains. Though there is smooth pasture on either side of the road from the hot springs to Fort Washakie, there's more roll to the landscape, more frequent interludes of bush and tree, and a sense, even with sun on your shoulder, that you have moved into the shadow of the exalted Wind River Mountains. They were right there before Washakie as he turned onto Highway 287 at Fort Washakie: a clown's hat of many peaks, ringed by hummocks of rocky moraine around the canyon mouths, and a soft-rising cuesta that turns abruptly upward where it laps against the hard granite of the range. In twenty minutes you could be up there in the pines, standing on a boulder casting to cutthroat trout. But first we had to visit the seat of reservation government.

Dick Baldes had been sitting on a seat of government—an orange plastic chair in the lobby outside the Joint Business Council chambers—for most of the afternoon, waiting to talk about Bull Lake and Bull Lake Creek. He had in his lap a 1986 study suggesting that fish had stopped reproducing in the lake when their shallow spawning beds dried out. This happened as the reservoir at Bull Lake was drawn down to water farmers' fields in the Riverton Unit. Next to him sat Eric Bergersen, the sandy-haired biologist from Fort Collins who had directed the study. The hour of their appointment had passed. Bergersen assured Baldes that he was in no hurry.

Outside the tinted glass doors of the tribal headquarters, spring was budding out along the Little Wind River, which runs along the northern edge of Fort Washakie. This is where the Shoshone settled in the 1870s, as they gradually cut back their roaming and accepted the reservation: the sheltering mouth of the valley, where streams gather after emerging from the mountains through steep-walled canyons. It's the kind of place a hunting tribe would naturally gravitate toward, the edge between plains and mountains where so many animals shelter in order to survive the winter. The plains are too exposed, icy and windblown; the snow in the mountains is too deep for foraging. The hills and escarpments around the canyons provided windbreaks, patches of snow-free vegetation, and irregular cover.

In addition to game, this upper end of the valley offered the Shoshone a quick escape into the high country if enemies should appear. It was laced with dependable streams to drink from and perhaps, given Washakie's interest in farming, to irrigate crops with. The military put up its first buildings at Camp Brown, then changed the name to Fort Washakie in honor of the Shoshone chief. From the earliest days of the reservation, this was where the white and Indian worlds connected.

Though established for over a century, Fort Washakie today feels as if it's only now becoming a town. The gas station and garage are new. There's only one restaurant, and you won't find it without directions. The small subdivisions south of town look unwanted; few residents have planted a tree or a garden, and those who can will eventually move out to a place in the country. But Fort Washakie does boast a grocery store, a rodeo and powwow grounds, a health clinic, and a bunch of government buildings, which, despite the departure of the Arapaho, provide a great many jobs. White rocks on the hill north of the river are arranged to read FORT WASHAKIE, but on rare mornings it says FART.

Especially in the spring, when the hills have the soft green glow of new buds and the trout are snapping at the first bug hatches, you feel lucky to be here. That's the way Bergersen felt, though he would have felt luckier on a riverbank than sitting in the lobby. He had some big ideas to pitch to the tribes: a plan to manage the whole length of the river from its sources near the Divide to the canyon where it left the basin, using what he called a River Continuum Concept. He saw damage along reservation streams from grazing and diversions, but it was not irreversible, and in fact there was an unusual opportunity: in his mind he could erase the sediment clogging the system and see a clear, boulder-cobbled stream. There were actually fewer disturbances here than on most rivers in the West, and a surprising variety of fish species. His plan would "develop a river in terms of what it should be," and he planned to devote the rest of his career to this watershed.

The thin-backed chairs in the joint tribal building lobby are joined together like airport seating, in a small rectangle across from the reception counter. The beehive-haired receptionist, Edith Johnson, looks as if she's been sitting there since the building was erected, behind a counter full of cupcakes and cookies that women have brought in to sell. The frosted battlements make it difficult to see what exactly she does, but now and then she talks into the phone in a gravelly voice.

In the early 1980s, when Bob Harris was running the council, Baldes and Bergersen would have been ushered right in. Though Harris had told Baldes it was a bad idea to return and work at Wind River with the U.S. Fish and Wildife Service, once he was back, Harris was eager to support his efforts to restore game and fish on the reservation. That was a little-known part of the FWS mission: to assist tribes. Even when that assistance was controversial—as when Baldes and his biologists proposed a game code that would limit tribal hunting in order to rebuild antelope and elk herds—Harris was there to exert his considerable political muscle on Baldes's behalf.

But in the late 1980s, Harris was back on his ranch along the Wind River, and the council was dominated by the cadre of brash young leaders with college educations and big new ideas—young men like Baldes. Water was high on their list: they were aggressively fighting for tribal water rights in the courts and pushing agencies like the U.S. Bureau of Reclamation, which managed Bull Lake Dam, to conserve water for the Riverton Unit, to balance the agency's irrigation mission with better protection of tribal resources.

A few years before, visitors had lowered their voices when they entered the lobby, as if it were a nursery of sleeping children; now the phones were ringing, harried secretaries dropped papers in the hall, and voices were raised in argument and laughter. There were also sudden trips to Montana and Washington, D.C., piles of phone messages on desktop spikes, and meetings trumping other meetings—a governmental thrill ride, some thought; a runaway train, thought others. In all this excitement the councils were sometimes too busy for courtesy or details, and they didn't always find time for reports like the study in Baldes's lap, the kind of scientific ammunition required for the water wars.

Baldes was sensitive to slights. What he brought to the council had been high-priority under Bob Harris. Now the style was to keep almost everyone waiting for hours—a view that was voiced, gingerly, whenever lawyers, businessmen, or reporters got up from the orange seats and stepped outside the building to commiserate in the squinty sun. They wondered whether it was proper to ask when in the afternoon their 10 a.m. appointment would be kept, and if so, who to ask: Edith, hunkered down behind the cupcakes? Every so often a council member would emerge from the double doors of the council chamber and swing quickly into a restroom, or greet an Indian family with restless children rolling on the lobby carpet. And now and then, if a waiting supplicant was bold enough to ask, the councilman might tell him, "Oh, sorry. Right now we don't have a quorum."

The joint tribal office building has two long wings running east and west, with shallow offices on each side of the hallway. At the center, the council chamber bulges out the back side of the building, and on either side there are exits through which members can slip outside for a smoke—or slip out into the parking lot and drive away, with no one in the lobby any wiser until the sun goes down and a custodian opens the double doors to air out the empty chamber.

When you gain an audience, other frustrations can follow. I once introduced a fellow from Habitat for Humanity to the Joint Shoshone and Arapaho Business Council. He knew from his research that the reservation suffered from a serious housing shortage, and was eager to offer his help. The council members sit on a raised bench that angles around the witness table: Arapaho on the right, Shoshone on the left. A picture of Washakie hangs on the left side, and one of Black Coal on the right. An American flag is prominently displayed. The dress is informal, and there are the usual boxes of doughnuts on a counter by the door.

The Habitat fellow gave them a good spiel, emphasizing the need for locals to take control with a do-it-yourself housing project using Habitat materials and volunteer assistance. When he finished, the chairwoman looked around at her colleagues, then thanked him, and that was it. No questions. As we left, most of the members' heads were bowed toward their desks. This lack of engagement frustrates some visitors and angers others. But what might seem hostility or indifference or inarticulateness is, I think, a cautious and touching shyness.

Tribal government is a mystery to most outsiders, partly because those double doors remain closed to the press and casual observers, and partly because Indians have found invisibility a useful survival tool since the conquest. The very idea of separate sovereign governments carved from the heartland of the United States is hard for many Americans to accept, and the Indians know that, so they do their business quietly. Even harder for outsiders to accept is the notion that within reservation boundaries certain parts of the U.S. Constitution don't apply—separation of church and state, for instance, or individual rights such as the right to bear arms or the right to a jury trial. That sounds positively subversive.

But reservations are not nation-states. Whatever a tribal government does can be trumped by the federal government, based on a paternalistic "trust" duty to protect tribal assets. U.S. Supreme Court Justice John Marshall, in 1831, called the tribes "domestic dependent nations," an interesting blend of autonomy and vassalage.

Actually, there's a rich history of Native American governance that predates Columbus, and some of it was borrowed by the founding fathers of the United States; for instance, the Constitution of the Iroquois League, written on a wampum belt in seashells, was a model for Ben Franklin's Articles of Confederation.

Among the many tribes of early America (more than five hundred, by some estimates), there were diverse styles of government. But some generalizations can be made: those tribes we know tended to be decentralized and, particularly in smaller bands, democratic in the manner of a New England town meeting. Leadership roles were often divvied up by clan, and spiritual leaders were consulted and deferred to. The Indians had a flair that the Europeans lacked when it came to titling their officers: in the Iroquois League, for example, there were Keepers of the Fire, who acted as moderators at meetings, and Solitary Pine Trees, who had earned the right to speak through acts of valor but couldn't vote at council meetings. Military and civil leaders often came from separate castes, and the latter often bent over backwards to understand and embody the will of the people; indeed, the most respected leaders styled themselves as self effacing *followers*. This tendency, carried forward into modern times, frustrated federal government officials who wanted in each tribe a single strong leader with whom they could make a deal. That partly explains Washakie's popularity with the U.S. negotiators: he exercised absolute authority. But this was not the style of the tribal leaders who came before and after him.

In 1927, for example, decades after Washakie's death, the superintendent of Wind River, Reuben P. Haas, came to the tribal Joint Business Council asking them to approve setting aside a small fund from tribal revenues to make loans to Indians for houses and farming equipment. The $15,000 would be repaid into a revolving fund. Haas kept asking the Indians for a vote, and council members kept saying they weren't ready. Federal officials were always approaching the tribes with a new deal: Okay, you've gotten a poor shake in the past, but I'm new, let's start over. Clean slate, the American way. Trust me, it's simple, it's for the good of your people. The Indians, of course, knew their history, and remembered it by reciting it, including a list of past wrongs that, it seemed to them, ought to be righted before they accepted any new ideas from the agent. So they asked, What about water rights, or welfare grants for older Indians, or per capita payments?

Finally, the exasperated superintendent said, "You councilmen were elected by the voice of your people, and in your election they expressed their confidence in you to transact their business, so it would seem to me that it is up to you councilmen as to what you want to do—whether it is best for your tribe or not."

The councilmen didn't immediately respond to this cranky notion of governance (perhaps smoothed out by interpreters), and the meeting droned on. The superintendent tried to call for a vote, but Charles Snyder interrupted him: "Mr. Haas, the Shoshone councilmen would like to take a vote among the Shoshone first, so that we will know what they want and they can't blame us for signing or rejecting anything they don't like."

Haas, nearing his breaking point, said, "You mean *all* the Shoshones here?" He took a glassy-eyed look at the many Shoshone leaning against the walls, and then surrendered. "All right . . . I think that will be all right for you to do that."

Another Shoshone spoke: "But Mr. Haas, I object because the Shoshones aren't *all* here."

Haas slumped in his seat. Objection followed objection. When the superintendent insisted again that the councilmen decide, he got this unruffled reply: "We are not ready to vote. We want to vote some other time."

By this time the tribes had a wealth of experience with the ways of the federal agents, and realized that many of the programs implemented for the "good" of the tribes had been thinly disguised mechanisms to dismantle reservations. Even Habitat for Humanity might have seemed a Trojan horse (several years later, it's worth noting, the patient Habitat folks have a program up and running at Wind River). Back in the 1930s, the federal Indian Reorganization Act ended the allotment program, which had been converting tribal lands into private ownership, and offered tribes more power to develop their economies and run their own programs . . . *if* they adopted a U.S.-style Constitution. The Wind River tribes rejected this, suspecting it would somehow be used against them. When they expressed their wariness, tribal members often referred to the 1905 agreement that created the Riverton Unit; they were promised then that if they gave up the land north of the river, their water would be secured, so why wasn't it? The Indian Reorganization Act had nothing to do with that, government officials argued. But it did—all the broken promises did. Mark Soldierwolf's father, Scott Dewey, voiced the tribes' distrust when he told a meeting on reorganization that historically "the policy of the government has been to rob and to cheat and to beat the Indian of his property." Old Yellow Calf got up and said, "The white people are smart and they can foresee things a long ways ahead and there might be a time when I will be lifted clear off this reservation and put somewhere else." Indian irony again.

The tribes were always at a disadvantage dealing with the federal government, which could at any moment exercise its "trust" responsibility and erase a tribal decision, so it made sense to hem and haw and skip meetings. Delay was a kind of victory.

When they weren't dealing with federal officials, though, tribal leaders moved at a brisker clip. The traditional people identified youngsters with a talent for secular government, and groomed them for the business councils. This included "breeds" like Bob Harris, and several women who took prominent roles, including Nell Scott of the Arapaho and Maud Clairmont of the Shoshone. Meetings were run efficiently, and non-Indians—as long as they didn't work for the federal government—were generally treated fairly.

Carroll Riggs, the Midvale farmer who had come from Oklahoma brimming with energy and ideas, took a lease on some reservation land in the 1950s. He came to the Joint Business Council because the tribal land office had leased the same land to an Indian farmer after one of their officials had said the Indian "needs it very bad" and ought to get it. But Riggs had built a road and cleared sagebrush to begin irrigating the land, and he still had a year to go on his lease, which he'd paid at the outset. "Being a stranger here at the time," he said, "I didn't know anyone well enough to go my bond, so I paid the whole rental in advance for the five years."

Pleading before the council, Riggs humbly asked them to put themselves in his position, appealing for fairness. But when he began talking about what he was doing with the tribes' ten acres—experimenting with a red-clover crop—he grew more animated.

Trying out new things excited him. "Of course, I won't get an answer on how it came through the winter until next year," he told the council. "So naturally I wouldn't want to break that up. As you know, it's quite a job putting sagebrush land into water the first year."

But the fellow from the land office kept defending the Indian lease, until Maud Clairmont finally cut him off. "I don't see any reason why we should give that any consideration at all," she said curtly. "I think we should give consideration to the person who leased it first. . . . Being fair, that is the only thing we could do."

The council agreed with her, and even invited Riggs to extend the lease.

The business councils were not a natural outgrowth of either Arapaho or Shoshone political culture. The system was imposed by the federal agents, so they would have a discernible governing body to deal with during the allotment period, when many tracts of reservation land were moving into non-Indian ownership. Before that, traditional government in both tribes was densely layered, with spiritual leaders like the Arapaho's Water-Sprinkling Old Men keeping a steady but mysteriously still hand on the helm while younger leaders acted and spoke for them. This ancient hierarchy began fading in the twentieth century, and few Indians today could tell you whether they belong to the Mountain People or the Nose Diggers (Shoshone clans), or the Kit Fox Men or Crazy Lodge (Arapaho).

Well into modern times, though, the traditional people still pulled the strings, while keeping their distance from whites by often using lighter-skinned tribal members of mixed blood such as Bob Harris as middle men. Anthropologist Loretta Fowler, in her book *Arapaho Politics, 1851–1978* proposed that the tribe has taken the new council system and, while appearing to accept a non-Indian model, slyly adapted it to their old ways. I'm not so sure. Sometimes, these days, it doesn't work.

The business councils, six-member bodies elected every two years, are not the topmost governmental branch of the tribes. Over them rule the General Councils, a legislature that includes every member of the tribe. "It's government by town meeting, the sort of thing Ross Perot advocated when he was running for president," said Dave Allison, a former BIA superintendent at Wind River. He used to attend General Council meetings, reporting from the federal government and sometimes wielding the gavel. He chuckled at the memory. "Obviously, Perot never sat in on a General Council meeting."

Neither have I, but I've interviewed participants and read some transcripts. In recent years, General Council meetings have sometimes become the stage for personal vendettas and political sparring among powerful reservation families. One group shows up to get a tribal employee fired because he disciplined a relative; another may try to throw out an entire elected business council. Many people vote strictly according to familial alliances. General Councils are held at irregular intervals and can extend for days, allowing organized factions to wait until tired opponents head for home before calling for a vote. Attendance has declined, whether from frustration or boredom. Members of both tribes tell me they simply don't go anymore, and the Shoshone have failed repeatedly in recent years to get a General Council quorum.

The mayhem at General Council meetings stems, according to some, from the decline of the traditional order, when elders quietly let the people know what was best for the tribe and the council followed their advice. With so few private jobs on the reservation, the government is now the biggest patronage operation in the valley, and family groups angle for control, demanding a piece of the action and sometimes using the General Council to bring down the officials who stand in their way. Dick Baldes was once fired by a Shoshone General Council because a member of a powerful family had been cited by the tribal Game and Fish Department. Baldes reminded the council that he was actually employed by the U.S. Fish and Wildlife Service, not the tribes, but they passed the resolution firing him anyway.

In 1991, three years after Gary Collins narrowly lost reelection to the business council, his successors were ambushed at an Arapaho General Council meeting. Collins was in on the well-planned attack, which was aimed particularly at Virginia Sutter, another college-educated Arapaho, who had charged into office that fall with blunt talk about cleaning up incompetence and financial chaos. In the go-go years after the oil scandal was uncovered, the Arapaho Business Council had trouble saying no, and money was disbursed for all sorts of business ventures and individual grants. Most tribal members had heard rumors that recent councilmen were being investigated by the FBI, and there was talk that $7 million had disappeared. (Though indictments were never brought, the FBI prepared charges that about $8,000 was misused by council members in the late 1980s.) Sutter was on to something, but she had the people skills of a drill sergeant, and she made enemies fast.

At the 1991 General Council, a motion was made to render null and void the election of 1990 and reinstate the previous council. Molly O'Neal, a young woman elected at the same time as Sutter, was warned ahead of time, but she sat in Blue Sky Hall and watched the coup unfold in disbelief. The only elder to speak at the meeting was Pius Moss, who rose and walked with his cane to the front of the room. Though elders once played a prominent role in General Council, not many attend these days, and it's uncommon for an elder to address a political issue directly, but Moss was uncommonly upset by the turmoil of recent elections.

Moss is a big bear, slightly bent by arthritis, and when he's thinking hard he squints and tilts his gray head to one side. Years of teaching small children at St. Stephens have softened his growl, but when he spoke to the council his face was furrowed and dark, his arm extended and imploring. Occasionally switching from English to Arapaho, Moss told the council it would be a mistake to boot the elected business council. "Now, when we have elections like this, it should be final, no argument, because I respect the thoughts of the people, every Arapaho voting member of the tribe. I respect your thoughts. Now, [this council has] just started. We haven't had time enough to voice our opinions on the selection. It takes two years before you can change your mind. And I believe at this time that the words I've said, you kind of ponder them, think about them."

They didn't ponder long. The proponents of the ouster had their votes lined up ahead of time, like skilled ward heelers. The council was ousted by a 203–134 vote. (Tribal enrollment for the Arapaho tribe in 1998 is about four thousand, including children.)

Molly O'Neal was in shock, unsure of what to do, so she spent the night at a friend's house to avoid the phone. In the morning, when she checked her messages, there was one from a tribal elder: "I don't like talking to a machine," said an old lady, who nonetheless went on: "When you get thrown off a horse, you get back on and ride. Only this time, use the spurs."

Flanking the lobby where Baldes and Bergersen waited for the JBC were separate offices for the Shoshone and, before their move to Ethete, the Arapaho. The Arapaho's departure is just one indication that all is not well between the two tribes. The Shoshone, who have fewer enrolled members, insist on splitting reservation revenues and federal support 50–50—which can mean smaller per capita payments and a lack of housing funds, among other things, for the Arapaho. During the most bitter periods, joint projects are often waylaid because one tribe may simply stop showing up for meetings. The Arapaho periodically propose dividing the reservation in half, sick and tired of second-class treatment.

A dinner more than a century ago illustrates the historic delicacy of tribal relations.

Washakie and the Arapaho chiefs Black Coal and Sharp Nose were among the most admired Indian leaders in the West, and they seemed to enjoy swapping stories with the army officers about battles on the frontier, like old football players remember the gridiron where they once banged one another around. Usually, the post commanders were careful to socialize separately with leaders from the two tribes. On one occasion, though, all three chiefs were invited to a meal in the officers' mess. Buffered by translators—which Sharp Nose and Washakie didn't really need—they ate and talked pleasantly enough, discussing, among other things, the Battle of Little Bighorn. Washakie and Black Coal had both warned the U.S. military of the Sioux strategy in 1876; though several Arapaho participated in the attack on Custer, tribal leaders stayed on the sidelines, trying to win support for their own reservation.

The Indians generally ate whatever food was put before them—all of it. As the storytelling and drinking went on, one of the younger officers, as a prank, filled Black Coal's glass with Worcestershire sauce. When a toast was proposed, Black Coal tossed it back, winced at the taste, and then, respectful of ritual, put the glass down and in a choked voice complimented his hosts on the strong drink. All this was done straight-faced, but more experienced officers recognized a dangerous moment. If Black Coal felt singled out for ridicule, equilibrium would be lost and the consequences could be dire. One of the officers surreptitiously filled Washakie's glass with the same Worcestershire. But before he lifted his glass, Washakie asked Black Coal, "Why do the tears come to Black Coal's eyes when he drinks the firewater of the soldiers?"

A bad moment, for sure. Black Coal had to wonder if Washakie had conspired in the prank. The Arapaho chief looked at him gravely and responded, "Because Black Coal is thinking of his dead grandmother."

The soldiers in the room were immediately watchful and sober. Indian kinship recognizes many grandmothers—and what if one of Black Coal's had been killed by Shoshone?

Then Washakie stood and drank his potion, too, as the officers watched with relief. As he finished the last drop, Black Coal asked, "Why do the tears come to Washakie's eyes when he takes the white man's drink?"

Washakie put down his glass, wiped his mouth, and said, "Because Black Coal did not die when his grandmother did."

After a moment's pause, everyone was laughing—uproariously, much harder than they had to.

Shifting the Arapaho offices to Ethete might actually have improved relations between the tribes, if the cooperation between the young leaders of the late 1980s is any indication. Also, the rigid segregation of half a century ago is now crumbling; there are many "Sho-raps" with relatives in both tribes, including Wes Martel.

There seemed no room for old grudges on the agenda that was

already building in the lobby. Martel, Collins, Washakie, and several other young leaders new on the council had the confidence to speed up change, and they had money to spend, thanks to a windfall of recovered royalties from the oil and gas thefts, and from new, more favorable contracts with several energy companies. They did a lot, maybe too much. Years later, Collins would wonder if "maybe we were just too aggressive." He's still dogged by a reputation for misusing his tribe's money, though an FBI investigation of several council members resulted in no charges. "The time was ripe, but we moved too fast, bought assets, equipment. The people lagged back, they didn't know what we were doing."

Meanwhile, the meetings lagged too. Baldes was embarrassed that Bergersen had to sit in the lobby all afternoon after his long drive from Fort Collins. Once they got in, he expected the JBC would be interested. Wes Martel could digest the study instantly and start citing it the next day.

Bergersen had photographs that showed how low Bull Lake got after the irrigators drank their fill. When the lake falls twelve feet below normal levels, the beds are eroded by wind and wave action. Ling cod spawn in the winter, broadcasting their eggs in the sandy shallows. When the ice broke in the spring, Bergersen and his assistants had trawled for larval ling in the shallows and retrieved empty nets. The ling may not have spawned at all in 1986.

When I walked into the lobby that day, all the seats were occupied—people in suits looking chafed, with folders in their laps. Baldes's and Bergersen's heads were together, elbows on their knees, talking. The results of the ling survey, added to past research, had prompted new ideas. Electrofishing and creel surveys told them the cold-water fish were diminishing in the Wind River, but it would take a big fish study on the entire river to tie that solidly to irrigation diversions or other factors. As the hours went by, their plans grew into a complete watershed study, ten years in the making, starting at the alpine lakes. Bergersen was enraptured with an idea that could be the capstone of his career.

My career at that point was working for a newspaper, and I wandered around the perimeter of the lobby, past the cookies and cupcakes on Edith Johnson's desk, reading the notices and posters on the walls, which formed an interesting collage of reservation life. Here's most of it, with my annotations:

Ladies Slow Pitch Softball League   (exciting to watch: these guys are good)

Farm/pasture leases due to expire   (many of these tribal leases for irrigable lands are held by non-Indians)

Whiterock Beardance Powwow   (the summer powwow circuit runs from May to September, all over the Plains, with some *big* purses)

"Speak Up for the Child" Special Advocate Program   (child neglect is a problem, despite—and some would say because of—Indian extended families)

Community Diabetes Screening   (Indian metabolism still hasn't adjusted to European diets and sedentary lives)

Teen Boys Basketball Tournament   (like the game you see on the best inner-city courts; these guys are *real* good)

Vehicle Registration Exemption   (to the chagrin of county treasurers, tribal members don't have to pay the fees)

Take Action! Demand Justice! End Sexual Violence!   (another very real problem)

Alcohol—We're Not Buying It!   (a bunch of hip, happy, hugging, hygienic, heterogenous teens, including a drop-dead gorgeous Native American girl . . . uh, can we identify?)

Wind River Indian Reservation Fishing Permits   (if you ask me, the most valuable license in Wyoming—or perhaps the country)

Then I heard Martel's voice booming up and down the hallway of the west wing, and I headed over. He waved me into his office, then leaned back and put his hands behind his big rooster's-head of black hair. I told him that I'd promised my editor stories from the reservation and now had to figure out where those stories were. The phone rang before he could respond, and he was on it, breaking someone else's eardrum. Martel's voice is huge without shouting.

Orville St. Clair came in, and we talked beneath the roar of Martel about basketball, which we'd played together once or twice. I mentioned that there were quite a few people waiting in the lobby, including some BIA officials.

Martel was off the phone. "Yeah," he said, "I think the superintendent wanted to meet with us today, he was over there. Might not get to that one." He and St. Clair smiled at each other, enjoying their mischief.

"So does he come over here, or do you go over there?" I asked. The BIA offices were across the road, a short walk past the post office.

"Oh, he comes to see us pretty regular," said Martel. "You know the BIA: 'Boss Indians Around.' "

Even a smart and sympathetic superintendent isn't likely to be popular with tribal leaders, because his job is to act like a parent, holding the keys to the reservation car and grounding the Indian government if it breaks the rules. In the 1950s, Monroe Marlowe told me, an angry tribal council marched across the road to the BIA offices, tied the superintendent to his chair, stuck him in the back of a truck, and drove him to the border of the reservation, where they sat him beside the road. Then they went back to the tribal offices and got on with their business. When I've asked old-timers if this is apocryphal, they roll their eyes and smile.

Sitting in his office at the end of the day, Martel leaned back and stretched, shook his head, and smiled. "Well, he'll just have to wait today. I don't think we have a quorum just now."

Then he remembered my question, and said, "You want some stories, huh? Well, if you want stories, follow the water. Just follow the water."

Dumb and dutiful, I wrote it down.

CHAPTER 10

Fort Washakie (Part 2)

A century ago, engineers followed the water of the Wind River Valley back into the foothills, where limestone beds were tilted up in angled sheets by the rising Rocky Mountains, then punctured by streams of snowmelt pouring off the peaks. They were looking for a place to put a dam. I went west of Fort Washakie looking for their footprints.

The engineers sought canyon mouths where concrete plugs might be inserted to make a holding tank; they looked for oxbows where water would gladly spare itself the turn and go straight off in a ditch; they looked for contours along the edge of the valley where canals might carry water above the bottomlands.

Some of these engineers had college degrees and crews of rod men and plane-table men; others were determined farmers who would squint at the land and guess at a reliable grade, then apply themselves with a shovel. To realize that the mountains just west of the Wind River Valley held off the worst weather took no special education, just a squinting eye and a winter's worth of patient observation. With its water, its wide valley, and its curving rivers, this potentially was the best farmland in the state, and there was the additional prospect of power-generating streams. "The [Little Wind River] has just emerged through a short canyon from the long rolling outlines of the mountains," wrote Captain William A. Jones of the Army Corps of Engineers in 1873, "and shows a broad, flat, and well-watered valley of rich soil. A large area of land in this valley could be irrigated with but little expense." Yet it belonged to the Indians, who were the furthest thing from farmers.

Cultivation was under way in the Americas before the arrival of Europeans, but not, from the archaeological evidence, in the Wind River Valley. Elsewhere, around the Great Lakes, in the South and Southwest, in Mexico and South America, Native Americans had been irrigating and raising crops for centuries before Columbus. The stratified, highly organized political and economic systems of the Aztec and Maya were supported by an extensive water-distribution system and farms that enabled them to feed large populations in their magnificent cities. In the Southwest, ancient civilizations like the Hohokam showed their engineering savvy in elaborate networks of canals, then mysteriously abandoned them.

But the ancient Indians of the Wind River Valley were not farmers. The earliest known residents traveled by foot in the mountains, leaving only their mysterious messages carved in the sandstone by the streams and lakes. They might have been distantly related to the Shoshone, who seem to have wandered like gypsies around the central Rockies, well before the Europeans arrived with horses and the buffalo culture took shape. Archaeologists have found shards of Shoshone-style prehistoric pottery around Yellowstone, near the Great Salt Lake, and down in what's now southeast Wyoming.

While the Arapaho had migrated west and south to the Wyoming plains, the Shoshone came east. They differed physically: The Shoshone were "short and stout," said the Episcopal missionary John Roberts, who spent his lifetime on the reservation, while the Arapaho were the "tallest and largest of the people of any race, except the Russians." The differences between the two cultures went deeper than appearance. The Arapaho, like most Plains tribes, were of Algonquin language stock, spreading west from the Northeast and Great Lakes regions. The Shoshone language springs from the same root as the Aztecs', and their closest relatives in North America were the scraggly nomads who lived in the Great Basin between the Sierras and the Rockies. These "Diggers" lived a mean existence, huddled in roofless brush huts, subsisting on roots and berries and small game. Bands to the north found a better life along the rivers, supplementing their diets with fish and allying with the Bannock. But the Shoshone who shifted eastward found greater prosperity in the territory between the Great Salt Lake and the Wind River Mountains, a fertile seam between the desert and the glaciers, rich with bison, deer, and fish.

They made early, friendly contact with white fur trappers, often an intimate contact that produced *metis* children, like the infant carried by Sacajawea (the child's father, French trapper Louis Charboneau, was also a guide on the Lewis and Clark expedition). The legendary mountain man Jim Bridger married, among others, a daughter of one of his Indian trapping companions, Washakie.

We can't begin to imagine how fast the world was changing for the Indian. The shock of the New World to European immigrants was nothing compared with this: In just a couple of generations, there came a four-legged animal that could run down game and carry a man far afield, an aggressive race of light-skinned people, lethal new diseases that wiped out entire villages, and the enormous mayhem of the gun. (In return, it's often noted, Indians gave the Europeans, among other things, potatoes, corn, loads of silver, tobacco, a cure for malaria, chocolate, and possibly venereal disease.) Indian communities were suddenly larger, suddenly uprooted, suddenly wealthy, suddenly at war!

The Shoshone were quick to adapt: With the horse, they bullied old enemies like the Blackfeet and roamed far east of the Rockies, pursuing the great bison herds. Over a system of beliefs and history rooted in the hardscrabble desert of the Great Basin, they pulled on the flamboyant culture and finery of the Plains tribes.

These warriors, with their colorful wardrobes and gladiator mettle, have long been the emblem, in the world's imagination, of the American Indian of yore. I wonder sometimes whether we've got the right people for the job. The Plains Indians' brief stardom—promoted by the whites who collided with them on the western frontier—might better be seen as a temporary aberration, even a delusion. Many tribes were pushed onto the Great Plains by the growing population in the East, like immigrants tumbling out of a crowded ship, and they adjusted nimbly to a region too arid and sparse for big settlements. But for the horse and rifle, it would've been a most ungenerous environment. Along with new skills, and a new community order, there seems to have been an enormous erasure and transformation of memory and beliefs—the Arapaho, for example, remember almost nothing of their farming history in the Red River Valley, only a few centuries before. In a new environment, a new explanation was needed for the way the world was. There were hints of a cultural ache, an impending exhaustion, in the eccentric cruelties and wanderlust of the Plains cultures, and perhaps this would've become more explicit if the invading whites hadn't brought it all to a quick, sad end.

By the late nineteenth century, the bison had been obliterated and the tribes defeated and banished to the reservations. Despite their perceived friendship toward whites, the Shoshone were punished alongside so many other tribes. A large camp led by Bear Hunter, who had lured the more warlike of the Shoshone away from Washakie in the 1860s, was massacred by the army in a four-hour battle at Bear Lake in what is now Utah, leaving over two hundred Indians dead and many more captured.

That defeat brought the loosely affiliated Shoshone bands closer to Washakie, and convinced various factions to follow him onto the reservation. That very idea—a reservation, with inflexible borders determined by law—took years of getting used to. In the 1860s, the Shoshone were moving as they always had, one step behind the game and one ahead of adversary tribes: they'd begin the spring along the Green River on the west side of the Wind River Mountains, go south in the summer to the Sweetwater country near Jim Bridger's trading post, then come north for a late fall hunt into the Wind River Valley, where they would stay until spring. The U.S. government had two more reasons for wanting the Shoshone to stay on the reservation: they wanted them far away from the settlements along the railroad line that now ran through Bridger's country, and they wanted them to serve as a buffer between whites and the Sioux to the north. But once the snows melted, the Shoshone would cross the mountains through what's now called Washakie Pass to Green River and begin the circuit again. They were reluctant to settle year-round by the Wind River until a promised military post was in place, fearing the more numerous Sioux would prey on them there. Besides, they liked to travel. It was their life.

Within a few years of signing the 1868 treaty, the Shoshone got the message. They saw the bison herds rapidly dwindling, they felt hostile white settlers crowding around, and they heard federal agents talking about the sedentary rewards of farming. The location of Fort Washakie fit their notions of a good campsite: next to a river, near the good hunting of the high country, and sheltered from the open blows of the winter. Though they had moved out onto the Plains, the Shoshone never lost their attachment to the mountains, particularly to this deep and craggy range that dangled south of the Yellowstone Plateau, where a handful of related Sheepeater Indians lived their secretive lives among the giants and little people of the tribe's stories. If white allies couldn't provide promised protection, it would be easy to escape enemy tribes by retreating into the forests and hills.

All that, and irrigation, too.

U.S. Army engineers were the first to map out the broad potential for harnessing the Wind River water. In the late nineteenth century, the military wore many hats in the West: park managers in Yellowstone, road builders for the pioneers, and peacemakers to protect everyone from everyone else. Their first priority was to protect the miners in South Pass from marauding Sioux and Arapaho, but those tribes were also harassing the Shoshone, who had now allied themselves with the United States. In 1870, the military post was moved near the present government center on the Little Wind River.

For some of the soldiers it might have been a lonely outpost, but they could've done worse. The daughter of one of the officers stationed there remembered lying in a hammock under stars so brilliant she could read by them, awash in the "perfume" of summer wildflowers. Her father sat nearby sucking on his pipe, and she listened to the gentle chortle of a ditch as she traced the path of the Milky Way with a finger held up toward the sky. At 9 p.m., lights-out time for the barracks, a bugler played taps, and as the last notes faded away, a coyote took up the job. From another hill came an answer, and then another, and soon the valley echoed like a hollow gourd with a riot of yelps and howls. Gradually, the coyotes quieted and there rose a new sound, faint at first: Indian drums, a steady rhythm that seemed to travel through the ground from the firelit camps across the valley. The song grew louder, and she lay in a trance, the chanting of the men and the shrill tremolo of the women bouncing off the stars.

When the army moved its troops onto the reservation in 1871, cabins began replacing tents as the Shoshone took the first step toward a domestic life. Chief Washakie, familiar with the Mormons' success in irrigating the Utah desert, was ready to give farming a try. The 1868 treaty also had nudged the Indians in that direction, through provisions that gave each adult Indian seed, $100 of farming equipment, land, and a cotton shirt, among other things. If a Shoshone farmed, he would get $20 annually; if he roamed, he got only $10. The Shoshone had plows, they had cows, and they had their very own farmer.

Finn Burnett was his name. He was really just a youngster from the Midwest adventuring on the frontier, newly married and already well stocked with hearthside stories of hand-to-hand combat with the savages. He arrived in 1871 and worked with other agency employees to finish fortifications and log homes for themselves. The stories he shared with his mates often featured Arapaho villains: he described a woman "old and gnarled like an oak" greeting an army major with a smile and then trying to clobber him with a war club hidden behind her back. This unsportsmanlike act took place in 1865 during an army attack in which Burnett himself turned a Howitzer on an Arapaho camp along Montana's Tongue River; the officer responded by "accidentally" shooting the old woman in the head.

Burnett would despise the Arapaho the rest of his life, but he admired the Shoshone. It was his job to teach them how to farm, and the effort focused initially on a 320-acre plot of land west of the new agency buildings. A friend of the superintendent's was hired to plow the land in 1870 and 1871, but nothing was planted until the third year, because government-promised seeds and equipment failed to arrive on time—a recurrent problem during the transition years at Wind River. Game was dwindling fast in the valley, so the failure to grow food was felt acutely by the Indians.

The first Shoshone attempt at farming was a Keystone Kops adventure. Horses were hitched to shiny new plows, and the men lined up in a row behind them on one edge of the field, like competitors at a track meet. Women with papooses sat on some of the horses. On a signal from Burnett, they all moved forward at once to plow parallel furrows. Neither the horses nor the Indians had any idea what was happening. When the horses moved, the plows either tilted up and furrowed the air, or dug deep and stuck. The ponies, which had never pulled anything but travois before, spooked and refused to move in a straight line. The teams collided with one another, then raced across the fields in a cloud of dust, harnesses flapping and plows bouncing, riders thrown and plowmen sprawling. When the Indians weren't bent over laughing, Burnett reported, "they were betting which team of runaways would be leading at the farthest limits of the field."

A day of laughter in the fields . . . and then it was time to return to life's more serious business: the Shoshone packed up their gear and headed for their summer hunt in the mountains. It was left to Burnett and his agency cohorts to plant oats, barley, potatoes, and wheat, as well as build the first irrigation canal in Wyoming, from the Little Wind River to the Shoshone farm. They built it, according to Burnett, under showers of arrows from the Arapaho, who then sabotaged the ditch by ripping holes in the banks.

Walking the laterals that carry water from the South Fork of the Little Wind River to the fields today, one can see breaches in the banks that set the water loose in glistening zigzags of blue fingerpaint on green fields. It's not sabotage by Indians, but probably by Black Angus, tromping along the unfenced canal banks until they break down and flood. Some get repaired, some don't. The budget for the BIA ditches on the Wind River Indian Reservation is minuscule compared with the investment in the dams and pipes and manicured canals of the Midvale and LeClair systems.

Today you can't tell exactly where that first hand-dug irrigation ditch was turned out from the South Fork of the Little Wind—the log structure has long since rotted away—but from descriptions of the time, one can guess that it was probably a short way downstream from the present diversion of Ray Ditch, the biggest of five small irrigation systems that service reservation fields today.

The irrigation supervisor for the U.S. Bureau of Indian Affairs at Wind River, Ray Nation, put a tennis shoe on the concrete crest of the little dam, shrugged his shoulders, and said quietly, "We can only operate on what we collect from the users." Indian and non-Indian farmers who use this water pay very little (about $12 an acre) and irregularly at that (the BIA collects less than 80 percent of the operation and maintenance fees). Some reservation projects qualify for federal subsidies, but not this one. Non-Indian projects get loans and grants from the state, but not a BIA project, though there are many non-Indian users on the ditches. Critics scoff at the leaky old wooden headgates, at the wallows where livestock have waddled into the water, at the clogs of accumulated trash; and farmers either flood their fields with more water than they're due or complain that they're not getting enough. Some of the ranchers on BIA ditches, frustrated by the agency's slow response, hire their own crews and do the work themselves.

Nation reacts mildly to the criticism, but behind the soft brown eyes there is, one suspects, a little concrete. "I think the problem in a lot of cases isn't that they don't get enough water, it's that they don't practice good irrigation."

The job of the six ditch riders who work for Nation hasn't changed much in a century, except that they now ride in Ford Broncos instead of on horseback. Farmers drop cards requesting water for their fields in boxes located along the ditches, and the ditch riders collect the cards and adjust the headgates, cleaning trash from the system as they go. If the BIA could afford to put the water in pipes (as Midvale is doing on the Riverton Unit), there would be less maintenance and less evaporation. Plus, Nation pointed out as we drove by a trio of shirtless kids splashing in the ditch beside the Ethete Road, there would be less risk of a drowning.

Many of the irrigated fields are simply growing grass for horses and cattle—neither plowed nor planted. Much of the allotted and tribal land is leased to a few larger-scale farms and ranches, which, Nation said, "use water efficiently, probably because they pay a lot of money for that land. They've got big water bills, they've got money in it, so they're often the best farmers." Many of those larger operations are non-Indian, too. Indian kids, like young people all around the country, show little interest in ranching or farm life, despite the lack of jobs on the reservation. "It's ironic when you think of the rural setting they've grown up in, but most people on the reservation don't know how to do this," Gary Collins said one day as we walked the irrigation ditch on his farm. "It's going to take at least a generation for them to learn . . . if they're willing."

I've stopped to chat with young people out haying their grandparents' spread or helping to vaccinate an uncle's cattle; it's just a summer job, and they sound anything but willing.

The first generation of Shoshone farmers got a glowing report in 1873 from the Wind River superintendent, who predicted they would "henceforth successfully till the earth, and raise stock, and that the time is not distant when the Shoshone mixed bloods . . . will be attracted to the rich valley on this reservation, on seeing the improved condition of the parent stock." But much of the tribe's brief prosperity at the beginning of the reservation era was handed to them by the federal government: a $10,000 annuity, and generous rations that included beef and flour. Though tribal members emphasize that these were treaty obligations and not handouts—just as the per capita payments of today are the tribes' own oil and gas revenue, not welfare—some also suggest that the cycle of dependency had begun.

Soon, though, the glowing reports turned grim. The Shoshone, reported the superintendent, work like "good stout white boys, twelve to fourteen years old, and unused to labor," and when the crops are harvested, each "returns to his old companions—his horse and gun." But crop losses weren't a flaw of Shoshone character: in 1874, there began a series of grasshopper plagues, outsiders stole free-ranging tribal cattle with ease, and the government failed to provide promised materials, like the wire to string between fence posts. By 1884, the Indians at Wind River were eating seed instead of planting it.

This was a dreadful turn of events for Washakie, who a few years earlier had reveled in the treaty that gave his people the Wind River Valley—the only negotiation in which an Indian tribe actually got to choose its own reservation. By the summer of 1878, it was apparent that there would be no farming miracle, and the Arapaho had moved in, too, demanding a share of rations and real estate. Though Washakie was generally optimistic, and a tactful diplomat, he was desperate enough to make threats.

"The white man kills our game, captures our furs, and sometimes feeds his herds upon our meadows," he told Wyoming's governor. "And your great and mighty government . . . does not protect us in our rights. It leaves us without the promised seed, without tools for cultivating the land, without implements for harvesting our crops, without breeding animals better than ours, without the food we still lack . . .

"I again say, the government does not keep its word. And so, after all we can get by cultivating the land, and by hunting and fishing, we are sometimes nearly starved, and go half naked, as you see us! Knowing all this, do you wonder, sir, that we have fits of desperation and think to be avenged?"

Washakie was an eloquent man, even allowing for the literary flourishes of his translators. He was also stunning to look at—you can see it even in the old photographs. He stood an imposing six-foot-three, with a strong jaw and a straight back that kept him upright into his nineties. He was "majestic in appearance" and manner, according to the whites who knew him, but in some pictures he has a jagged smile that suggests, contrary to most Indian portraits of his time, a man who was comfortable with his celebrity, a man who had *fun*.

In battles against the Crow and the Sioux, he was by all accounts courageous, and a sharp military strategist. Once on the reservation he was an absolute ruler, but he generally put his people's interest before his own, and was generous to outsiders. Yet among the many Indian leaders revered for their courage and dignity during the last years of their tribes' freedom—Tecumseh, Pontiac, Crazy Horse, Chief Joseph—Washakie stands a little less tall, for an odd reason. In the endgame of war and diplomacy, when leaders made desperate choices among allies and strategies, Washakie bet on the right horse. He chose the whites. A crafty calculation, as it turned out, but not the tragic stuff of warrior mythmaking.

One of the most intriguing things about Washakie, for an outsider trying to understand the character of tribal affiliations, is that the greatest chief of the Eastern Shoshone was not Eastern Shoshone by birth. Movement from tribe to tribe was not uncommon during the nomadic era, when a young Indian captured and enslaved by an enemy might eventually marry among his captors, or a woman might be exchanged as battle bounty (Washakie gained a Crow wife this way). Even today there is a fluidity of relations in Indian country, as witnessed by the Sho-raps of the Wind River Reservation and members of other tribes who live here.

Washakie was born around 1800 in the Bitterroot Valley, in what's now Montana. His father was a mixed-blood member of the Flathead tribe, and there are whispers of a French trapper in that line, which might explain Washakie's light complexion. His father was killed by Blackfeet when Washakie was a boy. His mother was probably Lemhi, a branch of the Shoshone that lived in what is now Idaho; and she lived with the Lemhi after her husband's death. (One tribal elder told me Washakie was actually a Crow, but I think he was pulling my leg; he also told me Washakie earned his chieftaincy by playing with white kids as a child.)

The sketchy details of Washakie's youth are the stuff of boys' adventure. Separated from his parents, he wandered for a while with a Bannock band that harassed immigrants, then partnered with white fur trappers before joining the Shoshone. Some of his descendants say he was first treated as a slave by the Shoshone who took him in, but he became a valued member once he demonstrated a gift for prophecy. The sudden death of an elderly Eastern Shoshone chief, and then his son, opened the way for Washakie to lead the band beginning in about 1843. Over the next half century he would consolidate various bands, and survive occasional defections, as chief of the Shoshone.

His success says much about the fluidity among Indian tribes, and the meritocracy by which leaders were selected. "It was truly a time when if you proved your leadership, people followed you," according to his great-grandson, John Washakie. "You had to prove it every day. Their very existence depended on it."

He proved it in battle repeatedly. The old Washakie would say, sheepishly, "As a young man, I delighted in war. When my tribe was at peace, I would wander off sometimes alone in search of an enemy." He fought the Crow, the Blackfeet, and the Sioux, and probably, as a juvenile delinquent hanging out with disreputable Bannock, he marauded white settlers.

The various names attributed to Washakie, like many Indian names, are descriptive—snapshots taken at different stages of his life. His birth name was Pina Quanah, which meant "Smells of Sugar" (his mother must have loved him). He was struck in the face by a Blackfeet arrow while peering from a Shoshone fortification, and because of the scar on his cheek (visible in photographs), other tribes called him Scar Face or Two Scar Chief. Eventually he became Washakie, a name so often heard and written in the West that you can find about thirty different spellings, among them:

Washikeek
Wash-Ah-Wee-Ha
Wash-o-keg
Wesha
Who-sha-kik

There are just about as many explanations of the name's meaning as there are spellings. One biographer said it was a tribute to his shooting skill in buffalo hunts ("Shoots on the Fly"), while another suggested it described morning sunbeams striking a newborn child. A grinning Arapaho, not to be trusted, told me, "The traders called him that, because that's the way he pronounced the drink he always asked for." Most commonly, though, the name is said to mean "rawhide rattle." When the young Washakie killed his first bison, the story goes, he scraped the hide from the animal's nape and blew up the hairless skin, put some stones in it and tied it to a stick, dried it, and thereafter carried it into battle, shaking it above his head to scare his enemies' horses.

Stories embedded in the landscape survive forever, and there is one about Washakie's courage and ferocity that I think of whenever I drive north into the upper Wind River Valley. In the wide curve where the Wind River sweeps east and away from the mountains rises a butte, visible from far away. It was here that Washakie fought hand-to-hand with a Crow chief, Big Robber, for hunting rights to the valley (an event recounted later in this book). Today no one is allowed to climb the butte, and it strikes me as a much finer monument than a cemetery headstone.

Early hagiography typically describes Washakie as "the finest specimen of an Indian I ever saw," and a lifelong votary of whites— the kind of praise that damns a historical Indian in today's world. But Washakie was a lot craftier and more complicated than that, shifting his alliances and using his leverage with whites to deliver goods and, finally, land to his people. This hardly makes him a toady; he was rather an early practitioner of realpolitik, maneuvering among the much larger powers that surrounded his small tribe—including the Sioux, the Crow, and the U.S. Army—for the best advantage.

The chief often took a few extras for himself during negotiations— a new horse, an annuity, a fifty-dollar "uniform jacket." When he was quite old, a fancy saddle was sent from the White House, a gift from President Ulysses S. Grant in recognition of his help against enemy tribes in the 1870s. Washakie accepted it quietly, but the federal agent insisted he send some word back to the President. Finally, Washakie responded, "Do a kindness to a Frenchman, he feels it in his head and his tongue speaks; do a kindness to an Indian, he feels it in his heart. The heart has no tongue."

His courage, like his eloquence, never flagged—well past sixty, he was leading his warriors against the Sioux and the Arapaho. In his seventies, he joined General George Crook in his campaign against the Sioux, and one of the soldiers described him leading his men in a mock charge: "The ponies broke into one frantic rush for camp, riding over sagebrush, rocks, stumps, bunches of grass, buffalo heads—it mattered not the least when they went over it—the warriors all the while squealing, yelling, chanting their war-songs, or howling like coyotes. . . . In the center of the line rode old Washakie; abreast of him the eagle standard."

He was close to a century old when he died in 1900. He had lived through the transformation of the American West, from the days of chasing the great bison herds, through the collisions with trappers and Mormons and Sioux and settlers, to the baneful disconnection of the reservations. He died the way most people die, only older: a scarred and feeble man on his bed, unable to rise, alone with himself.

Washakie's coffin was strapped on a cannon caisson and draped with an American flag. Rifles were shot, taps was sounded, and parallel lines of soldiers raised their sabers as the chief's body was carried from his cabin. The procession to the cemetery at Fort Washakie was a mile and a half long. One of Washakie's biographers wrote that it was customary to pile sagebrush by the flap of a Shoshone tepee whenever the Indian left on a journey. I like that image better than the raised swords: a mountain of sagebrush by the door where Washakie departed.

At his grave, a border of smooth river stones circles the mounded red earth, and there's a rough granite headstone speckled with orange lichen. Visitors have pushed quarters and dimes and pennies into the dirt atop Washakie's grave, so it looks in the springtime like a budding garden of coins. There is a motley array of artificial flowers, too, and the dried-out remnants of fresh bundles. On the front of the stone is carved WASHAKIE 1804–1900. And on the side: *Always loyal to the government and to his white brothers.* A little more than that could be written, and should be. You can lean on a sandstone wall that surrounds the old cemetery and listen to the Little Wind River rushing by.

A short walk down the road to the east, Washakie's great-grandson John chaired a meeting of the Joint Council's Water

Resources Control Board, to consider a proposal to protect Wind River streamflow from irrigation drawdowns. It was April 1990, two years since Dick Baldes had cooled his heels in the lobby with his Bull Lake report. Now in a much better frame of mind, he explained that if the tribe could protect instream flow and keep it colder, cleaner, and deeper, his agency would plant 140,000 fish over the next few years. The magic number was 252 cubic feet per second, the minimum amount of water needed to keep trout, ling, and sauger alive and healthy, according to an FWS study whose methodology was approved by the State of Wyoming. That study went into the record. So did a fifteen-page application from the tribal water engineer, Kate Vandemoer, complete with hydrologic analysis and detailed description of stream reaches, the source of the water, a monitoring program, and maps. Attorneys were present to explain why they believed water rights granted under the 1868 treaty provided a legal basis for the streamflow protection. There was even a report from an Arizona economist on the economic benefits of protecting streamflow, not just to the tribes but to the basin as a whole. When he spoke, Baldes couldn't resist a moment of personal testimony. "I lived by the river in Riverton when I was growing up. It was not unusual for Dad and I and my brother to set lines, which we did all the time, and also fished with the hook and line, and there was often times when we would catch ling, sauger, and trout on the same set line. I defy anybody in this room or anybody in the world to do that today. It's not possible. That is what we are trying to do: to get to that point."

Plenty of other people were in the room: farmers, BIA officials, fishermen, tribal members, newspaper reporters, and Jeff Fassett, who sat in the back of the crowded council chambers, dressed in a dark-blue suit, flanked by two attorneys. He was not happy. "You could say we brought a negative view to those meetings," he said.

Fassett was no longer the wide-eyed young consultant who visited Wind River Canyon in 1977. He had risen rapidly to become state engineer for Wyoming, in charge of dispensing water all over the state. This battle with the Indians had Wyoming politicians squirming, and it was Fassett's job to end it. He believed he had a talent for informal, face-to-face negotiations, and thought he could make progress if they kept it out of the headlines.

But this day had already started badly. An earlier meeting at the offices of the tribal water engineer had ended with folders closing, briefcases snapping shut, and no smiles. The problem was, on this visit Fassett had nothing to barter with the tribes—no money, no water rights, no authority to cut a deal.

He was the man who turned the spigots in Wyoming, and the state's position was that if the tribes wanted to protect instream flow, they'd have to go through him. He didn't enjoy waiting in the lobby any more than Baldes and all the others, and didn't like coming before the council as if he were just another petitioner with a grievance. The non-Indian irrigators who thought they would be hurt by the tribes' initiative, the farmers Fassett and the state had promised to protect, were sitting grimly around him. Under these circumstances, he could hardly smile or make small talk.

When he finally spoke, it was only to say that the state hadn't had enough time to prepare "substantial" comments on the instream-flow proposal, and he hoped the board would "look to some sensitivity of the enforcement of that permit different from the approval and dedication of the waters provided by that permit." Sumner Marlowe, who was sitting in the audience, was one of several who didn't know quite what this meant. But he could see that something big was afoot, and wished he'd paid closer attention at Vandemoer's workshops. Are we *winning* this one? he was thinking. Does that ever happen?

CHAPTER 11

The Courts

Though we've been following roads and pathways along the riverbanks from Wind River Canyon to the Continental Divide, Jeff Fassett and many of the people who gathered in the council chambers at Fort Washakie in 1990 arrived by a different route. Their journey was through the frosted-glass doors of old Wyoming courthouses, through the foyers of big city law firms with watercolor landscapes on the wall and twentieth-floor urban panoramas, through a few dusty small-town offices with cigarette smoke in the carpets and yellowing diplomas on the wall, all the way to the white marble steps of the U.S. Supreme Court.

Now it's time to interrupt our upstream journey and spend a while at the old oak tables in the attic of the Washakie County courthouse, thumbing through thousands of pages of evidence and testimony, tracing a twenty-year odyssey formally known as the General Adjudication of All Rights to Use Water in the Bighorn River System. While the arguments often seem abstruse and narcotic, the case has changed the order of things in some of the most beautiful landscape in the West—and before this is over, it will change the Wind River Valley even more, and maybe some other places too. Beneath the veil of legal maneuvers and obscure technical jargon is a struggle between two cultures that have been arguing for 150 years over the same beloved country, and trying to find a way to share it.

The tension that hovered over the Wind River Valley in the spring of 1990 was the result of a convergence: the legal wrangling over water rights that had been percolating through distant court-rooms for a dozen years was meandering toward *real* water. The massing of arguments by gray-suited litigators, the boggy weight of experts' transcripts, the ebb and flow of motions—all this was about to be felt in the streambed, and who could predict what that might do to the heave of the river, or to tempers on the ditch banks? The lawyers and politicians who'd stirred this pot were safe in their offices, but the farmers and engineers were out at the headgates.

Even people whose livelihoods were not closely tied to Wind River water had begun to pay attention to the incessant head-lines about the dispute, not so much because they understood the region's big economic stake in water as because they sensed a very real challenge to the power of the state. It had stirred tribal elders, too, who spoke of the historic and spiritual importance of water with a piety that irritated some state officials while it gave heart to Indians like Sumner Marlowe and Mark Soldierwolf and Merle Haas.

The pressure was building on Fassett to do *something*, but for the short term his hands were tied. In 1989, the state had quieted the tribes with money, cutting a deal where the Indians would back off on their water demands in exchange for tax breaks on oil produc-tion (the tribes had long disputed the state's right to tax oil pumped on the reservation) and funds to rehabilitate reservation irrigation projects. Now the public was telling the politicians that another arrangement of this type would amount to no more than a gussied-up bribe, and the politicians Fassett worked for were telling him, No more deals. He sensed that tribal people wanted, as he did, to get to know the other side better, to talk about their fears and hopes without the press or juris doctors in the room. But the media were all over the story, and they sold more newspapers by playing up the conflict. And to the lawyers it was a just a game, which they would argue endlessly, and expensively—without, it seemed, caring much about what was happening on the ground. Some of them had spent years on this case without ever visiting the Wind River Valley.

Fassett, on the other hand, had been a foot soldier since the begin-ning of the adjudication, gathering the raw statistics on streamflow and crop yields and performing the calculations that transformed that data into legal ammunition. Now he'd moved to the front line on the battlefield, while the lawyers moved their briefs back and forth like chess pieces. He dealt with real people, who wanted their problems resolved, while the lawyers debated and delayed in the safe confines of the courtroom, unaffected by the changes of season that marked, out here, the beginning and end of a farmer's hopes.

But if you like chess, this was quite a game: high stakes and cunning strategies, spiked by sudden emotion and human frailty. Even among *attorneys,* those pitiless pettifoggers, the case has taken an emotional toll. For some, it had consumed the largest chunk of their careers, a twenty-year diet of depositions and motions studied in the yellow light of motel lamps. A few moved on to other jobs, like Norman Young, the Fremont County attorney, or retired, or left the profession altogether. The judge who first heard the case is dead, and since then two other judges have sat on the case, not counting all the appeals-court judges and clerks who poured over the briefs and transcripts as the case climbed up and down the litigation tree. No one has compiled hard statistics, but there are enough bulky documents to build a small diversion dam and certainly enough money spent—estimates put the cost at more than $60 million so far—to build a much larger one. When you look at the Wind River—a rocky little stream overhung with scraggly cottonwoods, small enough to wade easily across in August—you wonder how it could be worth so much.

Some people claim that the tribes picked this fight. In 1975, when plans were announced to drill water wells for an industrial park near the Riverton Municipal Airport, the tribes objected. The airport west of Riverton—and the city itself—is on land that was part of the reservation before it was opened up for homesteading in 1904, and which, the tribes have argued and some courts have confirmed, is *still* part of the reservation, despite non-Indian occupation. The airport land no longer belonged to the tribes, nor to individual Indians. But the tribes held that their 1868 treaty, which said nothing specific about water rights, implicitly reserved for them enough water to farm their land, including, they argued, the groundwater under the airport.

Others say the state started it—that Wyoming was, in fact, itching for a rumble. What would the tribes have done if Riverton had simply gone ahead and drilled the wells at the airport? Probably nothing. But Wyoming rushed to the legislature and then into court. The state law setting up an adjudication process was "the fastest law ever enacted in history," according to Walt Urbigkit, a legislator in 1977 and later a judge on the state Supreme Court that heard the case. Urbigkit, who owns land in the upper Wind River Basin, voted for the adjudication bill, and many millions of dollars later, he and others felt the legislature had been duped by water lawyers who soon would be collecting fancy fees.

But the state's chances looked pretty good in 1977. A 1952 congressional act allowed state courts to adjudicate water rights, which in Wind River's case might be based on a federal treaty signed before the state existed. The Wyoming statute instructed judges to let the state Board of Control (its water agency, headed by the state engineer) act as special master for the court, gathering the facts and suggesting to the presiding judge who should be awarded water rights. This case would put Wyoming on the cutting edge of Western water law; it could be the first test of fully adjudicating federal, tribal, and state water in state courts. Best of all, Wyoming could assert its authority without relying on the federal courts, which tended to interpret Indian treaties liberally.

A decision for the home team seemed like a good bet. But the strategy began to unravel when the presiding district-court judge in Worland took the Board of Control off the case and appointed Teno Roncalio as special master.

Despite Wyoming's well-known appetite for government-allergic Republicans—its legislature has more janitors than Democrats—now and then the Cowboy State spits up a liberal Democrat in the governor's mansion or Congress. Roncalio was a former Democratic congressman who had once chaired the House Interior Committee, a panel whose many duties include authorizing federal water projects and overseeing Indian reservations. Wyoming Democrats get their votes from the descendants of the immigrants who dug the mines and built the railroads across the state's southern tier—from people like Roncalio himself. He was a bald, bearded, and boisterous institution before he retired after twenty years in Congress; a liberal, maybe, but a straight shooter and savvy wheeler-dealer who, as a powerful committee chairman with the majority party, had brought home some generous portions of Capitol Hill pork.

Like the state legislators, Roncalio didn't know when he took the special master job what a monster the case would become. He was in his sixties when he was appointed in 1979. The volume of technical and legal information to digest—the piles of briefs and platoons of experts brought in by both sides—nearly overwhelmed him. After a couple of years, he was lying awake at night with stabbing headaches, worrying that he might have a brain tumor. Certainly there were a lot of experts trying to get inside his head.

"A case like this is really a matter of teaching," said Jim Clear, a buck-toothed attorney from the Department of Justice who worked for twenty years on the Bighorn case. "You have to make the court understand not just the legal issues, but soil science, and then a series of other scientific disciplines, all of which build on top of each other. Teno probably wasn't expecting that."

The science and engineering were complex, and the legal issues momentous. At the heart of the case was the long-standing struggle between Washington and the states over the trove of resources buried beneath the windswept surfaces of the West. Western states generally feel squashed by the federal giant, which controls much of their land through national parks, the U.S. Forest Service, and the U.S. Bureau of Land Management. Indian reservations are a further insult: tribes have treaties with the federal government that bypass the states entirely. The Indians made their deals with Washington a century ago and think state taxes and laws shouldn't apply to them—including Wyoming's water laws.

When Wyoming proclaimed in its 1890 constitution that the state, not the farmers, owned the water running down the streams and through the fields, it was a radical idea—socialist, really. The state gained enormous leverage in controlling settlement and resource development, since it alone could decide which water uses were "beneficial." The state, which still takes enormous pride in its historic role in Western water law, chose to distribute that water using another radical new idea called the prior-appropriation doctrine.

The West was moving away from the English common-law notion of riparian water rights, which gave people who owned streambanks the right to use the water flowing by. The gold rush exposed the shortcomings of this approach in the West. It simply didn't work for the miners who invaded California in the 1840s—they needed a way to move the water away from the streambed, to work the gravels and blasted rock at placer claims that didn't adjoin streams. The vehicle for doing that was the prior-appropriation system: *First in time, first in right.* If you were the first to build a ditch and divert the water to some dry plateau miles away, you had the senior water right, even before the fellow who later built his cabin right there by the stream. This was a truly revolutionary idea: Water in the West would not necessarily be attached to the property through which it naturally ran. As long as you used water in a way the state deemed "beneficial," it was a quasi property right, which you could buy and sell like a liquor license.

The treaty-based rights claimed by the Wind River tribes were an affront to that system. If the courts gave them what they asked, it wouldn't matter whether they were using the water beneficially, or even whether they'd ever used it at all: they would forever have the senior right to the water in the basin. Tribal attorneys held that Indians could build a ditch tomorrow and take water that some white homesteader had been using for ninety years. And they were not only talking about irrigation but also dreaming up "beneficial" uses that the state rarely if ever allowed, such as instream flow and even, good grief, aesthetics.

Led by Denver attorney Michael D. "Sandy" White, the state team tried a preemptive strike: that the tribes, based on their treaty, had no water rights *at all.* The tribes, he told Roncalio, should have to wait in line for a state permit like anyone else. He pointed to language in a 1904 congressional act that opened the north side of the reservation to homesteaders; the income from those land sales was to be used, among other things, to buy state water rights. That clinched it. How could Congress have "reserved" any water rights in 1868 if it was telling the tribes in 1904 to get permits from the state? And even if the courts ruled that the 1868 treaty implicitly included water rights—not likely, thought White—then those rights should be limited to the amount of irrigation the tribes had done over the past century, and not infringe on the non-Indians who had been hard at work in the fields just as long.

Sandy White has the breezy, boots-and-pinstripes style of many successful Western lawyers, but above his busy mouth hovers an appraising eye. Like most successful advocates, he wears his losses lightly and doesn't let himself get ideologically attached; with a self-deprecating laugh, he calls himself a "legal whore." The state called him a "special consultant" in the Wind River adjudication. He had excellent credentials: experience as a special master himself in Colorado water cases, and Wyoming roots of his own, including distant Shoshone relatives from the Wind River Reservation. He insists he didn't sweet-talk Wyoming officials into bringing the lawsuit, and in fact only took on the Indian-rights portion of the case at the last moment, when another attorney left the state attorney general's office. "Everybody thought it was the right thing to do," he said years later.

White did most of the courtroom talking for the state during the first big trial and its appeals, while the tribes ran through several lawyers over the years; and another bullpen of lawyers appeared for non-Indian water users. But in the early sessions of the litigation, when hearings were held before Teno Roncalio, the expert witnesses were at least as important as the lawyers.

The tribes argued that they did indeed have a "reserved" right to water based on the 1868 treaty, citing as proof of the government's intent a passage in the treaty noting the Shoshone's "desire to commence farming." Now they claimed water rights for everything from farming to industry to fish and wildlife. And they wanted enough water to fulfill the agricultural *potential* of the reservation;

to measure that potential they designed a series of irrigation projects in areas that had not been farmed before. The job of designing the projects fell to Wold Mesghinna, the Eritrean engineer who toured the sagebrush plains with lawyer Harry Sachse.

The tribes' hopes hinged on convincing Roncalio to add up the reservation's "Practicably Irrigable Acreage"—both the old ditches and these "future" projects—and use the totals to figure how big the tribes' senior water right should be. Mesghinna spent months exploring the reservation and consulting with experts on soils, hydrology, and economics, and came up with five hypothetical irrigation projects.

Sandy White did his best in hearings before Roncalio to erode those ditches before they could be built—which he never believed they would be. They were far-fetched and impractical in an age when the government no longer invested in marginal water projects. Briefs filed by other nervous Western states supported this view: New Mexico attorney Richard Simms called the future projects "nothing more than a pretext to create large paper water rights as a form of wealth" and labeled the cost-benefits analyses a sham.

There was some concern among the tribes' and the federal government's legal teams—both of which supported the tribes' position—about how Mesghinna would come across in the courtroom. With the exception of Indians, people of color are a rarity in Wyoming, and this expert was not only dark but foreign, speaking with an accent. White was sure to go right after his lack of local experience.

When Mesghinna first learned he would be the tribes' primary witness, he began losing sleep. He was all too aware of what was at stake. "Water is life to the tribes," he said. "Culturally, religiously, economically. They have gas and oil, but that will end someday. I said to myself that the life of these people for the coming generation is on my heart, to such an extent."

Mesghinna expected to spend about two days explaining the design and capabilities of these conceptual projects; Jim Clear guessed it might take seven days at the outside. The Eritrean ended up testifying for two weeks, with White pounding away on every detail of Mesghinna's qualifications and calculations.

White: Have you ever actually, yourself, conducted sprinkler irrigation, done sprinkler irrigation, as an irrigator?
Mesghinna: Well, I did work when I was in school. I did
what's called experiment in the field for about one and a
half years.
White: Did you ever move a sprinkler with a tractor?
Mesghinna (brief pause):   No, by hand.

The courtroom was drooping with exhaustion, but White pressed on, trying to crack him. Instead, the extended testimony gave the neatly dressed engineer more chances to explain in his liltingly accented English the arts of hydrology and engineering. Special master Roncalio became an eager pupil. Mesghinna became more expansive, and White began to pull back. Roncalio made no secret that he was tired of White's endless questions. At one point he said, "You can't drill him to death on every point like this ad nauseam and prepare your case on cross-examination."

Mesghinna's growing confidence was such that he sometimes interrupted when the tribes' attorneys and the special master were trying to block White's questions. "This is—we can settle the matter very easily," he would say. Then, like a schoolmaster, "Let me start this way. Before we design our system we study the historical conditions in the area. . . ." And he was off and running, explaining, for example, why a future project was best served by an unlined canal. White tried to show the shortcomings of Mesghinna's plan by comparing it with Midvale: "Isn't it true that the Midvale Project District continues to line their canals?" Mesghinna answered, "Yes, of course, because the canal is getting old, and as it gets older you have to maintain it better."

Roncalio, who couldn't spell Mesghinna's name correctly when he first took the stand, was won over. "There's only so long you can keep anyone on the stand," said Clear. "I don't think Teno believed anything the state said after that. He liked Wold a lot." White did, too, later calling Mesghinna "one of my favorite people in the whole world." Weary courtroom observers dreamt of traveling to Eritrea to see what sort of culture produced this unusual package of politeness, intellect, and dignity. Feelings toward White were less positive, even among some of the state's lawyers.

Less likable experts from both sides followed, and Roncalio sat through them all. The briefs and motions piled up. His headaches had grown so disabling he'd had a battery of medical tests, including a brain scan.

At one point, Roncalio took a show-me helicopter trip around the western side of the reservation. There was some bickering among the attorneys about just where they would set down. The state wanted the special master to see that the "future" projects were in fact unredeemable, uninhabited wasteland. When the helicopter settled onto one of these barren plots, an old Shoshone appeared out of the sagebrush, grubby from fieldwork. "Teno! Teno!" he shouted, and he ran up to hug his congressman.

Roncalio intended to be strict about applying the law, but he was sensitive to the historic deprivations of the reservation. "Goddammit, I couldn't help but feel the neglect and abuse that had gone on for decades," he told me. " 'Roncalio, you're not supposed to think about this.' But it's awfully hard. I tried to stick with facts, statistics, the testimony from the professionals. What the hell else can you do?"

With luck, you can find a witness like Mesghinna. White talks about the need for "intellectual sex appeal" to win a case. Patiently and without condescension, Mesghinna gave Roncalio the facts and statistics and professional advice that he needed to follow his heart.

"On the stand, Wold explained how you study land to see if it can be irrigated—the quality of soil, the availability of water, evapotranspiration in plants," said Harry Sachse, who was the Shoshone's lawyer at the time, "and you could see Teno thinking, 'I'm going to understand this.' Wold taught a course on what you look at, and by the end of the day, Teno knew it was fully explained."

The experts for the state of Wyoming did not fare so well. Roncalio questioned the value of state testimony on soils, economics, and engineering and repeatedly found it inferior to what the tribes and the U.S. government put on. Jeff Fassett had designed a computer model that showed damaging impacts on other water users in the basin if the tribes were given a large senior water right. Fassett's model, Roncalio wrote, "left me with a distinct feeling that the inputted assumptions were carefully crafted to secure the desired printouts." Roncalio wondered, too, why the model hadn't been used to test more constructive possibilities, like a program of storage construction and cooperation among governments. "It is a comment on the disobliging nature of our times that such an alternative use of this vast and costly exercise was not engaged in," he wrote in his report. A frustrated Vandemoer would remember this a few years later, when she found Fassett stubbornly sticking to his ideas about impacts: "He was completely discredited."

Roncalio's 450-page report supported the tribes' claim to treaty-based water rights. He was a nimble writer, telling the story of his investigation concisely but sprinkling a little vinegar, too. Dismissing one of the state's arguments, he cited the opinion of another special master in a Colorado case, who said reserved tribal water rights couldn't be blocked by using something called the Equal Footing Doctrine. The Colorado special master was none other than Michael D. "Sandy" White.

The Roncalio report, while a major defeat for the state, was not a total loss. It gave the tribes a huge share, totaling more than 700,000 acre/feet of water per year, more than half the amount that flowed through the basin, but it restrained the development of those water rights over a long period of time, to give other users a chance to develop new sources, and it forbade the tribes to sell their water outside the reservation. Still, non-Indian landowners in the basin, many of whom had confidently stayed away from the proceeding, were in shock.

The report went to Harold Joffe, a frail, unassuming judge who was nearing retirement and was now being assailed with protests. He received letters from all quarters. A Riverton minister suggested this was a water grab by Texas agribusiness. Craig Cooper inveighed against the report as both the Division III water engineer and a private water user on the LeClair ditch. The Hoopengarner family, which had ranched for three generations along the Wind in the heart of the reservation, wrote that their place would be worthless without water, adding, "I realize that the Indians have been shabbily treated and taken advantage of, and perhaps it now seems like some sort of poetic justice for the white man to have been promised something by the government (water rights to the land he was urged to come in and settle here), only to have the government later on change its mind and take away that something."

Somewhat bewildered, Joffe decided to listen not just to lawyers' arguments about the Roncalio report but to the testimony of locals as well. In 1983, a parade of farmers took the stand in his courtroom to describe the devastation they would suffer if the tribes got Roncalio's big award. The straight-backed benches of the Worland courtroom were packed with state officials, tribal members, reporters, and people in blue jeans with red noses and troubled white foreheads.

Gideon Davidson was one month old when his family came to the valley in 1906, and he was still raising sheep north of Riverton, on what used to be reservation lands. "If you take the water away, the land goes back to desert," he said. He invited the tribes to talk. "That's the way we do when we have a dispute on our irrigation district, we go up and sit on the ditch bank and settle our disputes right there."

Starr Weed, the Shoshone elder who played Washakie in the pageant at the Thermopolis hot springs, arrived at the courthouse and saw visitors signing in by the door, so he wrote down his name. At the end of the day, when heads were beginning to nod beneath the high ceiling fans, he heard his name. He was being called to the witness stand. He'd accidentally signed up to testify.

The judge asked him, "Are you a landowner?"

Weed answered, "I am a landowner. I own a hundred and one acres of land. Then I have several other acres that I lease on the reservation. I have lived there all my life. Born and raised there since I was a little baby."

Weed is a tall, good-looking man in his seventies, polite and usually smiling, whose walk to the witness box was stiff and bowlegged from years of ranchwork and bareback horse racing at rodeos in Indian country. When Weed speaks English, he moves his hands in wide, unfolding motions. In the early years of the reservation, the tribes communicated across the language barrier with sign language, and when Weed visits Arapaho friends at the senior center in Fort Washakie today, they often talk with their hands. Sometimes he repeats words slowly—he's thinking in Shoshone, translating.

"And then I hear you all talking about my reservation and the water," he said. There was a long pause, and people who didn't know him raised an eyebrow, wondering if that was it. "I think the water goes with our land. And there is some seasons that it is a dry season there and you can't always get what you want with this water. . . .

"And then my old people always told me that they had several spots to pick from. They all moved to Fort Bridger." He paused, and then repeated, "Fort Bridger. And then they had a big meeting there. They always told me: it took them five days to talk with the U.S. Government and put so many things in the treaty. And then they had a chance to pick Pinedale. They said: It was too windy there." Weed waved his hand in the air, a slow Frisbee-throwing motion, vaguely in the direction of Pinedale, a town on the east side of the Wind River Mountains. "And then they went over into the Jackson area. They said: There was too much snow. And then they come down into this, they call it Warm Valley." His open hands curled toward his chest, as if he were gathering in a litter of kittens, and his smile widened. "There was no name for it then, it just went by the name of Warm Valley. And they said: There is headwaters there. There is a lot of good streams and water coming off the mountains. Lot of fish. And then they said: There is hardly any snow that comes in there. There is a lot of wild game there. Lot of wild game. And we always wintered there." He shook his hand in the air, as if sprinkling salt. "And there is a lot of minerals there. And then there is hot springs. And they say: Well, that's where we will pick our reservation.

"And then they talk about this water, which you say isn't reserved. They always told me, I sit down and listened to them, they said: As long as the grass grows and the river flows, that's your right. That's your water rights here. Whenever anything comes up, well, mention that and tell them about this treaty. They was having wars at that time. And then in the treaty, well, they talked about putting down their spears and no more wars. And then they pick up shovels and start in on farming, which was new to the Indians at that time.

"And so that's where we are at now, we farm and all that and we need water for our lands."

A river is obedient to the laws of gravity, obliging to the peculiarities of geology, and even in its most violent moments it suggests a consistent natural world, which both scientists and shamans study and follow to divine its messages. The laws of our courts are something different.

If you tried to map the journey of the Wind River through the courts, it would have none of the shape and logic of the valley itself. Water would run uphill, or disappear, or be transformed into straw or gold. But the legal system resembles the hydrological cycle in one sense: It goes round and round, and there appears to be no end to it.

When the perplexed farmers of Midvale and then Starr Weed talked about the waters of this valley, it seemed to me a stark juxtaposition of histories and beliefs, a clear enough choice for a judge to make. But finality is only for television trials. The report that emerged from Roncalio's hearings would circulate in the courts like a quilt at a bee, a new square quilted at each stop.

The job of the courts was to interpret the intentions and understandings of the people who wrote and signed the treaty over a century ago, then figure out how to uphold the deal in today's world. There was a lot of tinkering, first by Roncalio, then by Judge Joffe; after Joffe retired, another district judge reshaped the decree again; and then the Wyoming Supreme Court took a turn. The amount of water awarded in the decree changed, requirements to build new dams came and went, restrictions on how the tribes could use or sell water rights were imposed. But the heart of Roncalio's decision remained: The tribes had a basic right to enough water to wet the "practicably irrigable acreage" (PIA) on the reservation with an 1868 priority date. When the state argued that there was *no* 1868 right, Sandy White admitted, "we lost, every step of the way."

White had lost some of his luster, too, with his prolonged and ultimately fruitless interrogations during the trial, but he was not about to give up. Like a terrier clamped on the small end of a bone, he carried his objections to treaty-based water rights all the way to the U.S. Supreme Court.

By 1989, the litigation had been going on for a decade. The legislature was increasingly grumpy about paying the adjudication team's legal bill. Farmers on the Riverton Unit and farther upstream were losing faith in Wyoming's attorneys, putting up FOR SALE signs and cutting their losses. Though these farms were productive, they found few takers. There was grumbling on the reservation, too: When does this business end? Where do these water rights help us with the problems we face every day, like jobs and schools? How much more fighting in court can we afford? Political tremors were shaking up the business councils; some of the younger, better-educated council members, like Gary Collins, lost their seats in 1988. The team of tribal attorneys also kept changing. One of the new Shoshone lawyers was a striking young Sioux woman named Susan Williams.

"We didn't want to appear afraid," Williams said, "but we didn't think it was a great idea to take this case to the Supreme Court. Water is so esoteric. We could have counted our blessings and walked away." But the tribes had no choice when the U.S. Supreme Court granted the state a writ of certiorari to hear arguments on the validity of the PIA standard used in the Wind River decree. So in the spring of 1989, Williams packed her bags in Albuquerque and headed for Washington, D.C.

To figure out what treaties actually mean has often been left to the federal courts, and it's been their job to define the peculiar status of Indian nations living under the blanket of the stars and stripes. Historically, the federal courts have perhaps been the Indians' best friend in government, albeit one of those difficult friends—helpful, wealthy, changeable, controlling, sometimes vengeful. A short list of some famous Indian-law decisions is unbothered by the hobgoblin of consistency:

Worcester v. Georgia (1832)   A key decision on tribal sovereignty: The state of Georgia was bothered by the Cherokee living as a "nation" within their borders and tried to prosecute some hapless missionaries on the reservation who were spouting scripture in Cherokee. Justice John Marshall, who had called tribes "domestic dependent nations" in a Georgia case the year before, defended the tribes' sovereignty in the majority opinion: "a weak state, in order to provide for its safety, may place itself under the protection of one more powerful, without stripping itself of the right of government, and ceasing to be a state." That didn't stop President Andrew Jackson from driving the Cherokee west a few years later.

Ex parte Crow Dog (1883)   The federal courts step in front of the states on Indian matters: Crow Dog was a Brule Sioux chief who killed a tribal member named Spotted Tail and was sentenced to death by a state court in South Dakota. Indian against Indian, said the court, should be left to their own "savage nature," and Crow Dog was released. The U.S. Congress immediately made sure it wouldn't happen again, passing the Major Crimes Act, under which felonies like murder are tried in federal court.

Lone Wolf v. Hitchcock (1903)   Treaties are not cut in stone: In the treaty creating the Kiowa-Comanche reservation, there was a clause requiring a three-quarters vote of the tribes for any sale of tribal lands. But when the U.S. Congress wanted to sell some tribal lands, the Supreme Court said, Sure, Congress can change a treaty unilaterally, and will surely do it only in "perfect good faith toward the Indians." Uh-huh.

Winters v. United States (1908)   The key decision determining when water rights are implied by treaty: When settlers upstream of the Fort Belknap Indian Reservation started building dams and diverting water, the Indians who had settled on these arid plains in 1888 lost the irrigation water they needed to become "pastoral and civilized" (as the treaty put it) on their small patch of reservation land. This notion of a senior water right implicitly reserved by a treaty became known as the "Winters Doctrine," and continues to rankle non-Indian irrigators in the West.

Arizona v. California (1963) A "future" water right for tribes: This was a long-running fight for the Colorado River between two dry and mighty states, but the winners turned out to be Indians. The U.S. Supreme Court ruled that the states could divvy up the river, but only what was left after reservation tribes like the Navajo took the water they needed for present and future irrigation. The standard for calculating that need would be "practicably irrigable acreage." This was bad news on the putting greens of Scottsdale.

U.S. v. Sioux Nation (1979) Attempting to redress old treaty violations: When gold was found in the Black Hills, the federal government decided this sacred tribal place shouldn't belong to the Sioux Nation after all. Though it took a century, the U.S. Court of Claims and U.S. Supreme Court finally admitted this violated the 1868 treaty with the Sioux ("a more ripe and rank case of dishonorable dealing will never, in all probability, be found in our history," wrote one justice) and ordered the federal government to write the tribes a check for $122.5 million. No thanks, said the Sioux, we'll take the Hills. They're still awaiting the outcome.

Kids are taught in social studies classes that the Supreme Court sits loftily above the hurly-burly of politics, steadying the helm of government by hewing strictly to the law, unswayed by political pressure and popular causes. But no seasoned attorney expects to win strictly on legal merits, and that is particularly true when it comes to Indian-law and sovereignty issues, where the courts have zigzagged all over. The personal charm of attorneys can really make a difference, since the justices aren't likely to have read all the briefs in the dozens of cases before them each year. "They really want to hear what you say," said Harry Sachse. "And they can find a way to decide it your way if they want to."

"Think of the judge as a lifeguard in a rowboat with two drowning people, one on either side," said Sandy White. "The one that's the most appealing is the one he reaches for."

Some of us would never set sail in the first place, but lawyers who love their work are ecstatic at a chance to argue before the Supremes. John Washakie, who came with other tribal leaders to sit in on the preliminaries in Washington, remembered the relentless, jittery preparations. "We did ten days of practice sessions, acting out the roles," he said. "The buildup was really intense. For attorneys, it's like going to the World Series."

The script for those roles had to be cooked down from huge briefing books that the attorneys for the state and the tribes had prepared. Indian-law specialists around the country were following the case, and many showed up in Washington to kibbitz—tribal leaders, legal scholars, even attorneys like Harry Sachse, who were no longer on the case. The state got input, too, primarily from attorneys general from other Western states, because no water adjudication originating in state courts had ever been litigated this far, and there were reservations all over the West with "inchoate" water rights.

Saul Goodman, representing the Arapaho for the heavyweight Washington law firm Covington & Burling, wrote most of the tribes' brief, and it was assumed he would speak to the court. At the last minute, though, old rivalries asserted themselves, and the Shoshone insisted that since the Arapaho attorney had written the brief, the Shoshone lawyer should argue.

Susan Williams was about to bat in the World Series.

After graduating from Harvard Law, where she once took a class from Harry Sachse, Williams made several trips to the Supreme Court to watch arguments made by the partners at her firm. But on the day the Wind River case was scheduled, she felt more as though she were part of the wide-eyed sightseeing crowd climbing the broad marble steps and entering through the massive Corinthian columns. The tribal and U.S. attorneys ate in the cafeteria—there were Sandy White and his team, at another table—and then she and Saul Goodman wandered around, stopping, like tourists, to use a restroom. When Susan Williams's big moment arrived, she was sitting in one of the stalls and Goodman was pounding frantically on the door: "We're up *now!* We're going to be *late!*"

The attorneys were separated by a railing from the public gallery and sat at dark mahogany tables "in the hole" before the justices, who were arrayed on a raised bench that angled around at the ends. The faces of the nine justices seemed larger than life, like pale busts mounted atop black robes against the red velvet drapes on the walls. Once the arguments began, though, they would not sit silent; in the Supreme Court, attorneys can expect aggressive interrogation by the justices.

This can cut into the time they have to make their arguments, which is not much. The era when Daniel Webster could orate for days before the court is long gone. Below the red mahogany bench where the justices look down at the courtroom there are lights of white, amber, and red, and when your ten minutes are up, and the red light goes on, you'd better finish up your argument. Sandy White went first; then a bow-tied attorney for the United States, Jeffrey Minear; and finally Susan Williams.

The court had agreed to review only the PIA standard's validity, but Wyoming's attorneys hoped that the increasingly conservative personality of the court—William Rehnquist was now the chief justice, and President Reagan had appointed Antonin Scalia and Sandra Day O'Connor in the 1980s—might tilt it toward the states' view on reserved rights. All the lawyers kept an eye on O'Connor to gauge her reactions. She was from Arizona, where some key issues in water law and Indian law had been played out in the courts.

Given the uncertainty of much Indian law, and the new minds on the court, no one knew what to expect. Early in White's argument, O'Connor interrupted him to ask about state water rights obtained for the reservation around the turn of the century—reopening the basic question of whether Congress meant for the tribes to get their water rights through the state when it approved the 1868 treaty. The justices didn't hesitate to go beyond the PIA question if something intrigued them, and they expressed opinions when they felt like it. Brennan commented that the federal government let a lot of state water rights lapse after the Winters Doctrine was established, because "they didn't think they were giving up anything that couldn't be restored" as an implied treaty-based water right under Winters. Some of the justices seemed to be groping for even a basic understanding of reserved water rights and PIA. "If the Indians need more water, why, the United States will have to condemn it," said Justice William Kennedy at one point, as if the federal government could blithely claim an aquatic right-of-way where there was no surplus water to take.

There were so many interruptions that White couldn't finish his opening argument. He never got to expand on the "sensitivity" issue—consideration of the devastating impact on other water users, which some earlier rulings applied in water adjudications. Nor did he mention his certainty that the "future" projects—a big part of the tribal PIA—didn't have "a snowball's chance in hell" of being built. Nobody, he figured, not even the Supreme Court justices, was fooled by that claim. He hoped the justices and their clerks had read the briefs thoroughly.

When Minear spoke for the United States, the justices became more focused. Eyebrows went up among the attorneys when Scalia questioned the very idea of PIA. "Well, why—why is that such a natural conclusion? If you give somebody a certain amount of agricultural land, I assume you would think that he'd have as much water as everybody else around him." A glance between Scalia and Rehnquist put all the attorneys on alert: Were the daggers out for PIA?

At one point Rehnquist asked Minear, "You don't want the reserved right to ever be subject to diminution for nonuse?"

"Well, that's in the very nature of a reserved water right," said Minear.

"Well," said Rehnquist, "it doesn't have to be."

Minear, a little dumbfounded, started to respond, "I think—"

"It certainly doesn't," thumped the Chief Justice.

Williams argued last, and it was her job to stir up some emotion. Choosing her to speak might've seemed as if it was due to intertribal rivalry, but it also proved a smart move. Her youth was accentuated by her short black hair; she was Native American and a thin and beautiful woman—all those things that shouldn't make a difference but do, not least because they're so rarely seen before the Supreme Court. She was absolutely game for it, like a kid on the playground who doesn't seem to realize she's the smallest one out there. The justices weren't as inclined to interrupt her, and she took the state's argument against PIA quantification and wrapped it in a tragic history in a voice that never quavered. "Wyoming suggests that the tribes have had ample opportunity to demonstrate the amount of water needed for this reservation, ignoring utterly that over the last eighty years the federal government has funded irrigation projects at Wind River and throughout the west primarily for the benefit of non-Indians." All this was in the briefs. Even within the historic boundaries of the reservation, the federal government had invested ten times the money in non-Indian irrigation as it had in the tribes'.

She saw the light go amber; she saw it go red. Judge Rehnquist said nothing. He was letting her run long.

"For the first time in their history, the Shoshone and the Arapaho tribes are poised to build a sustained and productive reservation agricultural economy. This is what their ancestors envisioned in 1868 and what the tribes must do in 1989 to alleviate staggering unemployment and poverty-related social ills on this reservation."

She was finished. It was over. Everyone rose as the justices left their seats. In a daze, the attorneys piled their briefing books, clearing the tables for the next case, and made for the exits. Williams grabbed the quill pen—a memento for each attorney who argues there—and followed Goodman out, catching the tip of the quill on the heavy red curtain and breaking it off.

Was it an omen? she wondered.

Justice William Brennan was moved by the inequity described by Williams. "The court now proposes, in effect, to penalize them for the lack of investment on their reservations by taking from them those water rights that have remained theirs, until now, on paper," he wrote in a draft opinion.

But Brennan was writing a dissent. Four of the justices were siding with Sandra Day O'Connor, who was ready to give Wyoming a victory and send the case back to the state court to reconsider the method used to quantify the tribes' water. Her reasons were the very ones the state never got to flesh out in its oral arguments: the impact on non-Indian users of the "future" water-rights award for projects that, in today's world, might never be constructed. As attorneys on both sides had suspected, O'Connor wanted to make some Indian water law of her own.

But before any of that came out, a memo from O'Connor was circulated June 22, 1989: "The unexpected has become the order of the day this Term. I am a minority stockholder in my family's ranching corporation. My brother, who manages the ranch, telephoned me this week to let me know the corporation has been named in a river water suit brought by an Indian tribe affecting the Gila River, which adjoins a portion of the ranch . . . as of now I believe I must disqualify myself in this case."

A few weeks later, this Per Curiam: "The judgment below is affirmed by an equally divided Court. Justice O'Connor took no part in the decision of this case."

The Wind River decree was allowed to stand, on a 4–4 vote.

The tribes had won.

Even if O'Connor had prevailed, the court would not have ruled on whether the tribes could use their water rights for something other than growing crops. The Wyoming District Court had affirmed they could change the use of their water rights, while the state Supreme Court said nothing on this. And so the tribes, a year later, listened to Dick Baldes and Kate Vandemoer and Susan Williams explain how they could dedicate some of their water rights to instream flow in order to protect fish and prevent the dewatering of riverbeds by irrigators. At the same time, they listened to Midvale irrigator Mike Donelson, who spoke in favor of instream flow as long as it was accompanied by new storage dams upstream. Donelson, echoing other farmers, wanted to "leave the lawyers out of it and work together as individuals."

But it was too late for that, and from the tribes' view it was on behalf of farmers like Donelson that the state had engaged lawyers and gone to court thirteen years earlier. Now the tribes were intent on turning the huge "paper" water right they'd won in that lawsuit into "wet" water.

That was a direct challenge to Jeff Fassett. He, too, was not opposed to instream flow. He was willing to work with the tribes, and in the long term he could see some possibilities for large investment in water storage that would make possible instream flow and "all the things they're interested in doing" without destroying others' livelihoods. Short-term, though, he wasn't about to cut off farmers who held state water rights: they depended on him. The tribes, he felt, had put their faith in the federal government and turned against the state and their neighbors, undermining his authority in the process.

Once again, he was on the front line. He knew he would be accused of disrespect for the tribes, ignorance of the decree, perhaps even contempt of court. He could blame the lawyers for his predicament, and like a lot of others, he did.

CHAPTER 12

CHAPTER 12
CHAPTER 12
CHAPTER 12

North Fork

Everyone involved in this case, including the media, had put in long hours on the hard benches of the Worland courtroom. I had worn out my eyes reading transcripts, exhausted my questions in hallway interviews, gone numb from answers that got mired in the lingo of engineering, agriculture, and water law. It was time for all of us to flee, *out the courtroom door,* away from the old men in robes, away from the cologne-scented, hair-in-place, former debate-team captains jousting with words. There was still a world out there of cobble streams running beneath cottonwoods.

In the fall of 1989, when farmers in the Wind River Valley sat burnt-neck exhausted at the kitchen table at the end of the day wondering if they had any future left here, when the phones at the tribal water engineer's office and the U.S. Fish and Wildlife Service rang and rang with edgy-voiced questions from bosses who'd gotten edgy-voiced calls from congressional aides, when the Shoshone were fighting one another over who qualified for tribal membership and the Arapaho were fighting one another over where the tribe's money went, when the state engineer was trying to reassure farmers that he could protect them against a water grab by the tribes, Baldes took his son Jason fishing.

In late August, the rabbitbrush blooms yellow on the stream-banks in the Wind River Basin, the nose-clotting clouds of insects are quelled by the cooling nights, the cloven prints of white-tailed deer zig to the water and zag around the bramble of wild rose and under the willows to the beds of cool, damp earth, and you can see turning in the clear water the yellow belly and red maculae of the brown trout and the soft pink brush stroke of the rainbow trout. Baldes steered his truck up a two-track that climbed the ridge between the South and North Forks of the Little Wind River. They drove up the backslope of an earthen sea rolling west, a wave of tawny, dried-out ocean bottom combing toward the solid granite face of the Rockies. Here and there this westward surge of foothill is broken dramatically by a stream, which cuts through it like a surfer breaking through the back of a curl. Baldes stopped on the lip of one of these, the North Fork of the Little Wind River, and they descended on foot, he with his fly rod, Jason with his spin-cast rig.

The North Fork is not a big stream, but it's a healthy one, with firm banks, falls, and pools, its path skewed usefully by unyielding outcrops and boulders cast down in spring torrents. It's hard for anglers to get to, if they even know about it, so the fish do wonderfully well.

Father and son worked their way upstream, hooking a small trout now and then and throwing it back. One of the pools had a crinkly riffle where the current skirted a bison-sized boulder, and then a deep spot where the water smoothed. A small place with good possibilities. Late in the afternoon, you could see the little gulping rises of unhurried fish, methodically dining on mayflies. A spin-cast lure was useless when the fish were watching the hatches on the surface, so Baldes offered Jason the fly rod. The boy had been asking for it all year, rolling his eyes when his father told him he wasn't ready.

Small shrubby streams make a mockery of the graceful, spacious art of classic fly casting and respond best to a more cramped style of attack, which can look pretty artless but in fact requires precision, patience, and stealth. Of these qualities, alas, nine-year-olds often possess only the stealth. But there was space for one fisherman at a time on this pool, so Baldes offered Jason the old fiberglass pole he'd been using for twenty years.

First the son had to endure his father's casting demonstration, which he watched sideways with his raven head propped on skinny arms across his knees. It was a sunny, squinty day, with a breeze off the mountain putting a shimmer in the trees. He'd been quietly studying his father's moves for years, and knew, like most sons, the large difference between doing and saying.

When at last he was handed the rod, Jason positioned himself on a rock at the bottom of the pool—out from the bank, safer from snags—and began casting. The movement was stiff-armed at first, but his father watched and said nothing. Attached to the tippet was an elk-hair caddis. On what must've been his tenth cast, the fly looped up to the riffle and came bobbing over the small standing waves and into the deeper, smoother water.

In this clear water they both could see the trout rise to the fly, which it took with a sudden, sideways jerk of the head. The fish threw its heft against the line and darted upstream, and Jason could feel its pull from his wrists to his shoulders. His father fought the urge to step forward and add his hand to the rod, while Jason fought the urge to give his father a help-me glance. The rainbow dove with the fly, but when the pull on his jaw didn't give, he charged angrily to the surface, where he jumped and danced, slacking the line and trying to throw the hook. The fish was bigger than anything Jason had ever caught, over twenty inches.

"Just let it run," Baldes whispered, watching Jason's left hand pulling on the loose line and dropping it at his feet. The fish darted up and down the pool, erupting now and then for another head-flopping Charleston. Jason's eyes were narrow, watching the arc of his rod as he tried to steer the fish away from the accelerating current at the pool's outlet. For more than five minutes the boy and the fish pulled and gave. Then the trout made a final, exhausted leap and allowed itself to be dragged into the shallows, where it lay defenseless on its side with an unblinking eye taking in the sky.

"Nice fish, Jase," said Baldes. "Good fight. You ready to let it go?"

Jason shook his head no. Almost always, they released the fish they caught. Baldes was surprised. Was it because this was the boy's first catch with a fly, or maybe the battle to land it? His son crouched above the fish and stared at it—a husky trout with a bright red slash down its side.

The father ran a stringer through the trout's gills and placed it in shaded water. Jason left the rod leaning against the rock—no further interest in fishing, apparently. Let him think about it, Baldes decided. He took the rod and started upriver, and each time he looked back his son still squatted motionless by the fish. Baldes went from pool to pool, hooking a few small browns and letting them go, until his arms grew tired. The light was starting to fail when he headed downstream.

For a moment, before Jason knew he was there, he was free to watch his son, to study the shape of his head and the slope of his shoulders and to imagine the utter concentration of a mind trans- fixed by the very slight movements of the rainbow. It was like a vigil at a sickbed. Then Baldes said, "Okay, you want to keep this fish or turn him loose?" The boy was startled. Baldes believed in letting the big fighters go, but he held no principled opposition to killing; his freezer was full of game. Anyway, it was Jason's fish.

The boy said nothing for a moment, then: "He fought so hard. I think we better turn him loose."

Baldes felt a surprising rush of relief.

As they walked back up from the river, he tried in his mind's eye to see Jason's face and what was on it when the boy was crouched over the beautiful fish in the shallows, and tried to remember from his own youth the gifts that passed between boy and fish. That task could take a good piece of time.

From atop the ridge Baldes and his son drove up, you can see the green paths of the South and North Forks as they journey east to Fort Washakie, where they join. The steep sides of the canyons flare out and flatten like collars opening at the neck, and the bald, steep rocks smooth first into rocky hills and then green fields. Fences appear, then livestock corrals, sheds, and muddy pick- ups. The twisting path of the river is marked by tottering cotton- woods and thick borders of willows. Barely visible in this cover is a hump of brown canvas set back from the riverbank, with a trail of smoke rising from a smoldering fire.

Sumner Marlowe pulled his shirt over his head, freeing his long hair, and stripped to his swimming trunks. The first of four red-hot rocks had been carried by shovel to the door of the sweat lodge and placed in a pit just inside. The river was low, its bumpy surface dimpled with light from the setting sun. The lodge faced east, toward a clearing where burning cottonwood logs surrounded river rocks, heating them for the sweat. Clustered around were at least a dozen people, including shy teenage girls, an older white man with a cigarette dangling from his mouth, a Shoshone elder, myself, Sumner Marlowe, and leaders from both tribes, including Virginia Sutter and John Washakie—a motley, convivial group, moving about, shaking hands, talking and laughing. This might've been a weekend barbecue, except that only rocks were on the fire and the guests were in various stages of disrobing.

Every year, Zedora Enos's family erected a sweat lodge on their property along the North Fork, and people squeezed into the lodge to pray and purify themselves in a wash of hot steam and darkness and sweet cedar fumes. There was no set schedule. Someone who might be ill or overstressed or in need of a spiritual boost might call the family and ask for a sweat. Other people would hear about it, and offer help or support, perhaps to deal with some problems of their own. A core congregation showed up regularly; but others, like Sumner Marlowe, dropped in occasionally.

The lodge was built by anchoring green willow branches in the ground and bending them over to form a shelter. Several layers of blankets and tarps were then lain across the willows, until the lodge looked like a brown beanie cap or an enormous drooping mushroom. Facing the east, and the fire, was an opening with a blanket flap that could be closed or opened when people came in or left. Inside, at the center, was a shallow pit where the red-hot stones would be placed, a dipper, and a bucket of water; sitting at the rear, James Trosper, who would lead the prayers.

The variety of guests at these sweats increased the likelihood that old feuds and enmities might be circling the altar, but some of these folks were Marlowe's relatives, and he felt welcome. Sweats tended to diffuse tension. Anyone present was there because of a spiritual need or at least a wholesome, cleansing desire. They knew going in that they'd be asked to pray for others a chance, perhaps, to look on an enemy with fresh generosity.

During the four rounds of sweating, prayers would be offered both in silence and out loud. Marlowe had always had reasons to pray: for a job, for his family, for a plan to catch some wily horses, for ill friends. "It's not hard to think of people who need help, in the hospital or somewhere else," he said. During the long years when he drank and smoked dope, he prayed for help controlling himself, and sometimes it worked for a while. He always prayed for the children, and now he prayed for his daughter and his nephew, Michael Marlowe.

The sweat lodge has been called the "little brother of the big lodge," the big lodge being the Sun Dance, the most vibrant contemporary spiritual event in the lives of many Indians. Strength and insight, even visions, can be infused in a sweat or a dance, but on the other hand it's possible that *nothing* will happen. Some men who've gone repeatedly into the Sun Dance never have experienced the seizing vision that throws a man to the ground, unconscious or in a dream, and teaches him secrets—but their regrets are mild, because the days of thirst and prayer at least cleared their bodies and minds. "Sometimes you want the power strong, you want it to manifest," said Trosper, a Sun Dance chief, "and it just doesn't happen. It's not up to you."

In 1985, Marlowe was asked during a sweat with Arapaho elders to pour water. This is an important role and an honor: the one who pours decides how hot the sweat will be, by the amount of water turned to burning steam on the rocks. The process begins when the red-hot rocks are brought into the lodge—usually four rocks to begin—and people enter silently, hunched over as they circle the low-ceilinged lodge clockwise and seat themselves. There are four "rounds" to the sweat, between which you can leave the darkness of the lodge to stand in the open air. During Trosper's sweats, there is "doctoring" in the third round for people with ills, and a chance, for those who want to, to talk of their travails, their gratitude, their hard road. After three rounds of prayer and proximity, shy people lose their fear of revealing their pain, and in the darkness secrets are shared and tears are shed. When Marlowe poured the water for the Arapaho elders, he was asked to pray in the third round. He asked for help to go straight and quit his drinking and doping.

He had asked the same thing as a dancer in the Arapaho Sun

Dance. He wanted help, but he was still hedging his bets. He had a wife and a newborn and no steady paycheck, and it wasn't as much fun as it used to be. He didn't drink every day, but when he had a birthday coming up or some other excuse, he'd start a party that would last a week. His marriage was shaky—his wife drank, too—and Marlowe had trouble with her family. Only a month earlier, he'd vowed in the Catholic Church to quit his binges, and the priest at St. Stephens had had him sign a pledge that included abstinence from marijuana; he told the priest he wanted to quit alcohol but continue smoking. The priest crossed marijuana off the list, and Marlowe almost laughed with glee as he signed it.

So there was reason for skepticism when Marlowe lay on the ground resting after the sweat with the Arapaho elders. One of the old men came up to him and started talking about his own troubled times with the bottle. Marlowe told him he had taken a pledge. "A pledge is just a piece of paper," the old man said to Marlowe. "It's got to come from the heart." He tapped his chest. "The only way to quit is, you've got to have the *want* to quit." It was not that often that an elder opened his heart, and Marlowe felt abashed by the elder's generosity.

He was not sure at first that he believed himself. Weeks went by, and in his dreams he was still gulping liquor. But he would wake himself up—he could do that—and start another dream, changing the subject. As the landscape of his dreams changed, he became more uncomfortable with his waking world: the same troubled house, crowded with the family and friends with whom he had lived and hunted and slept and partied. When he wasn't drinking, there seemed to be more empty hours in the day, hours that in the past he'd been able to erase with drugs. Some of his relatives, the wilder ones, always seemed angry about all sorts of things. And he noticed disrespect he'd previously been deaf to—as when his nephew Michael, just a boy, cursed his grandfather when he was asked to help load hay.

Marlowe moved out and went to stay with his father. Monroe Marlowe was laid up with heart problems, so they had time to talk. He talked to his son about the reservation of his own childhood, a very different world. "We were a clan. Each morning we knew what was expected of us—to milk cows, whatever. Everybody in the clan disciplined us—our parents, our uncles, aunts. Our time was taken up, and then, then we'd ride our horses."

Monroe Marlowe wanted his son to get a degree in education, to come back to the reservation and work in the schools. He blamed the boarding schools for the trouble young people had today. He watched his son carefully, knowing he was only *just* sober, knowing how he missed his wife and daughter. His tried to take some of the blame off Sumner's shoulders. "My generation didn't learn the ways of the people, didn't learn the language. For so many of you, parents were never really parents. They came back from the schools, and they had kids, and they didn't have no family sense."

Sumner Marlowe resolved to go back to school. He assumed that this time his wife wouldn't leave her relatives to accompany him, and that his daughter would stay with her. There were other trials ahead that his father foresaw but didn't bring up. Monroe knew there would be envy among Indians if his son returned with a graduate degree. And he knew that while schools off the reservation would hire him, they would follow him and watch him as if he were a child. But as a boy Monroe Marlowe had run away from the missionary schools, and since then he'd devoted his adult life to building reservation schools where Indian kids could feel at home. And that's what he wanted his son to be part of.

Sumner went back to school on the West Coast alone, knowing that his leaving was driving a deeper wedge between him and his wife and daughter. He did well, but when he heard from Monroe that his daughter and his nephews were moving with a bad crowd, doing the same sorts of things he once did himself, he came home. He had no plan, just the conviction that it was time for him to be there. He got a job in Riverton. He stopped in at the house by the river, but was not welcomed. When his nephew shot Ray Brush, it swept over him like a black wave. If he'd fallen back into his old ways during this lonely and anguished time, people might have understood.

But when he ducked into Trosper's sweat lodge, years after the shooting, he was still sober and had been for ten years.

He was glad to be seated inside when the flap came down across the entrance and swaddled them in darkness. He felt the wet touch of the shoulder next to him, and heard the labored breathing of an old person on the other side. Trosper's voice came out of the dark sounding small and tinny, far away, giving thanks to the Creator. There was the fizzy sound of water pouring on the rocks, and the sensation of his own liquid core springing up to the heat, and the music of the river just outside.

Marlowe always had reasons to pray.

CHAPTER 13

Diversion Dam

The rivers climb out of the Wind River Valley into the mountains like the three toes of a bird—the Popo Agie to the south, the Little Wind in the middle, and the Big Wind to the north end of the range. Our journey now turns north, crossing over from the fine filament of the Little Wind to the thick artery of the Big Wind, the pulse of the valley, the prize of those who covet water.

In August, James Trosper drove north out of the valley and up onto the plateau drained by Sage Creek, on his way to cut down a tree. It was a hot, muggy day, and several people were with him, including an elder visiting from the Ute tribe. Trosper was headed to a grove of cottonwoods along the Big Wind where the water eddied in ponds. A forked tree would be cut and placed at the center of the Sun Dance lodge, and hung with buffalo skull, eagle feathers, and flags.

A Sun Dance happens because a dream says it will. The spiritual leader who brought the dance to the Shoshone around 1820, Yellow Hand, had a vision in which a buffalo taught him the dance. Each dancer who enters the lodge follows, similarly, a personal call. So does the Sun Dance chief, which makes it chancy: one year he might not have a dream instructing him to sponsor the dance. Some years there are several Sun Dances at Wind River, because several men had dreams. "Dream" may not adequately describe the trancelike, paralyzed state, neither exactly asleep or awake, in which power and wisdom are often received. Fasting in the mountains can lead to such dreams: That was what John Truhero, Yellow

Hand's grandson and Trosper's great-grandfather, was doing when he met Seven Arrows.

Seven Arrows was one of the "little people," or *nimimbe*, who inhabited the Wind River Mountains and can be both tormentors and advisers to the Shoshone. Beatrice-like, Seven Arrows led Truhero through a wall of rock and into a series of subterranean chambers in the heart of the mountain. In different rooms, men were racing horses and gambling at hand games. Those were evidently temptations, because the final chamber contained a sick person in a tepee, ministered to by an Indian doctor while a drum was played and a song was sung. Seven Arrows said Truhero must choose between two trails, the peyote church or the Sun Dance, and directed him to choose the Sun Dance.

Truhero has been dead since 1985, but visions continue to guide the dance. Trosper and his subchief each had dreams in which they saw the center pole, but they weren't sure just where it was in the corporeal world. Trosper trusted that he would recognize it, and he did, one day when he was out gathering willows that would line the encircling walls of the lodge. The Sun Dance lodge is about 100 feet across, with cottonwood spokes radiating from the notch in the center pole to the circular outer wall. Leafy limbs lean against the exterior frame, providing shade for the dancers when they rest. The lodge entry—wide enough for an audience outside to see much of what goes on within—opens to the east and the rising sun.

Once the center pole was located, Trosper gathered his crew and headed north again to cut it. The road rose from the snug valley of the Little Wind through stubbly, grazed hills and then leveled off. There is an anticline beneath Sage Creek, where the earth's surface has responded to subterranean pressure by bulging up a little, forming Winkleman Dome—shales and sandstones that then filled with underground pools of oil. Even before you see the oil pumpers on the ridge, you might smell them: hydrogen sulfide gas comes up with the crude. This field has been producing since 1917, and it's one of the reasons the Wind River tribes can afford modest creature comforts . . . and their legal representatives.

For most of those years, the tribes collected only a pittance, because they were locked in long-term leases negotiated by the

BIA. While oil companies were pocketing $40 a barrel after the international oil embargo of the 1970s, the tribes received the same $2 they'd been getting under their original leases. That changed after the oil thefts were uncovered; and luckily for the tribes, the field continues to produce, 85 million barrels later, long after geologists predicted it would run dry. It could be that as the underground stores of oil deplete, the huge volume of water that comes down off the mountains every year—much of it underground—repressurizes the dome and pushes up what's left. The geology of the Rockies is so faulted and flipped that most descriptions of what's underground are merely educated guesses.

Driving north, Trosper crossed the high, flat sagebrush steppes where the oil field sits. The small creeks were mostly dry by late June, but some of them open into steep little washes, barely visible, which drop like trapdoors through the level plain. In those washes you might find elegantly carved sandstone spires, blooming wildflowers, flint chips left by ancient hunters, and a trickle of water.

When Trosper first began leading the Sun Dances, they were held across from Winkleman Dome in a dry, sun-beaten area of sagebrush and greasewood, so remote and exposed that it undoubtedly contributed to the dancers' travails. There was some controversy in the early 1990s, because Trosper and his subchiefs were young, and other families felt they had a claim on the rite. Trosper's revered and long-lived great-grandfather, John Truhero had spent a good deal of time up north on the Crow reservation (the family is descended from Chief Washakie and his Crow wife), and when he retired from the Sun Dance, he gave his "doctoring" eagle feathers and other medicines to a Crow, Tom Yellowtail. But Truhero's granddaughter, Zedora Enos, kept Seven Arrows' medicine bundle at Wind River. Trosper was a teenager when his grandfather died, and the family had no clear idea who would ultimately receive the bundle. One year it became "really active" and the family became concerned about whether they were giving it the proper care. Zedora Enos sent her son, James Trosper, to visit Yellowtail in Montana, carrying the medicine bundle. The old man greeted him happily, and performed a ceremony. (Trosper, trying to preserve the old knowledge, asked to record it, but Yellowtail refused.) When he was finished, Yellowtail said, "I'll come down and help when you put up the Sun Dance this summer." Though Trosper had experienced some significant dreams involving eagles and a wolf earlier that year, he hadn't considered putting on a ceremony himself until Yellowtail spoke of it. On subsequent visits, the old man instructed him about the ceremony and told him where to get roots and other medicines.

There is no college of cardinals to select Sun Dance chiefs, nor a right by lineage. Still, there are symbols of legitimacy, and today they inspire both jealousy and awe, as they did half a century ago. That Trosper's family holds the medicine bundle that represents Seven Arrows is no small thing. Some would say "representing" isn't the right word, that the medicine bundle *is* Seven Arrows.

Curious white people sometimes attend Sun Dances. With me, it has more commonly been the Arapaho Sun Dance, a big affair in Ethete where I can eat and play Scrabble with Alonzo Moss in his arbor when he's not tending dancers as a "grandfather." Southern Arapaho from Oklahoma and Gros Ventre from Montana often attend, creating a large tent city around the lodge. Early in the morning, when a medicine man sings a gentle song, I stumble out with others, wrapped in a blanket, and watch the brightly painted dancers, bouncing on their heels at the lodge entrance, and raising the sun with their eagle-bone whistles. The Shoshone dances at remote sites are less populous, and there are differences of substance as well, such as the Shoshone style of dancing forward to the center pole—charging the buffalo—while the Arapaho dance in place. Each tribe—and at least a dozen other Plains tribes as well— claims to have had the Sun Dance first.

Here is a morning prayer from a Shoshone Sun Dance fifty years ago:

> *Tam Apo,* here we are, standing up and facing towards the sunrise. I am offering a prayer again, asking your blessing. The sun you made has come up, it is shining towards us, all over, and it is the light from you and we like to have this every day of our life, and we want to live a long time. Because we are suffering for our homes,

families, friends, and all kinds of nations, I want you to bless us. And I ask you to bless the service boys so that they will be safe and nothing will happen to them. . . . I ask you to see to it that there will be no war, make it that way through your willpower. And when we get to the end of these three days, when we get out, give us our water and our food. The powerful water will give us good strength, and so will the food—what we eat will give us good strength. For we want to live as long as we possibly can.

You can't think of the Sun Dance and not think about water, because the ceremony is *defined* by the absence of water; sometimes it's called "Standing in Thirst." At the end of the dance, singers by the lodge entrance sing the Water Song, and water mixed with a special white clay is ingested. Sometimes dancers who have collapsed—bowled over by the buffalo, it's said—awaken with their thirst spiritually quenched.

White people have occasionally gone into a Shoshone Sun Dance, but it's not encouraged, partly because some Indian participants will shy away from sharing the lodge with whites. (Visitors who want to sit outside the lodge are welcome at either tribe's camp, as long as they don't bring cameras.) Whereas Western religions proselytize, nourishing themselves on the capture of new souls, Native American religions don't; they survive by retaining their secrets.

Historically, they had to be secretive. The Indian Office outlawed the Sun Dance earlier in the twentieth century, offended by ritualistic mutilation (wood skewers were once pierced through dancers' chest or back muscles and tied to the center pole) and other "objectionable native customs" that diverted Indians from school and hard work. This sort of dance, according to a 1921 memo to reservation superintendents, encouraged sex, drugs, and "shiftless indifference to family welfare." Sounds a little like rock-and-roll.

The road from Fort Washakie follows the curve of the mountains north, and rises gradually to a panoramic view of the Big Wind River Valley—deeper and wider than the Little Wind, less cozy, more monumental. To the north stands Crowheart Butte, a great fez of sandstone that rises by the river in the center of the valley. And below, where the river takes a steep turn to the east, its waters are stalled by Diversion Dam, which supplies the Midvale/Riverton Unit.

Trosper drove down to the river and parked short of the dam, which was pouring small white tongues of water from its seven portals. Grasses, trees, and bushes grow thick here, partly because of the dam, which slows and spreads the river out just to the west, allowing it to settle into the ground and reemerge outside the riverbed in the low places. Wildlife likes it: There are deer nibbling in the marsh, pelicans billing in the ponds, and sandhill cranes flying overhead.

With the Sun Dance drawing near, Trosper had been anxious to find the center pole. When he returned with his cohorts to cut it down—*him* is the pronoun he used—they first prayed and burned cedar, standing in a circle around the forked tree. The smoke went straight up in the windless air, through the bushes and canopy, as if there was no uncertainty or difficulty in finding a path to carry prayers. The calmness of the place took hold of the group. They smoked a pipe. They rubbed the blade of the ax with sweet sage, then struck the trunk of the tree four times. They sang to the tree four times. Then they cut the cottonwood down, lowering it carefully into the back of the truck so that it never touched the ground.

Trosper had asked permission of Millie Guina, an old Shoshone woman who lived nearby along the river, and she'd told him he could go anywhere around her place. The land where the tree stood might have belonged to Guina's non-Indian neighbors, the Hoopengarners. Or it might have belonged to the U.S. Bureau of Reclamation, which built the dam back in 1924. But it never occurred to Trosper to ask the agency; for that matter, he seemed oblivious to the dam itself, though its dull roar followed him everywhere as he went about his work.

One thing I notice about a lot of Indian women is their forearms. Millie Guina has saggy eyes and the caved-in smile of a woman in her eighties, but when she slaps a fly in her snug home near the Wind River it sounds like a two-by-four coming down on the card table; from her elbows to her hands there's enough muscle to wrestle calves for branding. Which she used to do: rope and brand calves, ride and shoot and drag elk home through the snow, roam the wild country above Sage Creek and Bull Lake with a small band of Indian women who were, according to those who knew them, tougher than most cowboys. The day we met she wore a colorful flower-print dress with loose sleeves to the elbow, leaving her sinewy brown arms free. She still tans hides the old way in her backyard: scraping them, stretching them, coating them with a paste of cow brains. (She's mischievous: "I go into Safeway," she said, "and ask the guy, 'You got any brains?' ")

The old women of both tribes seem to age better than the men, who grow quieter and quieter, creaky and sad-eyed, until finally there is no voice for their knowledge. The old women are often talkative and boisterous. You can spend hours with Guina, or Helen Cedartree, or Cleone Thunder, and hear stories the way they were once told as bedtime entertainment, spiced with teasing asides. ("Those Arapaho," Guina said, "before they go in Sun Dance, they eat dog soup.")

People pay good prices for Guina's beadwork, and she teaches those who want to learn, though she complains that young people don't know anything, that they'll ask her for instruction and then not show up. She showed me a beautiful bird on a field of blue beads, a design she picked up in Oklahoma, from the Kiowa. "He lives in the water, and brings water or rain," she said of the image. "The peyote people use it—you pray to the waterbird."

But how much praying is there now? "The powerful prayers haven't been used since John Truhero," she said. Truhero was more than a hundred when he died in 1985. Few Shoshone or Arapaho now belong to the societies of each tribe that once were assigned duties and esteemed among the people. I've mentioned Arapaho lodges like the Kit Foxes, the Crazy Lodge, and the Water-Sprinkling Old Men. The Shoshone lodges included the Logs (*wobine*) and the Yellow Noses (*oho mupe*)—warriors who used inverted speech, answering no when they meant yes. Dances that were once important to the tribe have been forgotten, and when Guina named the medicine men and doctors who once lived along Sage Creek—Pine Tree, Sam Nipwater, Toody Roberts—she shook her head in puzzlement. Why had these old ones taken their knowledge, their songs and prayers, with them to the grave? The same question applies to the Arapaho.

Like her tanning methods and other traditional skills, a lot of what she knows may die with her. She knows no English words for some of the healing plants; "toy-yah-vee-tum-buck" (my phonetics) is her name for a tall weed found up in the mountains, which you boil and apply to infections. For Guina and some of the other older reservation women, there is a medicine cabinet outside her door: pain relievers from grasses for stomach problems, ground bark for headaches, even a root that helps a man catch a woman . . . but "it's bad to use that—you end up with a crazy woman." She smiles as if this might be fun.

Here are some more remedies used in the past and present by Wind River traditional people:

bawayump A dried plant rubbed on an infant's skin to alleviate rash.

cutnose Bush (*tabbicabiic* in Arapaho) Walnuts from this tree are worn on a string by children for protection.

dogtooth violet (*do yawitambok* in Shoshone) Used as a painkiller.

Griswold root Ground fine and used to heal open sores when applied as a powder and dusted on.

hacawaanaxu A root ground and mixed with earth by the Arapaho, drunk in boiled water for back and chest pain.

Indian home prairie flower The leaves are wide and long, and it's gathered in the summer, used to increase the appetite and growth of children.

Lichen from conifer bark Dried and reduced to snuff, and used for headache.

Niaata A ground root consumed in water by the Arapaho for cough.

pine bark Mixed with a mountain root called "Fine Root," it's brewed in tea and used for headache and bad coughs.

peppermint   Good for kidneys, brewed in tea.

pi yigwab wa   An herb used by Shoshone to induce milk in a mother, translates as "milk squeezing."

prickly pear (*Opuntia* in Shoshone)   The boiled pulp of prickly pear cactus, taken by pregnant women in ill health.

sweet grass   Found above ground in swamps, burned by medicine men during prayers, used by young women as shampoo.

water lily   Mixed with grease and used for ailments of the skin, has some supernatural powers.

wild parsnip (*paro za* in Shoshone)   Used as a painkiller.

willow bark   Boil it and drink for stomach ailments and pain relief.

Guina spreads her beadwork out on a card table in her new blue house, two snug rooms where she lives alone. The tribes take care of their older people with housing and meals, even recreational trips out of state. When an elder says prayers at meetings, or tells stories in the schools, a wad of bills is usually pressed in his hand. I shot some video interviews of elders a few years ago, and when the Shoshone man who was helping me slipped Starr Weed some money, I asked if I should make a similar gift. "Oh, no," he said, "it should come from me." Simply growing old confers grace and wisdom. Few elders have to live alone, though the more independent ones, like Guina, prefer to take care of themselves. A nephew who lives in an older house behind Guina's is supposed to look after her, but he isn't always reliable. Her nearest neighbors, Bob and Molly Hoopengarner, who live just upstream beside the dam, make a point of dropping by.

Hoopengarner, a semiretired rancher whose thicket of white hair looks as if it's been licked by half a dozen cows, was born by the Wind River in 1915, the year after his parents moved there from Nebraska. The Hoopengarners were encouraged to move in by the Office of Indian Affairs, which sold them land by the river for $4 an acre on a "dead heir" deed—a piece of reservation land allotted to an Indian who'd died without a will. "They were trying to get white people to move in here," said Hoopengarner, who would have been too young to know this firsthand. "They figured the more white people you got, the sooner you'd get rid of the Indians.

"They were wrong."

Hoopengarner is an old man without many illusions, except perhaps his notion that he knows more about ranching than his college-educated daughter, Pat. She keeps about three hundred cows on the place now, and he keeps an eye on things while she works two other jobs. Listening to him, you'd think she was doing just about everything wrong, misled by all that education. The old man keeps neither his opinions nor his small, poorly lit ranchhouse in decorous order: a bag of tin cans sits in the middle of the kitchen, dogs bring the smells of the yard indoors.

He talked to me about how the Indian women "breed" half a century ago wanted to marry white men and get away from their own people. He says it without meanness, not as a proof of anything—just an unfiltered remembrance of how things were with his neighbors sixty years ago. He grew up during a time when your entire world was a stream and the people who lived along it, when "everybody was poor, but the Indians were poorer," and you knew the business of each family, whether it was a father's weakness for pinochle or a ranch woman's knack for raising turkeys. Hoopengarner and his neighbor Harold Winchester (several miles away, up Bull Lake Creek) started school at five years old so there would be enough kids from surrounding ranches to employ a schoolteacher in a one-room schoolhouse. To put water on their fields, Harold's and Bob's families joined forces, and horses, to dynamite and clear a ditch through the glacial till that forms hills along the mountain front above the river.

That private, family-dug ditch is still running today, which may explain why Hoopengarner is not impressed by the big government-subsidized canal just down the road. Diversion Dam inundated some of the family's land when it was built in the 1920s. That wasn't all bad: The government paid the Hoopengarners nearly ten times what they'd paid for the same land a decade earlier, and the family picked up some additional revenue supplying the dam builders with food and goods. "Hay for those mules was like the gasoline business is now."

Hoopengarner's second wife, Molly, arrived in Wyoming as a teacher in the 1950s and, coming from Wisconsin, wondered why anyone would bother farming in such dry country. She has short white hair and a buck-toothed smile, and though she's a small woman, she recently qualified for the national Senior Olympics in the shot put. During the years when I was interviewing farmers on the Riverton Unit, she would sometimes show up at our meetings, fumbling with her hearing aid, and I thought her smiling presence made things go easier. Only later did I find that she'd written a 250-page study on the origins of the project, a manuscript chock-full of old newspaper clippings and government memos that show what a serpentine path the dreams of empire followed in the American West. Despite her friendly demeanor, she feels the project farmers have always distrusted her.

Yet her study is fairly sympathetic. She doesn't blame the farmers for the shortcomings of the project or the losses of the Indians; she simply navigates the labyrinth of speculation, government give-aways, hyperbolic promotion, and repeated failures that ultimately resulted in an irrigation project that, like many others in the arid West, can't pay for itself. The government, she concluded mildly, "erred in trying to undertake too large a project. . . . It is my firm belief that since the federal government created this mess, it is the responsibility of the federal government to make amends." That's the way a lot of people feel. But the federal government has been so slow to do anything, and its loyalties are so schizophrenic, that neither the Indians nor the white irrigators hold out much hope.

Her husband is more bluntly critical: "Midvale is inefficient. For every acre foot they take out, they lose one. The laws of physics enter into that. You run water from here to Shoshoni [a town near Boysen Reservoir], you lose a lot of it. . . . And when they put this [dam] in, they made a provision for silt."

Maybe what really bugs Hoopengarner is that he's more of a livestock man than a farmer. He likes to quote an old-timer who said to him, when Diversion Dam first went up, "God damn, they're ruining a lot of good sheep range with that big dam." He nods and smiles as he tells this, running a hand through the white prairie on his head.

Silt is piled along the Wyoming Canal on the other side of Diversion Dam like a series of diminutive pyramids. The "big" dam is quite small, comparatively; put next to Hoover Dam on the Colorado, it would be a pebble next to a boulder. It's much smaller than Boysen Reservoir, downstream, but that's partly because it's designed not to store water but to divert it.

In miniature, though, Diversion Dam and its related structures are typical of Western water development, perhaps more typical than the big hydroelectric dams on the Columbia or the giant Colorado River impoundments that supply Southern California. The idea over a century ago was that thousands of such small dams and canals would green the Western frontier. Eager settlers, and their eager hosts in the young Western states, expected an Eden of perpetually wet fields. They epitomized Horace Greeley's dictum "Turn your face to the great West, and there build up a home and fortune," and they were unafraid of going it alone on the frontier, as long as the government was practically giving land away.

Initially, Congress tried to promote water development the way it had railroads. The 1884 Carey Act (authored by a Wyoming senator) subsidized irrigation companies with big land grants to the states. That wasn't enough. The water speculators who made grand promises to Western homesteaders—in the case of the Wind River, the Central Wyoming Irrigation Company—failed right and left, and when they did, the settlers looked again to the federal government. Senator Francis Newlands—whose Truckee River Project in Nevada had lost him a fortune—joined Wyoming Representative Frank Mondell to pass a sweeping reclamation law that essentially handed the federal government the bill for irrigating the West.

A century later, only a small fraction of the West—a total acreage no larger than the state of Missouri—is irrigated, and the dream of cultivating a desert garden is fading. There is talk of tear-ing down dams on the Columbia; farms in some parts of the West are choking on salt after years of irrigation; and big impoundments on the Colorado are filling up with silt. A few years ago, during the Carter administration, the era of dam building was declared over, and the U.S. Bureau of Reclamation was reborn as a multipurpose water management agency that would look after not just farmers but ducks and water skiers and drinking fountains. A small project like the Riverton Unit might have continued on quietly, paying for its own upkeep (if not for its original cost). But when Dick Baldes and the Wind River tribes began attacking the project, it showed true Western character: one minute soldiering on with hardworking, go-it-alone yeomanry, the next whining like a hungry orphan for more help from the state and the federal government.

Irrigation projects in the West have three essential parts: an upstream dam to hold water during spring runoff for release during the summer and fall; a diversion structure to funnel irrigation water into a canal during those dry months; and a system of gated lateral ditches and pipes to put the water on fields. Often, a power plant is added to generate electricity from the flowing water; in the Riverton Unit, a small 1600-kilowatt plant was built off the Wyoming Canal at Pilot Butte Reservoir (and shut down in 1973).

The Wyoming Highway Department saw in Diversion Dam an inexpensive chance to run a county road across the river atop the 600-foot dam. That's a huge structure for such a small river, but it routes the river's current along the face of the dam from south to north, forming a bay that can empty either through the dam's spillways or into the outlet to the Wyoming Canal.

In a pullout next to the dam's roaring sluiceway, two pickups sat cab-by-cab on a late-summer morning. Bill Brown and Nick Harris were talking about silt. The silt that comes down the river to Diversion Dam, particularly during spring runoff, is a pale-brown mud sometimes brightened by a dash of cayenne red. It's much more beautiful to look at before it's stirred into this soup; the river-cut cliffs upstream are a geologist's dream, bands of chalky white volcanic ash, red clays, tan sandstones, purple slates. The soft sedimentary rock in the upper valley erodes into colorful badlands, but it erodes a lot, as the river drops steeply until Diversion Dam. Here the terrain flattens out, and the now-ugly silt settles down behind the dam, to the dismay of Bill Brown, Midvale's manager.

When silt builds up against the dam and the canal headworks, it blocks the flow of water and puts dangerous pressure on the structures. To relieve it, the dam tender will open the gates full some mornings and let a rush of muddy water surge downriver. It's done every fall, and other times as well. The settling muck from these purges coats the rocks and gravels downstream, to the dismay of Dick Baldes.

Silt also gets into the canal, which is scooped out by a dragline every fall and piled along the fence of the first farm along the ditch, the Harris place. When Bob Harris was chairman of the Shoshone Business Council, he threatened to sue Midvale over the mud that blocked his views. Now his son Nick is suggesting that Midvale pay him a princely sum to let the silt piles spill over onto his ranch. He and Brown part with smiles and no agreement, and Brown lights a cigarette and inhales deeply.

"There's no way I can give those people everything they want without just closing up this irrigation project and leaving it," he said to me with an exasperated sigh. "This project was a kind of show-and-tell for Indians. Here's what *you* can do. But they weren't interested."

Brown enjoys the show-and-tell. He's driven me all over the Midvale Project, from the far end of the canal by the Owl Creeks to the underwater gates of Bull Lake Dam. He's opened the files of the project, and set up interviews with Midvale farmers young and old. We've toured marshes where Midvale cultivates the waterfowl I've fired at from blinds on Midvale farms, and we've looked over the computers that trigger the gates at Bull Lake and Diversion Dam to adjust to the rise and fall of the streams.

But Brown is sixty-seven now, and his big frame has begun to sag, not so much with age as with discouragement. Beneath his black Baldwin Filters cap he wears a hearing aid, and he walks with a limp. Like many of Midvale's farmers, he feels unappreciated and hemmed in. His project has an annual budget over $1 million, irrigates over 70,000 acres, involves over 650 landowners, produces over $20 million in crops every year, and spins off who knows how many jobs in the local economy—but the project is getting squeezed from all directions. The farms that formed the backbone of the local economy half a century ago are being replaced by forty-acre "ranchettes." The federal agency that built the Riverton Unit, the U.S. Bureau of Reclamation, appears more interested these days in removing dams than in erecting them, and Brown can't get the time of day from the district manager. "That son of a bitch, I'll give him a good talk, and he just goes silent. He's just in the wrong camp, and they completely ignore the positive side." Indeed, the tone of the BOR's recent draft history of the Riverton Unit shows a decidedly negative attitude, describing a project that "as the years went by . . . became more of a salvage operation than an efficient irrigation enterprise."

It's an astonishing betrayal. For generations the federal government has promoted the Riverton Unit, from the time the first shovel of dirt was turned—paid for by Indian appropriations in 1918—to repeated efforts through the 1970s to lure new farmers into marginal lands at the far north end of the project. When Midvale couldn't pay back the federal investment in the project—over $75 million—the government kept the farmers in business by reducing the debt to less than $7 million.

Brown himself came out to Wyoming in 1951 from his parents' farm in North Dakota, a strapping kid of twenty who married young and was looking for some chances. "Riverton was a nice clean little town, and there was jobs around for young folks at the time. My wife worked for the Bureau of Reclamation as a draftsman, and I worked in the oil fields, and then for contractors.

"I was thirteen years in construction, traveling all the time, and my kids were growing up. When I bought my place on the project, an old fellow out here I got acquainted with, he said to me, 'What were you doing before you come out here? What kind of money were you making?' I told him, and he said, 'Young fellow, why don't you go see if you can get that job back.' It tickled me. I wasn't afraid of work. I had a place in town, and I traded places with old Mrs.

Williams, gave her a substantial amount of money, too. And it's worked for us."

We drove from Diversion Dam along the dirt road that follows the canal, then out through the open fields that stretch back toward the north side of the valley, walled by the Absaroka Mountains, which dangle south from the Yellowstone Plateau, and then the Owl Creeks, which dangle east from the Absarokas. We stayed away from the Riverton area and the fancy suburban homes that have crept into the farmlands around it and instead arched north toward Pavillion, a muddy cluster of homes that is barely a town anymore. Where the road cut 90-degree turns around a neatly cropped field, Brown pointed to some malt barley that was his. "The place has paid for itself. We don't have any money. It's really hard to start talking about turning it loose. But you have to sell. I spent thirty-two years—every one of these fields, put in pipe, got it level enough. My wife, she's out there with her shovel and her little dog, she can irrigate this place by herself. She's sixty-five, and she actually enjoys it. I'm kind of particular about who gets it."

It won't be his own children. "I wouldn't want them to farm. There are too many regulations. You can't get enough for what you raise. For a farmer, the rewards are kind of small."

But when Brown described the rewards, they sounded kind of big. "You just step back, put your hands on your hips, and look and see what you've done. You've paid your bills, and you got your kids educated. And a farm kid . . . he's got more concept of life, he puts a value on it. He sees birth and death from an early age. He knows the smell of soil and learns to like it."

He looked at me sheepishly. He was trying to convince me that Midvale farmers had their backs against the wall, but he couldn't escape the satisfaction he felt with the way his own life had played out. I wanted to reassure him that it *helped* his argument, because it suggested a way of life that might actually be *worth* subsidizing. Driving along the open road next to the ditch, with the big mountains up above us to the west and antelope on the hill to the north, he said, "I don't hunt. When my kids got old enough, I'd haul them up to the mountains, and I'd be the camp cook. I fenced thirty-five acres on my place for habitat, my own money.

"Me and my wife, after dinner at night, I'm not fooling, we'll get in the pickup and we'll get out and drive over my farm. Just to look at the wildlife. That's all."

CHAPTER 14

On the Wind

When Dick Baldes was in high school, he and his friend Richard Brown sometimes walked home together, and they'd stop at Dick's house for some of Juanita Baldes's homemade tortillas and beans. Sometimes they'd go to the house of Richard's older brother, Bill. "I fed him. He was just a nice little Mexican kid," Bill Brown remembers with a smile.

So years later, when Baldes returned to Wind River with a biology degree to work for the U.S. Fish and Wildlife Service and Bill Brown took over as Midvale's manager, both figured they would be able to work together. It didn't last long.

"We started off good," said Brown. "Then one time we had a terrible silt bar behind the dam. He saw them working in there, and he called me. I never got such a goddam ass-eating in my life. He just came apart."

Silt is the great enemy of Western dams. In arid regions where vegetation is thin—sometimes because of grazing—the roots' grip on the soil is weak, and a heavy rain can send tons of topsoil into the streams. As the river reaches lower elevations and slows down, the sediment settles to the bottom, only to be stirred up again and pushed farther downstream by the next surge of spring runoff. Theoretically, some of the mud scoured from the badlands in the Upper Wind River Valley is now settling in Louisiana, a state that is essentially a large, soft glop of Mississippi mud.

Diversion Dam, though, stops much of the Wind River's silt—a matter of both location and design. The grade of the river becomes less steep here and the river slows, so suspended sediments naturally begin dropping to the bottom; then the river has to find its way through a large pool behind the dam that diverts the water along the concrete face—slowing it even more, so that less silt will arrive at the canal and end up in the mud pyramids along the Harris property. The dam would build up a tremendous weight of mud if the operators didn't open the gates every September, when the canal shuts down, and flush the silt. This used to turn the Wind River brown for as much as fifty miles downstream. The silt would settle on the bottom of the river, damaging what might otherwise be good fish habitat, according to Baldes.

An FWS biologist named David Vogel did turbidity studies above and below Diversion Dam during the flushing process in 1979. Wyoming water-quality standards for pollution discharge limit the amount a single source can raise turbidity to 10 NTU (Nephelometric Turbidity Units), and federal standards are more stringent. When the silt was sluiced from behind the dam, Vogel took samples to see how much the cloudiness of the water increased. The NTUs just below it jumped from 2.2 NTUs to 41,600 NTUs, about 41,590 NTUs over the limit. Luckily for the dam operators, regulations cleared up that turbidity simply by refusing to categorize a dam as a pollution "point source."

The years were going by, and Baldes didn't feel he was making any progress. His opponents found that when his complaints went unaddressed, he became more strident and righteous, and less effective against them. He tried to make his arguments in scientific terms, but when that got him nowhere, his badgering of farmers and state officials often erupted in angry denunciations.

Wyoming is still a big empty space with a few outfits scattered around, and the people who run the state maintain a kind of open-range etiquette, as if government were a matter of keeping a respectful distance and never speaking ill of another man's horse. Ranchers and farmers dominate the state legislature—they have free time in the winter—and so they shaped the water laws to fit their needs, passing bills like the Surplus Water Law, which allows them to take double the amount of water they had rights to if the state engineer declared a "surplus." Routinely, then, irrigators took a lot more water than their basic right, and state officials "worked with them." The engineer for the Wind River Basin, Craig Cooper, describes a flexible system where he tries to be sensitive to the particular needs of particular crops on particular farms, an exercise of subtle fine-tuning and cooperation in which being a good neighbor is as important as the law. Baldes, on the other hand, describes a corrupt system of special privileges, lax management, and disregard for the rules that allowed irrigators to cloud rivers with silt and drain them dry. The Wyoming way of regulating requires a veneer of politeness—a skill Baldes lacked—but Cooper was not above taking a few swings himself in bitter letters to the higher-ups at the FWS: "Mr. Baldes has single-handedly polarized the [irrigators and the FWS] to the extent of animosity." Some tribal leaders, too, were put off by Baldes's confrontational style.

Frustrated and depressed, he found consolation talking to conservation activists outside the basin. Tom Dougherty, a representative of the National Wildlife Federation in Denver, met Baldes at a workshop and became interested in the wildlife potential at Wind River. Reservations were blank spots on the maps of most conservation organizations, which had little experience dealing with tribal governments. Dougherty, who soon became a close friend of Baldes's, saw big wildlife potential in the 50 million acres of relatively undeveloped reservations in the lower forty-eight states. His first visit to Wind River was "the shock of a lifetime." He saw what he thought was world-class habitat, stripped of its wildlife by lack of management from Indians and whites alike. He visited Baldes frequently, fished along the Little Wind, and watched from the sidelines while the FWS worked with Bob Harris to install a new game code on the reservation. He wanted to help, but he was just getting to know the tribal leaders. There has long been an uneasiness beneath the superficial affinities of conservationists and Native Americans.

From an economic and social perspective, farmers like Bill Brown might have more in common with Indians than environmental activists. They had themselves suffered the meddling of outsiders, and they weren't generally wealthy. Often they soaked up local history, feeling more at home with the homesteaders of the frontier past than the comfortable second-homers of the future. And they were sympathetic, too, to the wrongs Indians had suffered, though they were a little tired of hearing about them.

At times, the past seemed to provide Indians with more excuses than useful lessons. Now and then, the non-Indians lose patience with demands for reparations for past wrongs and—in the manner of conquerors, or the sons of conquerors, the world over—suggest it's time for the tribes to get on with the present, starting from where we are now. "They got snookered on a whole lot of deals," said Bill Brown, "but that was before we got here."

Indians took enough of a snookering, though, to create some residual paranoia in anyone with a memory. It's even harder to forget when you have a big concrete reminder, a weir dam taking water from the reservation's namesake river and carrying its beautiful blue cargo away to non-Indians who make their living off some of the best farmlands within the reservation's borders. And if memories reach back far enough, the tribes might remember it was Indian appropriations that got the project started.

There's no evidence that the use of Indian funds for the Riverton Unit back in 1918 was part of a comprehensive plan to siphon off assets that belonged to the Wind River Indian Reservation, but it could look that way—one bad act among many in a period when reservations were fair game for legislators, grifters, and interlopers.

Most of the damage was done early in the twentieth century, when the tribes were reeling: Indians had failed as first-time farmers, their spiritual and political elders were dying off, cultural traditions like the Sun Dance were banned by their federal overseers, and the Indian Service was managing their assets with careless aplomb. The only certainty in their lives was their land, the reservation itself.

But between 1900 and 1930 they lost much of that, too. First there was the sell-off of lands north of the river, ostensibly to put some cash in the tribes' pockets and build an irrigation system on the reservation. The Indian-occupied portion of the reservation should have been strengthened by this, but there were other destructive forces at work. On what land remained, Indian allottees were losing individual plots they had only recently acquired. Though the original allotment law would have had the federal government hold the allotted lands in trust for twenty-five years—to give Indians time to adjust to the rigors of individual ownership— the law was amended to allow the issue of patents much earlier to Indians "deemed capable of managing their own affairs." They often *weren't* capable of paying property taxes, or the O and M (operation and maintenance fees) for the ditches.

The Indians thought they had paid for those ditches through the sale of lands north of the river, and few anticipated a monthly bill for ditch water. In 1914, the federal government passed a law that said Indians nationwide would reimburse the government for irrigation projects "where the Indians have adequate funds to repay the government." That included Wind River, according to Interior Department lawyers. Another great sell-off of Indian lands was soon under way at Wind River. Indians who couldn't pay their O and M fees or property taxes found ready buyers among the whites, and the Indian Office helped them along with "dead heir" sales to people like the Hoopengarners. The list of sellers of land to the government around 1920 reads like a *Who's Who* of reservation families: Hopper, Bearing, White Plume, Ridgely, Washakie, Antelope, Goggles, Redman, Shakespeare, Quiver, Moss . . . Big newspaper ads placed by the Department of the Interior invited bidders to Fort Washakie, where they could submit sealed bids for these "inherited and noncompetent" Indian lands. The whites weren't just moving in north of the river, they were also taking over the best lands in the reservation to the south.

Almost immediately, the new white landowners started lobbying to be exempted from the construction costs of the irrigation ditches that watered their recently acquired lands. The Indians they bought from wouldn't have been required to pay—remember, construction was to be paid for by sales of reservation lands north of the river—so why should they? Such pleas found sympathetic ears at the Interior Department, which issued "Goodwin certificates" (named after an assistant solicitor at the Interior Department), exempting non-Indians who bought in 1920. What a deal: some of the best reservation land, sold cheap at government sales, and all the benefits of an irrigation system the Indians had paid for!

To linger in the past isn't constructive, not in forward-looking America. Anyway, a lot of the records at Wind River were destroyed in fires or left disordered in the basements of moldering old government buildings at the fort. Still, even in the present Baldes found plenty to complain about. His brief against Midvale—silting up the river, taking more than its fair share of water—finally found a sympathetic ear in a 1989 hearing before a congressional committee. After listening to testimony from Wind River officials, Senator Dennis DiConcini pointed a crooked finger at the Bureau of Reclamation regional director, and said, "You gentlemen have just as much responsibility to protect tribal fishery resources as you do to provide water to irrigators. It's obvious you have taken care of the irrigators and ignored tribal fisheries."

This was not the kind of treatment Midvale farmers were used to. They hadn't even been invited to testify.

For most of Midvale's existence it had been the king of the river. The state recognized its enormous share of Wind River water rights while denying the tribes' claims; the Bureau of Reclamation forgave the huge investment that brought the farms water, and tolerated the flushing of the dam and the dewatering of the river; the farmers themselves were regularly praised for their crucial contribution to the economic health of the basin. (The Riverton newspaper produced a collection of profiles titled "Remarkable Men of Midvale"; Bob Harris, a Midvale water user himself, used to call them "the Mighty Midgets of Midvale.")

But in 1989, and the years that followed, Midvale's fortunes seemed to change; it was skewered in the 1989 congressional hearings, and embarrassed by articles in the statewide *Casper Star-Tribune* about the project's finances and practices. The Bureau of Reclamation began a halting shift toward goals broader than just irrigation, including a responsibility to assist the tribes in improving the fisheries. The snowpack had been unusually low the last couple of years, which meant water shortages were inevitable. The tribes, which had done little to disturb the white farmers over the last century, were suddenly aggressive, attacking on two fronts: claiming damages to the river by "sluicing" at Diversion Dam, and claiming destruction of the fishery by the irrigators who periodically emptied the riverbed.

But none of these assaults was likely to shake the farmers' confidence that Midvale was anchored firmly in the soils of the valley. What accomplished that was the court's decision to award the tribes substantial water rights.

"Everybody was watching Wind River," said Charles Wilkinson, an authority on Western water law at the University of Colorado Law School. "It showed deep cracks in what has been perceived as the traditional way of Western water management. The old water establishment is giving way."

What made the moment doubly frightening for non-Indians was the kind of talk they were hearing from Vandemoer and Baldes and tribal leaders. With the U.S. Supreme Court decision in his pocket, Wes Martel was talking expansively about water marketing (selling tribal water rights to downstream users) and integrating water-quality and water-supply management. Though Martel said the basin could become a model for state-tribal relations, and promised benefits for the entire community, outsiders heard something else: The tribes were planning to *take charge*.

And it almost happened.

In April 1990, Wyoming state engineer Jeff Fassett had sat stone-faced in the back of the room while the tribal Joint Business Council held their hearing on applying 252 cubic feet per second as a minimum water level in the Wind River. The tribes knew that he wouldn't shut off the headgates of non-Indian irrigators to protect their instream flow. He questioned not only the process they used to dedicate water rights to instream flow but also the meaning of the court decree, then warned them he wouldn't help: "Dedication? Fine. Enforcement? That's different."

When he could get the ear of tribal officials, which was rare, he pleaded for less posturing, more negotiation of the cordial, across-the-fence sort. He would do his best to protect the tribes' instream flow because he certainly didn't want fish "flopping on the bank," but his first obligation was to people who held state water rights. "The tribes could be incredibly statesmanlike," he said. "My point is, 'Golly gee, why can't you just give us a break on these four miles?' "

Vandemoer reminded him that the tribes had the courts on their side and didn't feel they needed his approval. "The tribes aren't limited in the use of their water—they can use it anywhere and for whatever purpose they want," she said. "It's plain and simple in the decree. If the state engineer is not interested in protecting Indian water rights, that's why we need our own code."

Fassett had a point, though. The tribes could issue a permit protecting instream flow in the Wind River, but they lacked the manpower to enforce it, especially when rumors of gun-wielding irrigators were circulating on both sides of the ditch. The decree from the state Supreme Court affirmed the tribes' water rights and said the state engineer should enforce it, but Fassett insisted the tribe's "process" to protect instream flow was wrong and said he wouldn't cut off non-Indians.

Then in May, a new twist: The U.S. Fish and Wildlife Service planted 50,000 hatchery-raised brown trout fingerlings in the Big Wind River: the Denver FWS office told its Washington headquarters that the Lander office would plant 140,000 brown trout and 20,000 rainbow trout in the Wind River from May to September, supporting a request from the tribes to "establish a fishery after decades of no water in the river." It was one thing to ignore the tribes' instream-flow dedication and let the river dry up, as it had in past years; it was quite another to have fish carcasses bloating in the dry bed while Baldes and Vandemoer shepherded reporters to the scene. Fassett was caught by surprise, once again, by the tribes' aggressiveness. Then he sent a message through the press to Wyoming politicians in Washington: "I'd hate to see the federal government waste an investment until there is some true certainty . . . when the tribes' rights, by their own definition, can change tomorrow and are for sale today."

Republican Senator Malcolm Wallop went immediately to FWS chief John Turner, who happened to be a Wyoming dude rancher from the Jackson area. Wallop said that the Lander office—namely, Baldes—had acted without the approval of the FWS Denver office (despite the memo mentioned above), and he questioned the stability of the tribe's instream-flow protection. He told me in a phone call that he didn't intend to interfere with FWS operations, only that "some chains will be tightened a little bit on the process." In the meantime, Denver FWS officials reversed themselves, announcing that they would plant no more fish in the Wind River.

To tribal members who knew their history, it was a familiar scenario. The government fulfills its "trust" obligations to Indians in various ways, with welfare programs and housing grants and resource management. But tribes who depend too much on the federal government to defend and protect them will feel the other edge of that sword if they step on the wrong toes or act too independently; the federal government's "trust" relationship allows it to quash tribal actions it doesn't like . . . for the good of the Indian people.

That the congressional delegation had put a stop to the FWS fish planting wasn't surprising. What was, a month later, was that a hatchery truck loaded with rainbow trout backed down to the Wind River.

On June 15, Sumner Marlowe drove an Arapaho elder from the east side of the reservation to join a motley group of people on the banks just below Diversion Dam, near an old swinging footbridge across the river. The elder was supposed to say a prayer, but beyond that Sumner didn't really know what the gathering was about.

Talking excitedly in the dapply sunlight were fishermen from groups like Trout Unlimited, tribal officials like John Washakie and Wes Martel of the Shoshone tribe, Burton Hutchinson and Joe Oldman of the Arapaho, and Dick Baldes and Kate Vandemoer. There were also about 6,000 rainbow trout in a truck from a private hatchery—and television cameras. Tom Dougherty had finally found something he could do.

Dougherty had grown up in Wyoming, outside of Laramie, but only in his fifties, long after he had moved to Colorado, had he become aware of the reservation, through Baldes. "You know, when I was young, it was there for the Indians, but it wasn't a *place*."

When the FWS balked at planting fish, Dougherty decided it was time to mobilize the wildlife community. "We'd put reservations on the shelf before this," he told me later. "There was this huge potential for wildlife and fish. And now we found we shared the same vision of the river—tribal members, sportsmen, and conservation groups. People who never shared a common goal before. It wasn't to us a state rights versus tribal rights—it became a biological issue.

"I try to be a realist. But it really was a magic day. I don't normally talk like this, but suddenly a lot of curtains fell down. It had a totally unrehearsed karma to it. I wish we could bottle up what happened when they stocked the river."

Vandemoer knew that the farmers and the state would see the camera crews as a ploy to embarrass them. That was about right. The cameras rolled as the fish splashed into the river, as the old men prayed and blessed the water. Sumner Marlowe saw something the cameras didn't—an elder wiping away a tear. Roger O'Neill interviewed Vandemoer, John Washakie, and Joe Oldman, and the story ran on the *NBC Nightly News*.

But for Dick Baldes, the moment that mattered most was when a dark-eyed, skinny-armed eleven-year-old in stonewashed jeans and a baggy black T-shirt carried the first batch of trout fingerlings in a white bucket to the edge of the river. The tribal elders and conservation officials stood by, waiting their turn. His arm trembling with the weight of the load, Jason Baldes tipped the bucket, and rainbow trout streamed like falling coin into the river. Then he looked up wonderingly at his father. Did I do it right?

Kate Vandemoer, standing nearby, felt for the first time in weeks that there was nothing for her to do, nothing to say, and it was a relief. She felt what Dougherty did: This was something larger than she could ever have orchestrated, beyond any one person's control.

It relieved an intensifying fear that she had gone too far out on a limb, alone. As the first buckets of fish wiggled in the shallows, the activity on the banks mimicked the busy splashing, with tribal leaders and their supporters lining up to release a bucketload and television crews maneuvering for a good camera angle, trying not to miss anything. Laughing, milling about, the tribal leaders and the conservationists and the media jostled. In their midst of it, Vandemoer found herself speechless and a bit dizzy.

Her reverie was interrupted by a tribal lawyer, who pointed to the other side of the truck that had hauled in the fish and said, "Hey, whose dog?" There stood Honey, Vandemoer's faithful border collie, front feet in the river, lapping at the tumultuous water. The dog raised her head and held Kate's gaze with her moist, adoring eyes. Then the fish tail hanging out the side of her mouth slapped her chin and brought her attention back to the meal at hand.

CHAPTER 15

Courts Redux

Did you imagine that after the lawyers had argued their case in the Worland courthouse, in the State Supreme Court in Cheyenne, and in the U.S. Supreme Court in Washington, D.C., that after hundreds of boxes of transcripts and evidence had been stored for posterity in the Washakie County courthouse, that the lawyers were finished? They thought so in the Ivy League: At the Harvard Indian Law Symposium in 1989, attorney Reid Peyton Chambers delivered a paper that declared the long and costly adjudication process over: "a positive result from the tribes' standpoint and, perhaps, from everyone else's as well."

Not a chance.

The decree that gave the tribes a huge treaty-based water right in the Wind River Valley was only a piece of paper. A judge has no army to enforce a ruling. Every move the tribes made to use their water rights, and every move the state didn't make to enforce those rights, sent the lawyers scurrying back to the courts. The tribes had in hand the first adjudicated tribal water rights tested and supported by judicial decisions at every level of the nation's court system (water cases are often settled by negotiations, ending litigation before it reaches the U.S. Supreme Court), and it gave them rights to about half the water in the Bighorn Basin. Given water's importance in the arid West, those rights could vault the tribes into the driver's seat—or at least a copilot's seat—in the state's economy. But the court decisions were vague about some of the particulars, and the tribes would need the state's cooperation to enforce those water rights, particularly if water was to be shut off to some farmers with rights junior to the tribes'. When the tribes decided they wanted to keep water in the stream that had been going onto farmers' fields, the state water engineer refused to shut off the farmers' headgates.

Jeff Fassett gave numerous explanations for why he would not enforce: He questioned the legality of the tribal water code, he claimed lack of due process, he revived lost legal arguments like "sensitivity" to other water users. His stance for the summer had been that since the court decree gave him the authority to administer tribal water rights, the tribes had to apply to his office to use the water, not to their own "self-permitting" water board. When one argument fell short, he came up with another.

Even when the chief solicitor from the Interior Department—a Republican appointee from Wyoming—weighed in and told Fassett he had to protect instream flows for the tribes under the court decree, he refused to budge. He asked Vandemoer to give him "wiggle room," and held out the carrot of "big money" for a long-term settlement. He would work with the tribes to keep water in the stream, he said, but he wouldn't give them control, and he wouldn't recognize the right as it was interpreted by the tribal water board.

Years later, when I talked with Fassett and his wife Liz over lunch, he regretted the headlines and the hostility. "It was really not a fight about fish; it was about process," he said. "Kate never got past the issue of control."

Liz Fassett, a champion fly fisherwoman and one-time president of the Wyoming Outdoor Council, a conservation group based in the Wind River Valley, took her husband's arm affectionately and said, "*You* couldn't get past the control issue."

Since nobody could, the courts were back in the picture. The tribes sought to have Fassett cited for contempt. The state and the lawyers for non-Indians again made their arguments that the tribes had no power to protect instream flow.

In the fall came a recommendation from the special master (no longer Roncalio, who had retired, but a mountain-climbing young attorney named Terry Dolan) to Hartman clarifying that the decree did indeed allow the tribes to change the use of their water from future agricultural projects to instream flow. Fassett expressed relief that he wasn't cited for contempt. Also, by now it was October, and there were no headgates to close.

The lawyers trekked back to Worland in December, arguing for and against Dolan's interpretation before Judge Hartman. The audience included Midvale farmers, tribal leaders, and more lawyers. Everyone by now was familiar with the high-ceilinged courthouse—knew to grab one of the red seating pads before sitting on the straight-backed pews, and not to sit too close to the bright venetian blinds. Often, the Indians sat on the south side of the room; the whites sat on the north.

Lawyers for the state no longer seemed so cocky and sure, though they continued to voice the same arguments Sandy White had begun with ten years before; the institutions that they thought would bolster their authority, their own courts, had been unimpressed with their swagger, and now they were fighting a rearguard action, trying to stave off greater losses.

The most energetic arguments came from Richard Simms, a New Mexico lawyer who had worked on water litigation in the Southwest. It was unclear how many of the non-Indian farmers he represented, whether he was full-time counsel or just getting a tryout, but the farmers brightened when he stood to speak. The state had made lots of promises, but Wyoming's lawyers seemed to lose at every turn. Nor did the farmers want the state to "buy off" the tribes, as it had in 1989, with a package of tax breaks and ditch rehabilitation funds. The tribes' price tag would just go up, they figured, and non-Indian farmers would slowly be squeezed to death, so why not take off the gloves? No more Mr. Nice Guy.

Simms was not Mr. Nice Guy. The lean, gray-haired lawyer worked the way small birds feed—agitated, intent, quick, never resting. The collegiality of the lawyers long on the case was absent in him; in fact, he seemed contemptuous of the whole proceeding, and never smiled in the courtroom. The attempt to protect the fishery was just a ploy, said Simms, and the tribes "have done an end run around the treaty. . . . Instream flow is leverage to try to squeeze money out of the state." His new weapon was unwavering cynicism.

But Hartman wasn't swayed to discard Dolan's recommendation. "I thought we needed to shake people up," he told me later. "I had some general ideas about where we wanted to go, both from a policy and a practical standpoint. . . . There were no precedents, so I knew that any decision I made might not be the final decision, but we'd at least get people's attention."

That he did. On March 11, 1991, Hartman ruled that the tribes could indeed use their water rights to protect instream flow, and then he went further. Writing that state engineer Jeff Fassett had "difficulty in assuming a neutral role," the judge ruled that the tribes would henceforth be in charge of administering all water rights, Indian and non-Indian, within the reservation's historic boundaries, including Midvale and the city of Riverton.

"We knew there would be a reaction," Hartman said later. "We knew we'd hear the shouting from the reservation clear up here."

They couldn't hear Wes Martel shouting, because he was driving in his car in Colorado when he got the news—but shout he did. Kate Vandemoer was in Tucson, on winter leave, and when she got the call she didn't at first believe it. The surprise announcement created an air of hysteria at the usually laid-back tribal offices, where officials started scrambling to assemble a river-management team—did they have the equipment, staff, and knowledge? They were levelheaded enough to express the right sentiments to the press. "We're not out to hurt anyone," said Crawford White, a member of the Arapaho Business Council. "We just wanted the state to understand the court awarded us that water."

Legal scholars around the country who study "Indian law"—the interpretation of treaties, federal-tribal relations, and the sovereignty of nations within—sat up and took notice. It wasn't simply that a state judge was recognizing the tribes' right to make their own judgments of what uses of their own water were "beneficial," at the expense of non-Indian farmers; it was that Hartman had appointed a tribal agency to carry out a decree governing white water rights as well. "It's an extraordinarily important decision," said Charles Wilkinson. "A judge in a heartland state like Wyoming—an independent, objective observer—has given verification that Indian tribes have come a very long way in terms of expert management of resources. He's saying that they can be good and fair."

A letter to Hartman from the state engineer's office, which went out the day after the decision, suggests that Fassett had no idea how far out of the court's favor he'd fallen. It must have been written before the ruling, and perhaps mailed inadvertently. In it, Fassett told the judge that as long as there were still some other, unrelated water rights in the basin working their way through the courts, the Wyoming Supreme Court decree of 1988, upheld by the U.S. Supreme Court in 1989, was "not to be considered final." Under those circumstances, wrote Fassett, "decrees cannot be enforced prior to their finality." Therefore he would simply run the river as the state engineer had always run it, without enforcing the tribal water rights affirmed in the decree.

Fassett's obstinance, in spite of all the arguments he'd lost, showed a peculiar fortitude. And it would be rewarded. At a moment when Kate Vandemoer appeared to be victorious, and Jeff Fassett soundly defeated, their prospects were about to reverse.

The first reaction to the tribes' sudden new authority, from Fort Washakie to Washington, D.C., was amazement. The second thought was: Can they handle it?

U.S. Interior Department internal memos questioned whether the tribes had "the manpower, experience and expertise to administer the river, especially when many of the facilities necessary for administration belong to the state." In fact, the tribes wondered themselves, though they immediately set out to reassure the public by announcing they had a competent, calm hand at the helm of the tribal water engineers office.

When Vandemoer got word of Hartman's decision, she was still the tribe's water engineer, and she rushed back to the valley to take charge. She felt strangely unsure of herself, and to calm down she drove up to a campground on the Little Wind. That fall, aware that the conflicts over water had added to political turmoil in both tribes, she had thought about quitting her job. The livelihood of a non-Indian tribal employee can be precarious. When a powerful family in either tribe makes a move, consultants have to scramble for allies—and sometimes, to save themselves, they collude in the bloodletting of other consultants. Vandemoer was tired of the political hassles and had only a few friends in Wyoming; at times she felt quite lonely. If she left, it would be with a record of solid accomplishments. At Wind River she had set up environmental-quality and water programs, shaped the argument for instream flow, and begun training tribal members in the technical skills of her field, all in a few short years. She would be in demand and could take a job in a friendly city.

There was still snow along the banks of the Little Wind. She got out of the pickup, kicked at the crust of ice, hunched her shoulders, and jammed her hands in her pockets. She felt short of breath, having lived at a lower altitude for over a month. She looked around, feeling, as she often did, that she was being watched. I should be euphoric, she thought. We're actually *winning*. Instead she felt guilty, as if she didn't deserve this or had done something wrong.

But she wasn't ready to leave.

She was now fully aware of a campaign to undermine her within the tribes, painting her as a headline-grabbing prima donna with an agenda of her own. Members of her own staff were involved, and she was paranoid enough to suspect that state officials were saying things about her to their contacts on the reservation, questioning her science, her temperament, even her lifestyle. She still had friends in high places, particularly among young tribal leaders like John Washakie and Wes Martel, but they were not all-powerful; they too had been accused of conceit and agitation. She knew that knives could be unsheathed in reservation politics. She had experienced it in the fall of 1990, during a hearing at Fort Washakie about instream flow, in front of non-Indian irrigators and the press.

At that hearing, Vandemoer and Dick Baldes had finished offering documentation to support extending stream-flow protection into the fall. A couple of Arapaho rose to support instream flow, and one mentioned the possibility of moving ahead on an irrigation project east of Riverton designed as a "future" project by Wold Mesghinna. Non-Indian farmers sighed as Vandemoer explained that to do so would require that even more than 252 cubic feet per second be kept in the stream—using all of the tribes' senior water rights. Then the matriarch of a powerful Shoshone family got to her feet.

Eva McAdams, a descendant of Washakie's, said she just didn't know what this whole thing was about, this instream flow that was causing so much trouble. Chief Washakie, she noted, could always get along with everyone, and that was why the Shoshone got their fine reservation. Decisions about water, she said, should be made by the General Council, not by "the big Water Queen here. . . . Instead of coming to the people," said McAdams, "she goes to the newspaper, and she certainly is flamboyant about this, and it is hurting the tribes."

That was when Vandemoer started seriously thinking of looking for another job.

It had been Mesghinna, actually, whom Hartman had had in mind when he excused Fassett and put the tribes in charge. Like everyone else, he had been impressed with the Eritrean when he testified at various stages of the adjudication. "I wanted fair administration, no doubt about it, and he seemed capable," said Hartman. "I didn't think it was proper for the state to have control over the tribal rights, which are federal, not state. And how do you do a joint administration with state water rights on one side and tribal water rights on the other? We'd be in court every week."

Weren't they already?

Wold Mesghinna arrived back on the reservation certain that he could manage the water supply for the basin but uncertain about the political climate. He had gotten to know only a few tribal leaders, and the man he was closest to, Bob Harris, had retired, on less than friendly terms with young leaders like Martel. Mesghinna moved into a two-room house at Fort Washakie. "I was in a war zone," he said. "There was confusion in the entire drainage basin; there was hatred between Indians and non-Indians. You cannot conduct business in this kind of atmosphere."

In the upper reaches of the Wind River, there was talk of Indian and non-Indian facing off over a ditch with shotguns. "We've been abandoned by the powers that gave these rights away twice," said a rancher near the town of Crowheart. "My land isn't worth a dime." Midvale farmers were demanding that the state buy them out, so that, as one put it, they "could get out from under the dominance of a foreign country."

When Mesghinna invited the disgruntled irrigators to meet with him, he noted that the usual boxes of doughnuts went untouched. He was dressed impeccably, as always, in a gray suit and red tie, and he listened, smiling attentively, to the farmers describe their fears that the tribes would mistreat them, cutting back their water while Indian farmers flooded their fields. "People were very tense. I told them: The tribes are peace-loving people, but they've been pushed around. There's enough water. One of them asked, Is this just you talking, or do you speak for the tribes? I told him, I am the tribal water engineer. People started to talk. We started to develop relationships. They ate some doughnuts."

Talking to the newspapers, Jeff Fassett finally acknowledged that the tribes had "the keys to the car," but he reminded them that they now had to administer state as well as tribal water rights. "They're on a steep learning curve to find out what they've just inherited," he said. "It's the full body of state law, and that means the hundred years of history that's guided us. They are in my shoes. And they can't pick and choose."

Actually, quite a lot of people thought Mesghinna might be the right shoe size. Off the record, even some of the non-Indians, who were tired of the state's bluster, wanted to see what he could do.

But the lawyers were at work, and Mesghinna would never get the chance.

Almost before the ink was dry on Hartman's ruling, and well before the ditches were wet in spring of 1991, the Wyoming Supreme Court issued a stay to block the tribes, at least temporarily, from taking over management of Wind River water.

And so it became a lawyers' game again, with higher stakes than ever before. Many of the faces had changed, there were more briefs, and there were more elaborate arguments, but the choices were essentially the same as Teno Roncalio had faced twelve years earlier. The adjudication had now cost over $50 million in legal fees, and the arguments were now accompanied by some fairly harsh characterizations. It wasn't easy for either the tribes or the state water officials to hear themselves described as unreasonable, duplicitous, incompetent, and greedy.

Elected leaders grew short-tempered, from the governor to the tribal councils. Wes Martel, who usually kept a smile on his face, lost it one day when I passed along a state official's comment that there was nothing spiritual or cultural in the tribes' attempts to protect the water. They were making it hard to get, this official claimed, so they could sell it or cut a deal with the state. "We're very serious about this," Martel said. "Part of what non-Indian people don't understand is the cultural relevance this has to our people. They make it sound like it's about money, but it's fisheries and wildlife, too. They're our relations, and we want to see them thrive, just like us. If they start going, we're gone. So maybe we'll just never go back to the bargaining table. I don't care if we ever get any money out of the state or not."

Jeff Fassett, who felt beat up by the years of challenge to his authority and expertise, also got a little short tempered. "I've had those lectures. I've tried to know them better. They're not very motivated to understand the other way. And our way is certainty. Their government is not designed that way. That may be good for some things, but not water."

It took until June 1992 for the Supreme Court justices to digest all the briefs and arguments and agree with Fassett. By a 3–2 vote, they reversed Hartman, not just on the question of putting the tribes in charge, but also denying them the right to use their water rights for instream flow. The latter decision shocked legal scholars: On instream flow, the judges had taken their own decision of a few years earlier and tossed it out the window, and each of the three who voted to overturn Hartman offered a different reason why. This decision was so tormented by contradiction that lawyers still scratch their heads as they thumb through the separate logic of each judge.

"Water is the lifeblood of Wyoming," wrote Chief Justice Richard Macy in a "majority" opinion which only he signed. "Wyoming's founding fathers also recognized the necessity of having state control over this vital resource. . . . Water is simply too precious to the well-being of society to permit water-right holders unfettered control over its use." The court's earlier decision, wrote Macy, allowed the tribes to use their water rights "solely for agricultural and subsumed purposes and not for instream purposes." In fact, various precedents acknowledged the tribes' right to change the use of their reserved rights under federal and tribal law, and the previous state Supreme Court decree, in which Macy participated, held that "the decree entered in the instant case does not require application of state water law to the Indian reservation." What that really meant, Macy now wrote, was that state procedures didn't have to be followed to determine the tribal water right; when it came to *using* the water, he wanted the state back in charge, and the state wouldn't allow instream flow.

The two justices who voted with Macy to block the tribes' instream flow and put the state engineer back in charge actually disagreed with this argument. One of them simply couldn't live with the thought of more than one administrator in charge of water rights in Wyoming (a fairly common occurrence on watersheds that cross borders), so he wanted the state engineer back in charge; and as long as the state engineer was in charge, he continued, any instream flow would have to follow state rules, which provide that only the state itself can designate and hold water rights for instream flow. The third justice decided the tribes first had to divert the water rights awarded for future projects, and only *then* could they dedicate those rights to instream flow. That would mean building multimillion-dollar irrigation systems, briefly running the water into them, and then changing the use to instream flow—leaving the brand-new irrigation ditches as dry monuments to waste and futility. Justice Joseph Cardine also proposed joint state-tribal administration of water rights, noting that his opinion rested primarily on what he believed *ought* to be done rather than on what had been said and done in the past. "Therefore I cite little established precedent."

Because Wyoming is a state of few people, and not a very busy state, you can drive down to Cheyenne and walk into the governor's office, or the office of the Supreme Court chief justice, and say, "Hey, how are you, why'd you do *this*?" Which I did. Richard Macy was wearing boots and a plaid shirt that day, as if he were about to ride home on a tractor. He sat me down and talked freely about the case. A round little man with slicked black hair, he was feisty and confident. He didn't mind saying that he, like Cardine, was less concerned about legal precedent in Indian law than about social consequences.

"I haven't always been a judge," he said. "You know from practice and experience where society should be headed. I don't think we violated any treaty. The water was to be put to beneficial use. My attitude is, we don't have enough water in Wyoming, and I don't think sending it downstream to Nebraska is a beneficial use." He stuck his chin out and raised an eyebrow, waiting for my reaction.

I suggested that his own court had determined earlier that a federal treaty granted Indian water rights at Wind River, and federal laws governed. Federal law would allow the tribes to use their water to protect fish in the streams. The eyebrow went up again. "We say the state owns the water."

I stopped in to visit with several of the other judges, too, the last being Michael Golden, who hadn't been appointed to the court when it first approved the decree in 1985. He had had the last word in the 1992 decision, and ironically, he used his dissent to defend eloquently the decision his fellow justices had made without him seven years before.

Golden told me he'd tried to put himself in the position of the Indian leaders back in 1868, to imagine just what they'd understood was being "reserved" in the Wind River Indian reservation. "Given the limitations of language, of their understanding, I think we're fairly sure they didn't contemplate giving it all away." Golden would have upheld the tribes' right to use their water for instream flow, and also would have upheld Hartman's decision to let them administer water within the reservation boundaries. In the last two paragraphs of the court's opinions, he quotes another attorney, Joseph Membrino, before finishing with his own words:

> If one may mark the turn of the twentieth century by the massive expropriation of Indian lands, then the turn of the twenty-first century is the era when the Indian tribes risk the same fate for their water resources.
>
> Today some members of the court sound a warning to the Tribes that they are determined to complete the agenda initiated over one hundred years ago and are willing to pervert prior decisions to advance that aim. I cannot be a party to deliberate and transparent efforts to eliminate the political and economic base of the Indian peoples under the distorted guise of state water law superiority.

Most attorneys and judges who read the decision agreed that because the majority judges arrived at their decision each by different logic, it was so weakly argued and contradictory that it would carry little weight in the historic march of Indian law. Judges who had participated in the earlier decree appeared to misinterpret parts of their own decision. Most agreed it would never survive an appeal.

Tribal officials were crestfallen, and anxious about how their constituency would react. People were impatient with the endless litigation and had more immediate concerns. What did these council members have to show for all this time and money spent? Some, like Gary Collins, were already out of office. Others, like John Washakie and Wes Martel, soon would be.

They could appeal this back to the U.S. Supreme Court, but Susan Williams and the rest of the legal team were nervous about that. They consulted experts around the country, met, and fretted over their next step. They missed a deadline to file for a rehearing. The first time the U.S. Supreme Court had looked over the Bighorn adjudication, they'd let the tribes' water award stand, on a 4–4 vote. In 1993, though, it was a different court. The lawyers remembered how close Sandra Day O'Connor had come, before recusing herself, to throwing out the formula that determined the tribal water right. If she got another chance . . .

They say hard cases make bad law. The small cadre of lawyers that dominates Indian law debated whether the chance of overturning the latest Wyoming decision against Wind River was worth risking a U.S. Supreme Court decision that might harm Indian interests in water and sovereignty nationwide.

"I don't trust courts when it's Indians getting benefits," said Susan Williams. "I've been practicing law for fifteen years, and there are certain biases in the judicial system, and one area is Indian sovereignty. Any time you give an Indian a valuable property right, people take a real hard look at that in the court system. . . . So we didn't want to set a precedent. It was not a slam-dunk decision by any means."

What made it even harder to decide on a course of action was that leaders of the two tribes were barely speaking to each other. "Compare it to a Third World country," said Wes Martel. "The councils weren't getting together, there was no sense of order or urgency to the thing. They didn't discuss it until the eleventh hour. Intratribal politics kills off a lot of good things."

There was no appeal.

Their former antagonist Sandy White's comment: "I was flabbergasted, because they lost it all, right there."

And it's still not over, though it might never again capture the attention of headline writers in New York. The minutiae of water rights in the basin continue to be sorted out and argued by a small militia of lawyers. As special master Terry Dolan told me in 1994, still tying up the loose ends of the adjudication, "The party's over, we just can't get the drunks to go home."

But the big issue—the tribe's ability to take charge of their substantial water right in the Wind River Basin and change the ways of the valley—lies quiet, and the state engineer runs the river.

CHAPTER 16

Bahwitchyagaqt

Above Diversion Dam, the Wind River and its tributaries are thinner, swifter, and wilder. There are fewer people, living farther apart, and the roads following the streams into the mountains change from blacktop to gravel, then weedy two-tracks, then footpaths, then game trails. The valley compresses in the tightening grasp of two dramatic mountain ranges, the Wind River Mountains to the west and the younger Absarokas to the east, which draw together like the flanges of an arrowhead, pointing northwest to the Yellowstone Plateau.

Once a traveler follows the river's upstream bend to the north, he is wrapped around by snow-capped mountains, with no sense of the open-ended vastness of the plains. Rather, something grander: cottonwood groves on the riverbanks, meadows and furrowed fields on tiered benches, motley-colored pinnacles standing like a gang of chess pieces, elk and deer hemming the grassy skirts of the foothills, all encircled by armies of snow-helmeted peaks. Chinook winds sweep down this high valley and melt winter snows, no doubt the idea behind the Indian name Warm Valley.

The Wind River originates in the notch where the two mountain ranges meet and embed in the Yellowstone Plateau, a deep and trackless redoubt that tolerates human settlement only on its perimeter. The Wind River begins as a trickle off the battlements of this fortress wilderness, running south and east along the face of the mountain range that bears its name, picking up streams like a ticket collector walking through a train.

I drove up one of these streams, Bull Lake Creek, with Bill Brown, the Midvale manager. Diversion Dam was not far behind us, and the big river, which is stone-dotted and tumbly above, seems to take a big breath here, flattening and slowing down where Bull Lake Creek joins it. There is a modern, solar-powered rest area by the highway, and off to the north rises Crowheart Butte, alone in the middle of the valley like an inverted bucket of sand left on the beach by young castle builders. This is a story worth telling in some detail.

Before there was a reservation, in the 1850s, the Crow came down the Wind River and set up a large camp. They had claims to the Upper Wind River Country under the Fort Laramie Treaty of 1851—a treaty the Shoshone had been left out of—but that concerned only the U.S. government. Among the tribes, things were often still worked out on horseback, with bows and arrows and rifles. The Shoshone spent more of their time in those days on the other side of the mountains, at Green River, but in the winter they came across to the Warm Valley, where there was less snow on the ground and a few surviving buffalo roamed about. The rival presence of the Crows, especially when hunting was crucial for survival, made warfare inevitable. The Crows were camped along the Big Wind River, while Washakie was to the south, probably along the Little Wind.

When he got word of the intruders, he sent an unarmed warrior to tell the Crows to move along, but instead they killed the emissary. The fighting began with belligerent taunts, hit-and-run skirmishes and sharpshooting from bluffs along the river, with lives lost on both sides. Rather than mount an all-out attack against the Crow encampment, Washakie stalled, waiting for reinforcements from a Shoshone-Bannock band camped farther south. The Crow chief Big Robber called Washakie a cowardly old woman—perhaps we should picture them on opposite sides of the river, hurling insults—and Washakie challenged him to fight, one on one, for hunting rights in the valley. The fireside in an Indian camp could be a noisy, chest-thumping scene, and the night before, the Shoshone chief told his people that when he bested the Crow, he would eat his enemy's heart. Thus the two chiefs met alone and fought without guns on Bad Medicine Butte (later renamed Crowheart Butte). As a cloud of dust rose from the butte, women wailed on the valley floor. Late that afternoon, Washakie strode down the slope carrying the heart of Big Robber on a spear.

Many years later, not long before Washakie's death in 1900, Dave Love's father asked the chief if he'd actually eaten the Crow's heart. "Johnny," Washakie said with a wry smile, "when men are young and full of life, they do many strange things."

Well. A Shoshone storyteller tells me an elder once advised her that when white people ask for stories, "You tell them what they want to hear. Tell them anything you like. It doesn't matter." Washakie certainly enjoyed in his later years the way whites pressed forward to hear his stories, and who can blame him for a few embellishments? The Arapaho, too, like to make a good story better.

Certainly there were skirmishes between the Shoshone and other nomadic bands 150 years ago, but historians place the battles further downstream than Crowheart Butte; the antagonists were not necessarily Crows, but in some cases Arapaho and Cheyenne. And the notion of two chiefs battling alone on the butte is questioned even by some of Washakie's descendants. Some say he never ate Big Robber's heart, just displayed it on the spear point. Others say the fiercest conflicts between the tribes occurred nowhere near the butte, and that the Crow chief was actually slain farther north, near where the town of Cody is today. No archaeological evidence has ever been gathered from the butte, which some Shoshone will not climb for reasons of magic and medicine.

But the Upper Wind River Valley is in any case a land worth fighting for, a seam of striking landscapes where wildlife flourishes between mountain and plain—badlands striped by pink and mauve bands of mineral, bighorn sheep cresting the ridges above, bouldery mounds of glacial moraine, the thick green robes of fir and pine draped on the mountainsides, and the glittering, cobble-bottomed stream that runs to our left as we drive in Brown's pickup to Bull Lake. Bull Lake Creek pools and riffles in artful turns that any trout fishermen can appreciate. Sumner Marlowe brought his nephews here when they were young, and the cutthroat trout were too big for young boys to lift from the stream.

But in 1988 Bull Lake Creek went suddenly dry, and Gary Collins and John Washakie met at the hot springs near Ethete to figure out what to do. Someone had closed the gates on Bull Lake Dam, and that could only be the Midvale farmers. The next morning, when Bill Brown drove up the bumpy dirt road along the creek, followed by a flotilla of backhoes, front-end loaders, and semis, he ran into a roadblock of tribal vehicles, with Washakie, Collins, and various BIA police and tribal Game and Fish agents standing behind it.

"I still don't really know what it was all about," Brown said, as we drove up the road almost a decade later. "They kept saying, 'We want to make a point.' I don't know what the point was. We were shut down for three or four hours."

John Washakie remembers it as more like ten hours. His point, and one that Dick Baldes had been making for years, was that from the tribes' perspective Midvale had been operating Bull Lake Dam with cavalier disregard for keeping enough water running through Bull Lake Creek for fish. This was a federal project, but the U.S. Bureau of Reclamation had turned its operations over to the irrigators, since it had been built in 1940 to provide water storage for the Riverton Unit. That morning, Midvale planned to conduct a mandatory "safety of dams" inspection and do some maintenance work on the outlets that release water at the base of the dam, and the damkeeper had shut the gates completely the night before. BOR officials, who had come out for the inspection, insisted the shutdown wasn't *their* fault—and then Midvale officials blamed it on a damkeeper's error.

Dave Allison, the reservation superintendent, came roaring up in his dusty station wagon just as the confrontation began. A big man with a beard and boots, he clomped back and forth between the tribal officials by the pickups and the Midvale folks by their heavy equipment. "Let me take care of it," he said to Brown. "I don't want a damn war starting." If it hadn't been costing about $500 an hour in standby time for the equipment, Brown would have been amused. For years, Baldes had been raising a stink about the dam—not just about keeping enough water in the creek, but about fluctuations in the lake level as well, which the biologist claimed prevented fish from spawning—and Midvale never felt seriously threatened.

Brown had a file cabinet full of letters and legal opinions from the Bureau of Reclamation and higher-ups supporting Midvale's right to manage the reservoir for irrigation, and he had his own biologists to argue that occasional shutdowns wouldn't harm the fish. Despite Baldes's claims that Midvale had damaged the lake's spawning beds, thirty-pound lake trout were showing up in creels.

Before long the lawyers arrived, and eventually the tribes agreed to move the pickups. Midvale promised to keep water flowing from the dam while they did their inspection and repairs, though Brown noticed enough leaks in the dam that the stream would keep running even when the outlets were completely blocked.

The Bureau of Reclamation, which had offered little help to either side in the conflicts over its own Diversion Dam, likewise kept to the sidelines in this one, though no participant could have been more central. The agency was born with concrete in its veins, building huge dams for power and irrigation all over the West; but to survive in the late twentieth century, when the federal government got out of dam building, the BOR tried to transform itself into a "natural resource management agency," friendly to fish and waterskiers and other critters. An operation like Bull Lake Dam, right in the heart of a reservation, is triply vexing: the BOR also shares the federal trust responsibility to protect such tribal assets as fish and wildlife. The decades-old law authorizing Bull Lake Dam declares that Indian hunting and fishing will continue here as always, but notes that the purpose of the reservoir—water storage for irrigation—comes first. That might've been easier to swallow if the dam had been built, as it was originally intended, for watering Indian crops. After all, Bull Lake Dam was authorized in 1918 by the Secretary of the Interior as part of an Indian irrigation system. But two years later, Congress switched it to BOR and attached it to the Riverton Unit serving the reservation lands opened to white homesteaders in 1906. The major reclamation projects, and the major dollars, had a way of sliding off the Indian side of the ledger and onto the non-Indian side. Through it all, the BOR tried to straddle a very uncomfortable fence.

The tribes began seriously to challenge the way Midvale was managing Bull Lake Dam in the late 1970s—not coincidentally, when Dick Baldes came to work for the U.S. Fish and Wildlife Service and tribal claims to treaty-based water rights were first being heard in the courts. Since it was built in the 1940s, the 81-foot earthfill dam at Bull Lake had been Midvale's savings account—a stash of 150,000 acre-feet of water to draw on late in the summer, when the river was down and other irrigators had senior claims. It was a kind of riverbed shuttle: The gates were opened at Bull Lake, the creek carried the water to the Big Wind, which carried it to Diversion Dam, where water was diverted into the Wyoming Canal, some of it headed for the fields, some of it to another storage reservoir at Pilot Butte. Some of the Bull Lake water continued downstream to LeClair. When the gates were open, Bull Lake Creek was a wide, rollicking stream. But as soon as the irrigators shut the ditches in the fall, Midvale would start saving up water for the next year, and that meant, in years of low precipitation, only a trickle of water running down the creekbed. Water was also drawn from the creek by a private ditch, the one built by the Hoopengarners and Winchesters, which Baldes felt took more water than it needed or had rights to, while state regulators looked the other way.

While Baldes papered the desks of tribal leaders and federal officials with reports and fishery plans and memos complaining about the damage Midvale was doing to the lake, the creek, and the Wind River, Eric Bergersen was sending out graduate students from Colorado State University to provide scientific data on the drainage. Baldes's passionate campaign got the attention of the media, and Bull Lake proved to be a much more attractive poster child for tribal fisheries than the muddy lower stretches of the Wind River. The deep blue water twists back toward the mountains between glacial moraines left by retreating glaciers, and at the end of the eight-mile journey from the dam to the lake's inlet, a steep canyon rises into the mountains like a Bierstadt painting, with small beach coves and steep canyon walls and, above, the layers and layers of peaks receding in the misty distance. Fishermen from around the country would step forward for Bull Lake; while it holds cutthroat and brook and rainbow trout, it's best known for trophy-size lake trout and freshwater ling cod.

Dam builders often take credit for enhancing fishing lakes,

because a dam deepens the pool where the lunkers reside, and also makes it easier to manage seasonal changes in flows and precipitation. Opponents of the tribes' claims to the Bull Lake fishery suggest there might have been no more than a few deep ponds before the dam was built. But recollections of tribal elders differ, and an early investigation by a federal engineer in 1911, before the dam was built, described "a magnificent body of water, abundantly stocked with food fishes."

Whether ling would be viewed as a "food fish" by the average epicure is open to question. A ling cod looks like a jaundiced eel wearing camouflage gear, with a wormy pattern of dark brown over yellowish scales so minute they might be mistaken for skin. The dorsal fin is low-slung and set to the rear, and ling have a single Confucian whisker under their chins—a barbel—to feel and taste a potential meal before dining. They've been here forever, unlike many of the trout (only cutthroat are native to the Wind River Mountains), so the old-timers eat them, either boiled or pan-fried. When tribal and federal biologists netted ling during fish censusing, they'd throw them in a bucket and take them to Starr Weed. (Weed told me that the reason the Shoshone were sometimes called Snakes was that they ate the snakelike ling.) On one of those gill-netting trips, we brought the fish into shore, where Baldes lifted a three-foot ling out of the bucket and cut an incision around the body just below the gills. He then peeled the skin off like a sock, revealing a long tube of naked white flesh.

Other names for ling, some of which might come in handy: burbot; *lota lota* (Linnaeus's Latin); freshwater cod; *loche* (the French); methy; Alaska luch; eel pout; lawyer.

Ling are pretty casual about parenthood. The females drop millions of eggs in the shallow gravels of small bays along a lake's edge, where the eggs roll around on the bottom until they hatch, after about a month. Reproduction takes place in the winter, under the ice, sometimes in a writhing mass of excited fish. If the lake level was lowered during a dry year and sandy shallow gravels were left exposed, Bergersen wondered what impact this would have on the ling's reproductive cycle.

Because ling stay active in the winter, Bull Lake is popular with ice fishermen, who drill holes and drop set lines baited with carp meat or some other delicacy; they leave the lines overnight and return the next day to see what they've hooked. Mark Cook, though, followed a different schedule when he went to work for Bergersen. A dozen ling had been gill-netted in the fall and implanted with tiny transmitters. The surgery is fairly simple. Using as little anesthetic as possible (clove oil has recently become a popular and inexpensive way of numbing fish), the ling are placed in a cradle with fresh water sprayed over their gills. An incision is made on the abdomen, slightly off-center, and after a tag about two inches long is inserted, it's then sewn up with gut suture. Cook's job was to wander around on the ice in the middle of the night, drilling holes and lowering a "hydrophone" into the water, where he would turn it around until he heard the submarine-sound "ping" of a ling's transmitter. Then he would drill another hole fifty yards away, and another, until he could triangulate the fish's location.

He learned a lot about the nightlife of ling, the most salient fact of which is that the ling is an aquatic couch potato. At least that's how it was in 1985, the year he did his study. He was sure that one of his bugged ling was dead after it *pinged* from the same spot for ten days. "I was looking for a carcass, in about ten feet of water," he said, "then all of a sudden, on the twelfth day, it was half a mile down the lake." That was why the Indian ice fishermen kept relocating their lines: You had to take your bait to the fish, since they weren't coming to you.

Another low-water year was 1985, and most of the ling's spawning and nursery areas were exposed. In the spring, Cook and Bergersen trolled the shallow areas when the ice broke, but they found no larval ling. The resultant paper cautiously suggested that "habitat changes associated with the extreme drawdown in Bull Lake negatively influenced burbot spawning activities."

It was a solitary winter for Cook, but he enjoyed his work out on the lake. At one point he found a fresh deer kill out on the ice, and bloody coyote paw prints leading away from it. In the spring, when eagles and swans came flying back from lower elevations, and fishing boats returned to cruise the deeper waters with sonar gear, the lake seemed to come alive. But it was the dark nights of winter

Cook remembered years later, after he had moved to the Great Lakes region. Even on an overcast night, the ice had a faint gray glow, and there were shadows in his footprints on the snow. When it was really cold, the ice would pop and groan as the temperature differentials made the surface heave, and the wind would howl down the length of the lake. "It's one of the loneliest sounds you'll ever hear."

There are different versions of this story about the winter sounds you hear coming from Bull Lake:

It was a long time ago, when there were giants and little people and people without mouths in the mountains above the Warm Valley. It was winter, and the people were camped in the trees by the river, and it was very cold. A hunter left his family and went up into the hills to find food, and he came upon a great shaggy beast. The buffalo was plowing the snow with his head to get at the matted grass. The bison's coat was as white as the snow.

The hunter approached the bull, who looked up at him, then turned and began walking away. He knew he could not bring the bison down with his arrows, but he was mesmerized by the great white mound of fur. The bull broke a deep trail through the snow, and the hunter followed in this firm path, saving his energy while the buffalo plowed. The buffalo was not running away; he had encountered hunters before, and always he tested them, as if he were looking for a particular man. The hunter kept a respectful distance, and left his bow unstrung. A bond formed between the beast and the man who trailed him, a feeling that grew stronger as the plodding pursuit stretched out: the lives of hunter and prey were now intertwined, as the bull lured the hunter on, wearing him down, so that in the end he would understand he wasn't worthy to take the white buffalo's spirit.

The hunter followed the bull at a respectful distance,

learning the shift of the animal's haunches and the switch of its tail, thinking of all the hunts he had ever been on. Storms of flying ice and deep drifts of snow came and went. At night the branches of the trees froze and snapped. They climbed up over the hills and into the mountains; they broke the crust of ice and splashed through the chill water of streams; they traveled day and night, farther and farther from the hunter's camp. He wanted to sleep, but he kept walking. He forgot why the journey began—that he had wanted the white pelt to wrap around his family in their tepee down among the trees by the river.

Finally they came to a lake. By now the hunter was exhausted and cold, dragging his bow on the ground. The great white buffalo, too, was tired, too weary to turn west along the lakeshore, too weary to turn back on the hunter and drive him away. He stepped out on the ice and began to cross the lake.

The hunter hesitated, looked back at his trail, which led across the ridges and through the fir forests and down the steep canyons, and he thought for the first time in days of the camp of his people by the river. Then he turned back and looked at the rump of the buffalo and the great mound of its shoulders, disappearing into the blowing snow at the center of the lake. He stepped out onto the ice. He began walking in the buffalo's tracks. Then he began running. As he neared the buffalo, it turned to face him. He tried to lift his bow; the bison slowly lifted his shaggy head and horns.

Then, as the two drew together, there was a sharp crack in the ice. The crack ran like a flying arrow from the shore to the center of the lake, and then other cracks radiated from where the hunter and the buffalo stood, in all directions, breaking the ice like a great spiderweb. The buffalo threw up his front hooves, and with a huge roar he fell through into the frigid lake. The Shoshone hunter went down with him.

The people at the camp missed the hunter, and when the weather was clear, they came looking for him. They found the wide trail of the buffalo, and the footprints on top of it, and they followed them to the lake. They made a camp on the shore of the frozen lake where the tracks ended. That night, they were awakened by a moaning sound from beneath the ice. It grew louder. Then they heard a second voice—the cries of two great bison, beneath the ice. They named the lake Water Buffalo Lake.

In later years, when a Shoshone sought to become a medicine man, he would spend a night by the lake, to see if he would be driven away by the wail of the drowning buffalo. The cry from the lake in the black of night is eerie—you might find it haunting, or angry, or sad. I would call it lonely, certainly.

Stories like this get collected by anthropologists and folklorists, visitors who are quite familiar to the people of Wind River, who are generally good-humored hosts. They know these young scholars want to stake out a little cultural homestead in the West. There is not a lot of indigenous culture left in North America, not nearly enough to match the number of graduate degrees being pursued. The better ones help with the arduous work of trying to save what's left of the language, the dances, the stories. Now and then there's even a little competition among families on the reservation to see whose viewpoint will most color a visitor's thesis. Just as I've embellished the story above, without changing its essential truth, some playful creativity informs the exchanges between Indian subject and non-Indian student.

Increasingly rare, though, is a quality that goes to the very heart of a culture: Belief. That was what struck me when Starr Weed told his stories about Bull Lake; it wasn't simply that he remembered the stories that the old people told him, but that he knew they had *seen* the footprints by Bull Lake, and *seen* the serpents and giants and white water buffalo.

"My dad used to tell me about them giants. Way back, there was some there. The people come to the lake and they saw some fish bones piled up. That's what them giants was living off. They come up on this giant and he was asleep. And they all thought they'd get on top of him and tie him up. But when they rushed him, he just brushed them off and got up and walked away."

Such things are rare in the lives of people today, but not absent. "The little people, I've had some people ask me if they exist. I've been told by some members, how they got lost in the mountains, and it took these little fellas to guide them out of there.

"My father-in-law used to ride horses and go see his cows. And this little fellow told him, I don't want you to cross my pass. Find another route. And he ignored him. He found himself with an arrow in his shoulder. So he went to a medicine man, and he took it out.

"It's just got to happen, and then a person would know. If I just tell you, you won't believe me." And then he laughed.

Bill Brown saw a giant at Bull Lake in 1997—a huge boulder that got stuck in the spillway. He wanted to close the dam outlets and clear it out, but this time he contacted the Bureau of Reclamation, and the agency said no. To build a diversion and keep the water flowing cost Midvale an extra $20,000, and a tribal Fish and Game agent—big Terry Myers—stood silently by with a gun on his hip, watching.

By 1997, the threat that the tribes would flex their water rights to cripple Midvale had diminished, but the irrigation project nevertheless seemed to have lost its preeminence in the valley. The public seemed less impressed with the economic importance of agriculture and more impressed with scenery—not just at Wind River but throughout the West—as more transplants moved onto forty-acre ranchettes paid for with telecommuting jobs. Brown's calls to the Bureau of Reclamation went unanswered, like a rent-control tenant calling the unfriendly landlord. The tribes had lost the last instream flow round in the Wyoming Supreme Court, but relations between the state and the tribes and the non-Indians who farmed what had once been reservation land had been altered for good; tribal leaders were more outspoken and aggressive than they ever had been in the past. Midvale continued to make improvements that saved water—computer-automated gates, pipelines replacing open ditches—but to a lot of the newcomers in the valley, they wore the black hats, while the tribes were the friends of wilderness and wildlife. That hurt the most.

On our last trip to Bull Lake, Bill Brown sounded almost wistful. Before he retires, he wants to put a mission statement together for Midvale that will voice the dedication of its farmers to the betterment of the valley's environment and economy. Perhaps it would be a statement of defiance, too, of the meddling and inconsistent policies of a government that won't simply let these farmers farm. "If you want this thing for the Indians and the fisheries," he said, "relocate us. Don't starve us out."

And Brown is resigned to an essential cultural difference between the farmers of Midvale and tribal members. "The white man thinks he's got to possess material things," he said. "The Indians don't feel that way. Everything's got to belong to everybody."

In the blockhouse at Bull Lake Dam, I descended eighty feet down into the dam on a black spiral staircase to a room that looked a little like a domed wine cellar. Well below the reservoir's water line, this is where the automated valves open and shut to release water through the spillway. The system is clean and well kept. When I came back up, we looked down at the lake to where it narrows between jutting headlands; in the hazy distance, out of our view, the lake backs up to an inlet that comes sweeping around the last curve in the smooth stone mouth of a canyon. Hike above this first canyon and you come to forest-fringed cliffs squeezing deeper canyons and hanging valleys and alpine lakes cupped in the deeply lined granite palms of the mountains.

Though the water that flows through Bull Lake Dam to Diversion Dam to Brown's farm begins in those high places, Brown has never visited them. "I've heard it's really nice," he said as we stood on the dam, looking west, "but I just don't feel welcome there."

CHAPTER 17

The Divide

Above Bull Lake, where the streams become steep and fine, and the granite rises vertical, the trails fade and lose their purpose, buried under rockfall and mud, overgrown by wild rose and elk thistle and monkey flower, lost and found among misleading game trails. Now the streams become our only trustworthy guides upward into the wilderness, threads to follow from room to room in this rock house of aloof and dwarfing summits.

The small string of horses climbing the steep-sloping crests on the south side of Bull Lake Canyon might be Dick Baldes and the biologists on their way to the high lakes to plant trout, combating the lake-choking brook trout with native cutthroat and rejuvenating lakes made barren by deep winter freeze-outs. Or it could be Kate Vandemoer following a pack train of sampling equipment to the backcountry lakes to float around in rubber rafts, collecting water samples to see if acid rain is upsetting the delicate balance. Or it might be scientists from the U.S. Geological Survey, bound for the shrinking glaciers at 12,000 feet above sea level to drill cores that will tell them, in a language of ice and dirt and frozen bugs, what the weather was like centuries ago, what the weather reports might be a decade from now. Or it could even be the ghosts of earlier visitors, like Millie Guina and her wild women friends dragging an elk back to Sage Creek, or young Bob Harris trailing sheep down through the high meadows all summer long, or the Tukudika, the Sheep Eaters, the elusive relatives of the Shoshone who made rough stick homes in the high country. From the shadows of prehis-

tory, it might be the mysterious people who turned the great sandstone walls above the streams and lakes into the history books of
their civilization, pecking with flint tools to create murals of men
and animals and fantastical spirit shapes.

There is room for all of them, and then more room to be alone.
The Wind River Mountains form a broad and bristling range, its
peaks of 12,000 and 13,000 feet packed together like snow cones on a
tray, with deep lake beds set down amid their cirques. The glaciers
that form their skirts are still another apparatus in the machinery
of water, storing centuries of moisture and releasing it in the late
summer months. Their retreat—the big ones, like Fremont and
Knife Point, could be gone entirely in just a few more decades—is
another impetus for worry about Wind River water, because farmers have come to depend on their late season melt.

But it was not a hydrologist riding the horse above Bull Lake; it
was not a geographer or a biologist or an archaeologist. It was
Sumner Marlowe, his ponytail tucked under a beaten hat, his loose
body sliding side to side, his mind downshifting, searching for a
gear that would match the relaxed tempo of falling water.

Below and behind him were the paint-peeling trailers, the heavy-
lidded boys of the housing projects, the harsh morning-after voices
of home, the suspicious questions at work. He was heading for the
high country on a fishing trip. He would camp by a lake high up
near the Continental Divide, a glacier-fed lake as secure as a bank,
with a vault full of microbes and tiny shrimp and hatching bugs and
cutthroat and golden trout. Though his rod was strapped to the
saddle, he was thinking he might not break the still security of
the lake's surface with a lure. It was a strenuous two-day trip in,
and the reward was stillness. His mind would be unburdened because
the indifferent strength of the mountains would belittle his losses,
and they were the repository of his happiness and hope.

Climbing the dizzying trail to the rim above Bull Lake Creek, he
looked down at a pocket of marsh and meadow between the first
canyon feeding into the lake and a higher, steeper, almost impene-
trable canyon that led to smaller lakes above. Here, many years
before, he had taken his nephews, Michael Marlowe and Ray Brush,
on their first camping trip. They rode through a drizzly June rain to

get there, the boys complaining all the way. Marlowe would say to them, "You can't do nothing about it. Go ahead and get wet, have fun. We'll get dry when we get to camp." And because they were five years old, and it was not too cold, they *did* begin to have fun, putting their heads back to catch the rain in their mouths, grabbing at pine branches to shake the drops off, teasing each other about who was the wettest.

They set their camp near the top of the lower canyon, beneath a cliff face where pale columbine peeked from a small spring. A box canyon to the north produced a small stream that had cut a bed in the red soil. The rain grew heavier while Marlowe unsaddled the horses and pulled out the poles for the tent. His nephews were throwing sticks in the small, red-clay creek that ran into Bull Lake Creek right where it dropped into the canyon.

Michael approached him a bit shyly and asked, "Where's the bathroom?"

Sumner Marlowe stifled a laugh. He held out some toilet paper and said, "Here, we just go out there in the bushes, that's the bathroom." The boy looked at him crossly, thinking it was a joke. When he saw it wasn't, he looked at the thick stand of bushes and trees about 100 yards off and imagined mountain lions and bears and things that bit you when you squatted. When he looked back at Marlowe, his uncle could see he was scared.

"Be like a bear," he said. "*They* shit in the woods." And he growled playfully.

With a dubious gait the boy went off, but he came back strutting with success, and there was giggling and chatter when the boys burrowed into their nests in the tent. Marlowe was right there, the sun had gone down, and nothing was going to happen. He took pleasure in the way they trusted him, the way they lost their fear when he told them what to do.

The rain kept getting heavier. He told them about the people who used to live in these mountains, not in tents but in homes made of sticks, with brush piled on top. He told them about the traps they made to catch the mountain sheep, and he rotated his finger to show the curl of a bighorn's horn. The boys were nodding off when Sumner Marlowe realized that water was rushing around the tent, pulling at its corners, mounding up against the wall that faced the box canyon. Water spouting off the cliff face above began to strike the top of the tent. The boys woke when he turned on the flashlight. They heard the noise of water all around, saw the edge of the tent rocking up, and looked at Sumner Marlowe wide-eyed.

It was just what he had told them. "Be humble. In the mountains you're not in control, not of the wind, the snow, the rain." But he was terrified himself. The prying fingers of the flood lifted the upstream edge of the tent and rolled it half over, and Marlowe lunged at that side of the tent, bending the poles so that the wet fabric slapped down on the boys. They screamed, and he called them to him where he lay with his feet jammed against the floor and his back against the pressing wall, using all his weight to hold their ground. They were only fifty yards from the canyon, and if they rolled into that water, they wouldn't have a chance. The boys piled on top of him, adding their weight, and when they looked at him he tried to keep his eyes calm.

The rain subsided within half an hour. The boys were wet and exhausted, and he wrapped them in an extra blanket. Then he stepped outside under a clearing sky, the stars as dense as pebbles on a stream bottom. He looked for the horses and found them in the trees, still hobbled. For the rest of the night he sat by the door of the tent, and in the morning, when the sun came up and steam rose from the valley, he smelled the musk of torn-up sagebrush and the fruity sweetness of mud and manure and, finally, the indescribable scent of fresh water.

When Michael and Ray came out of the tent, rumpled and bleary, he made them hold still for a moment. "Just smell it," he said, and they stood there trying to do it right, raising their noses in as dignified a way as they could, nodding to Sumner Marlowe as if, yes, they got it.

Then Michael Marlowe said to his uncle, "Give me the toilet paper, I need to take a growl."

It had been more than a decade since that camping trip, and now Sumner Marlowe awoke in a tent near the top of the world.

Imagine a series of nested bowls, each one tilted slightly so that when it fills up it then pours into the bowl just below it. Marlowe camped in the highest bowl, where the trickles of ice melt from the beards of snow on the Continental Divide were gathered. From bowl to bowl to larger bowl the water falls, until finally it empties into the Gulf of Mexico.

No river begins in just one place, though explorers are always searching for the magical source of the Nile or the Amazon. Along the Continental Divide you can find hundreds of likely suspects for the headwaters of the Wind River Basin. The lake where Sumner Marlowe camped will do: the beginning of the water's journey, and the end of ours.

He had slept well, and he awoke thinking of a white woman from Billings who had come through Ethete recently, selling magnetic bands. Concrete has covered so much of the world, she said, that we don't get enough magnetism, except in the mountains, the only place where energy is still high. Her sales pitch made him smile, but that was close to how Sumner Marlowe felt: There was an energy in these high places that renewed him for the concrete world. He was always a little afraid when he went in alone, because he knew he would be at the mercy of his own thoughts, but that was just the first phase of getting through. He would think about his daughter, about his relatives who had passed away, about his nephew Michael in prison.

He had been coming to these mountains since the days when his father was a game warden and he rode behind him into the backcountry, and he knew that after that first anxiety he would be soothed and reassured. This was a gift he wished he could give to all the young people on the reservation—so many of whom had never been in the wilderness that belonged to them, or even slept on the ground. In their homes someone was always cooking for them, the television was always talking to them, their teachers asked nothing of them except that they sit still.

Here it was different. Here you had to take care of yourself, keep yourself warm and dry and fed. You had to admit all that you don't know and can't control. When you accepted that, the place accepted you and you felt safe, like a boy in a tent with a trusted uncle. The world below took that away. This world gave it back. He wished all the young people could experience that, and know it would always be here for them.

He stepped out of the tent and smelled the crisp, sweet smell from his childhood, a smell he had never been able to describe: water, tumbling fresh at the lake's inlet.

It was possible, he thought, that his nephew, in the prison where he now resides, remembered the smell too.

Epilogue

Six years after the Wyoming Supreme Court denied the Northern Arapaho and the Eastern Shoshone of the Wind River Indian Reservation the power to oversee water rights in the valley or to use their own rights to protect instream flow, negotiations continue between the state and the tribes. According to Jeff Fassett—who as Wyoming's state engineer shifted his attention from Wind River to negotiations with Nebraska over the Platte River—relations between the state and the tribes are cordial, and much progress has been made toward sharing management responsibilities.

Wold Mesghinna still works for the tribes, though he spends more and more time in his native Eritrea. For a few years, he regularly told me that a settlement very beneficial to the tribes was imminent. As of January 1999, no deal had been struck. Susan Williams continues to practice law in Albuquerque, and plays drums in a rock-and-roll band.

Richard Baldes has retired from the U.S. Fish and Wildlife Service and still lives near Trout Creek on the reservation. Bill Brown has not yet retired, though he talks about it. Kate Vandemoer is in the Pacific Northwest, working for the U.S. National Marine Fisheries Service. After many years in private business, Wes Martel rejoined John Washakie on the Shoshone Business Council in 1998. Gary Collins now works as the assistant tribal water engineer.

Sumner Marlowe is teaching again on the reservation, and in the summer he takes another set of young nephews and nieces on camping trips into the mountains.

An astonishing number of the tribal elders who talked with me over the years passed away in the 1990s. Anthony Sitting Eagle, Pius Moss, Francis Brown, Bob Harris, and the man I call Monroe Marlowe are all dead now. So are several other Shoshone and Arapaho elders whom I've spoken with over the years. For people who grew up knowing them, and relying on them, they were key links to the past, and the spiritual life of the tribes, and the loss is almost unbearable; even with the short time I knew them, I miss them too.

I still live in the Wind River Valley, though I say too often that I might pull up stakes and go looking for stories elsewhere. If vehicles are a kind of destiny, I no longer own the green Land Cruiser. These days, I sometimes drive a dented old Mercedes convertible.

A year after the Wyoming Supreme Court blocked tribal control of the Wind River, I took my young daughter backpacking on the reservation, hiking from St. Lawrence Basin up along the base of Lookout Mountain and Wolverine Peak to an array of deep lakes that pour out of bouldery pockets into the Little Wind River. We saw only a few other hikers, which is how it always is on the reservation. These ones complained of black bears harassing their camp.

One night lightning crashed back and forth in the cirques above us, a tent-shaking, ear-battering slam dance of violent noise. The next day was windy and overcast, but the sun made a yellowy smudge in the clouds, so I left my daughter with a fishing pole on the bank of Sonnicant Lake and headed for the Continental Divide.

It was a hike of a few miles and a thousand vertical feet, but as the wind whistled stronger and clouds began to bunch, I worried about Genya and considered turning back. The path had contoured along a steep slope until I reached the treeline, and then it braided into a half dozen game trails. There was a rough little canyon just in front of me, and a slope of open scree, though there was no mountain above, only the sky—as if these high mountains, which look so hard and unbroken from below, were really just huge piles of loose rock. But there was a lot of rock, steep and unstable, and I was running out of time.

I sat by the trail eating an apple and gazing at the lakes below—Heebecheeche, Kegavah, Solitude—and when I looked back up the trail I noticed the deer. She didn't look healthy, not for early August. Her ribs showed through a coat that seemed to be shedding handfuls of fur. She was just standing there, and when I got up and moved toward her, she turned and looked back at the canyon, but didn't flee. Then, when I was much too close, she began walking slowly west, into the canyon and up toward the Divide.

So I followed her.

For a while I couldn't see her against the brown rock, so I just turned up the drainage, which was really just a wet-streaked indent of scree. As I climbed, the grade softened and the little canyon opened at the top the way a lily's petals spread outward, sloping over backward to become the wide back of the continent. This can be deceptive—the grade lessens as you near the top of the divide itself, making it difficult to see the topmost ridge, which may actually lie several false summits beyond. Worried by the falling light, I was ready to turn around—and then the scraggly deer appeared again, walking stiffly up and over the last hump.

She disappeared above me, where no deer ought to be. About half an hour later, I arrived atop Photo Pass. From here I could look west into Utah and east across the Wyoming plains to Nebraska. For a short time after 1863 the United States government considered most of this extraordinary view the property of the Eastern Shoshone Indians.

The sky above was like the bottom of an overturned ocean, and below I could see the dark opals of lakes. The ridges that separated the drainages splayed out like the tassels on the edge of a rug, passing through the foothills and then flattening onto the plains. It was one of the higher spots I'll ever achieve in my life, but I didn't stop long; thunderheads were gathering, and the light was leaden.

As I started down, though, I paused by a small patch of shaded snow beneath a freestanding rock. I put my hand beneath the brown, retracted lip of the snow and dampened it in the melt that stained the rock, then touched my finger to my tongue.

No taste. I headed down the trail to my daughter. When I got to camp it was dark. She had built a fire and made some tea, but there were no fish for dinner. The rod leaned against a tree, and the pulpy novel in her hand was plump with turned pages. I could see the fly was embedded in the cork exactly where I'd left it.

Later, I described the deer to Starr Weed, and he said, with a smile, "Like there is *somebody* around, eh? It's just got to happen, and then you know." I'm still not sure I know.

NOTES

Prologue

5   "domestic dependent nations": U.S. Supreme Court Justice John Marshall first described reservations as "domestic dependent nations" in a ruling on the 1831 case, *Cherokee Nation v. Georgia*. The Cherokee, one of the Five Civilized Tribes of the South, had permitted a group of missionaries to preach among the Cherokee and translate Biblical passages into the tribe's tongue. The Georgia legislature, however, had banned the translation of scripture into Cherokee, a rather peculiar law among many designed to undermine the Cherokee attempts at self-government. The missionaries were arrested and convicted, and their case was appealed to the nation's highest court. Marshall defended the tribes as "distinct, independent political communities" within certain limits—they couldn't, for instance, have an ambassador in Paris. Though his opinion is still debated, it defined the tribes' relationship with the federal government: "a weak state, in order to provide for its safety, may place itself under the protection of one more powerful, without stripping itself of the right of government, and ceasing to be a state." For a good description of this case and others in the unique body of jurisprudence called Indian law, see *The Nations Within* (Pantheon), by Vine DeLoria, Jr., and Clifford Lytle. Many of the key judicial opinions in Indian law are collected in *Documents of United States Indian Policy* (Nebraska), edited by Francis Paul Prucha.

Chapter 1: Wind River Canyon

8   Shoshone Indian Reservation: It's a little confusing to refer to the Wind River Indian Reservation as the Shoshone Indian Reservation, but that's what it was called in 1896 when McLaughlin visited. It was renamed the Wind River Indian Reservation in 1937, when the federal government finally paid the Shoshone damages for having placed the Arapaho on their

reservation in 1878. For $4.4 million, the Shoshone recognized the right of the Northern Arapaho to live at Wind River, though some still gripe about it today. See Loretta Fowler's *Arapaho Politics 1851–1978: Symbols in Crises of Authority* (University of Nebraska Press), page 197.

8   Indian Inspector James McLaughlin: McLaughlin doesn't offer much description of his journey to Wind River in his book, *My Friend, the Indian* (Nebraska) other than to note that it was 150 miles overland from Rawlins to the reservation. There are other roughly contemporary accounts of what the landscape looked like then, including a report on McLaughlin's visit to the hot springs by a military man, John Small (*Annals of Wyoming*, vol. 8, no. 1), and the reports of various other schoolteachers, missionaries, and travelers, including an 1883 expedition through the valley by President Chester Arthur. But a good deal of the description is my own: the landscape has not been filled in much between Rawlins and the Wind River Valley since McLaughlin's time. Get out of your car on Beaver Rim and you'll see a view very like what McLaughlin saw (then you'll get back into the car to escape the biting wind). His description of Wind River Canyon is on page 297 of his book.

10   McLaughlin considered himself: McLaughlin takes great pride in his long association with Indians, his understanding of their ways and interests, and his concern for their welfare. Between 1896 and 1906, he negotiated dozens of agreements, almost all of them ceding lands to the white men. "It has been simply a matter of showing them, by illustrations they would understand, that what was proposed would be best for them in the long run. They are simple-minded people, and direct arguments must be made to them." For another perspective on McLaughlin, particularly his long feud with the Sioux Chief Sitting Bull, check Dee Brown's *Bury My Heart at Wounded Knee* (Bantam), page 400. In McLaughlin's own book, I found this passage worth repeating: "The Indian wars generally have been in the nature of fierce reprisals for injuries sustained. That the Indian has not always discriminated between the innocent and the guilty in taking his revenge, is certain. . . . If his sense of justice had led him to fine discrimination in these matters, the red man would long ago have made an attack on the national Capitol."

11   the legendary Shoshone chief Washakie: There's no record of any such speech by Washakie in the various journals of the 1896 negotiations. The pageant was written by Marie Montabe to entertain the annual convention of the Wyoming State Federation of Women's Clubs in 1925. Dick Washakie played his father. When the pageant was revived in 1950, it was sponsored by the local Daughters of the American Revolution. The story of the park and the pageant is told in *The Gift of Bah Guewana* (Frontier Printing), by Dorothy G. Milek.

14   Rocky Mountain geology: Every road-cut in Wyoming exposes some interesting geological history, and the Northern Rockies have inspired a number of "roadside geology" books that allow you to drive along and smartly

identify anticlines, thrust faults, and an occasional iaccolith. For Wyoming, my favorite is the *Traveler's Guide to the Geology of Wyoming* (Geological Survey of Wyoming), by D. L. Blackstone, Jr., which describes the Wind River Basin as a "rhomb-shaped topographic depression," and then confesses: "Nothing about the area is simple." To help me understand the language of geologists, I consulted my old soccer coach, Professor Donald Zenger of Pomona College.

16 The descriptions of the conflict—sometimes called the Bates Battle, after U.S. Army captain A. E. Bates—were assembled from the collections of the Fremont County Pioneer Museum in Lander, and mostly published in the *Wind River Mountaineer*, vol. 7, no. 1, a fine local history magazine edited by Tom Bell. The battle site is in a remote area of the Owl Creeks where two-tracks disappear in the sagebrush. I drove there with Henry Jensen, an elderly historian from the tiny town of Lost Cabin; several times it seemed we were lost, and I worried that Henry would have a heart attack as we bounced through the sagebrush and he rattled on about boyhood friends who'd collected a cigar box of human bones and spent cartridges from the site. Then we came over a bluff above the little draw, and as I walked down into it I understood how historians must feel when the landscape speaks to them of the past: it was so unmarked by man that it was easy to imagine the tepees along the creek, the soldiers on the hill where we stood, and the battle itself.

17 An Arapaho woman: It was Doris Oldman who heard the cries of her people while shearing sheep in the Owl Creek Mountains. Her memories were recorded in the 1970s as part of an oral history project titled "Valley of the Three Worlds," now stored at Central Wyoming College in Riverton, Wyoming.

17 Sharp Nose: the first treaty: Much of the material about historic Arapaho leaders is taken from Loretta Fowler's excellent *Arapaho Politics, 1851–1978*. The 1863 treaty described "Sho-Sho-nee Country" as bounded on the north by the Snake River Valley, on the east by the Wind River Mountains (*Peenahpah*, in Shoshone), the north fork of the Platte and the north Park, and on the south by the Uintah Mountains. "The Western boundary is left undefined, there being no Sho-Sho-nees from that district of the Country present; but the Bands now present Claim that their own Country is Bounded on the West by Salt Lake." That seems a little indefinite, doesn't it? Geographers estimate it would have encompassed about 44 million acres. Probably more important than boundaries to the white negotiators were articles promising that the Sho-Sho-nee would not attack emigrants passing through their lands, and that the Sho-Sho-nee would provide protection for stagecoaches and telegraph lines. In addition, "if depredations should at any time be committed by bad men of their nation, the offending Shall be immediately seized and delivered up to the proper officers of the United States, to be punished as their offences Shall deserve."

18 "fenced by posts alone": The description of fence posts without wire

comes from a U.S. Department of Commerce Census Report of 1894. I
found it quoted in a Ph.D. thesis by Thomas Hoevet Johnson, written in
1975 at the University of Illinois Urbana-Champaign.

19 McLaughlin, the Indian agent: Various descriptions of the negotiations
were written contemporaneously. One that was particularly interesting,
and quite different from McLaughlin's, was by Captain Richard H. Wilson,
who was acting agent at the Shoshone Agency at the time. He noted sadly
that "the amount paid was absurdly low for the finest hot spring on earth"
(*Annals of Wyoming*, vol. 8, no. 2).

20 Chief Washakie led his people: Teacher James Patten's vivid description of
one of Washakie's last hunts was published in the *Bighorn County Rustler*,
March 26, 1920.

21 they were being pushed toward extinction: In Dee Brown's *Bury My Heart
at Wounded Knee*, page 254, he notes that of 3.7 million bison killed between
1872 and 1874, only an estimated 150,000 were killed by Indians.

Chapter 2: The Community Hall

26 *Youa die:* The Shoshone name for the Wind River Valley was given to me by
Pat Bergie, an enrolled Eastern Shoshone.

29 irrigation project: The failure of the Wyoming Central Irrigation Company is expertly detailed in an unpublished manuscript called "To Make the
Desert Bloom: How Irrigation Came to the Ceded Portion of the Wind
River Indian Reservation," by Molly Hoopengarner, who lives on a ranch
along the Wind River herself. With variations, it's a story repeated
throughout the arid West during the homesteading years. Another source
of information on the history of non-Indian irrigation in the valley was a
draft history of "The Riverton Unit—Pick-Sloan Missouri Basin Program,"
for a book on historic reclamation projects in the works by the U.S. Bureau
of Reclamation. It's yet to be published—I got a copy from a local historian
who was sent a copy for review (and wrote an angry letter denouncing it
for alleged factual errors and its negative view of the Riverton Unit).

It was in this history that I first discovered that the early surveying and
initial earthmoving on the Riverton Unit had been paid for out of federal
Indian appropriations. This seemed a bit startling, suggesting as it does that
funds meant for the benefit of the Wind River tribes might actually have
been invested in a non-Indian irrigation project. The share paid out of
Indian appropriations might seem insignificant—a couple of $5,000 appro-
priations for preliminary surveys, then $100,000 in 1918 to begin construc-
tion (the projected full cost of the project at that time was $3.7 million). But
the vehemence of Senator Mondell's letter, which I found in the National
Archives in Washington, D.C., suggests this was a questionable use of funds.

38 the reservation's Indian population: Census figures for the tribes, and
descriptions from reports from Wind River to the commissioner of Indian

Affairs, were researched and skillfully distilled by Hank Stramm in an unpublished 1995 thesis at the University of Wyoming.

38 more than a hundred Shoshone: The letter from 120 Shoshone to the Commissioner of Indian Affairs is mentioned in Fowler's *Arapaho Politics, 1851–1978*, page 104.

39 Grace Coolidge: Coolidge's version of the meeting is recounted in a story called "The Man's Part" in *Tipi Neighbors* (Oklahoma), by Grace Coolidge. In the preface to this book of short stories, Coolidge wrote a description of reservation neighbors that's worth repeating:

> In the first place, the Indians are surrounded by white people mainly of two unfortunate attitudes of mind. The first is the man who hates the Indian. He lives generally across the boundary line of the reservation; he toils on his side while the Indian idles on the other; he pays his grudging taxes while the Indian exists free of charge; he sees loads of government freight driven into the agency for free distribution, and he envies. Of course this freight was bought with the Indians' own money at the discretion of the government, not the Indian; without indeed the consent or even knowledge of the owner of the funds. His mind is full of the old evil stories of the past, told always from the side of the Indian's enemy. . . .
>
> Then there is the far larger class of neighboring whites whose attitude toward the Indian is one of absolute indifference and uninterest. Familiarity of an entirely external sort has bred in them a kind of comfortable contempt.

Chapter 3: Riverton

45 Michael Marlowe: Young Michael Marlowe did not open his heart to me the way his uncle did, though we've had a nodding acquaintance. The only way I could get inside his head was by attending his trial, reading transcripts of the trials of other young Indian men, talking to psychologists, and conversing with various older Indian men who had some of the same experiences. The circumstances I describe are not the exact events of his life, which I've changed in order to protect his and his family's privacy. To understand his success as a firefighter, I recalled conversations I had with young men on all-Indian firefighting crews when I was covering the 1988 fires in Yellowstone National Park. The violent events at Double Dives, and the people who participated in them, blend a series of true incidents recounted in trial testimony and in interviews with attorneys and U.S. Bureau of Indian Affairs police and FBI agents who investigate major crimes on the reservation.

Working for public television and newspapers, I've interviewed a fairly large number of Indian teenagers about their lives. Often I've had the help of Indian colleagues, particularly during television interviews. But I'm still an older white male, and my presence undoubtedly creates inhibitions. I've had much more success talking to Indian girls, some of whom were willing to describe in some detail the bad behavior among their peers; the boys tend to joke around nervously, or go monosyllabic when asked about the dark side of their lives, as if they might incriminate themselves to a reporter. I've used those interviews to flesh out my portrait of Michael Marlowe and his friends.

48 gunshots had been fired at Double Dives almost a century earlier: I relied a lot on the *Riverton Ranger*'s archives for information about the town's early days, and I have talked at some length with the newspaper's publisher, Robert Peck, about the history and character of his town, where his family has played a significant role for generations. Peck will not agree with much of what this book has to say, but as a publisher and legislator he epitomizes the kind of character he ascribes to the town: optimistic, hardworking, not prone to feeling guilty about the past, a strong advocate of economic development, and iron-willed about achieving his goals. He has been helpful and courteous to me, even though we are sometimes at odds.

Chapter 4: Lower Arapahoe

66 dog-eaters: According to Virginia Cole Trenholm's *The Arapahoes, Our People* (Oklahoma), the Arapaho once considered dog flesh a delicacy, and the Shoshone called them *Sheridika*, or "dog eaters." One of the most senior men's societies in the Arapaho tribe was the Dog Lodge or the Dog-men's Lodge, but anthropological records don't associate this group with eating dogs.

71 Water-Pouring Old Men: Much of the tribes' oral history and many customs were lost with the move onto the reservation, and various anthropological reports use different names and ascribe different attributes to the age-graded societies that were a key part of tribal structure. The Water-Sprinkling Old Men are described in several different studies, including an essay by Henry Elkin in *Acculturation in Seven American Indian Tribes* (Peter Smith) and Alfred L. Kroeber's *The Arapaho* (Nebraska), an enormously detailed study of the tribe's customs, costumes, and language that was originally published in the *Bulletin of the American Museum of Natural History* between 1902 and 1907. Some contemporary experts find fault with Kroeber, particularly his analysis of the Arapaho language, but his detailed observations of dances and clothing from a century ago provide a valuable record.

74 "utterly valueless to the Shoshones": The resolution is in the records of the legislature, but I let Molly Hoopengarner do the work of finding it for me. She reproduces it in her unpublished "To Make the Desert Bloom:

How Irrigation Came to the Ceded Portion of the Wind River Indian Reservation."

75   a special vocabulary: Some of this hydrologic lexicon came from Vande-moer's materials, but I relied on Elizabeth M. Shaw's *Hydrology in Practice* (Chapman & Hall) and the *Wyoming Water Atlas* (Wyoming Water Development Commission), edited by Richard A. Marston, for additional help. Since I've modified these definitions to make them more accessible to laymen, I'm to blame for any misinformation.

Chapter 5: Leclair and the Lower River

83   electrofishing: The biologists don't electrofish often on the Wind, because the practice can fatally damage a fish. I've never seen fish killed unintentionally on these floats—carp, this does not mean you—but apparently the effects of shock can linger in the nervous system, and death can occur months later.

88   LeClair was no Indian: There is some confusion over the bloodlines of Edmo LeClair, just as there is over many tribal members and in-laws from the early days of recordkeeping in the West. From French trappers to Irish engineers, there has been plenty of intercourse between Native American women and white male immigrants to the West; there has also been a lot of genetic interchange between tribes. In the case of Edmo LeClair's mother, Wyoming historian Tom Bell describes her as a full-blooded Iroquois, while a 1929 document written for the Federal Writers Project history collections (stored at the Wyoming State Museum in Cheyenne) says she was Bannock-Shoshone. Much of my account of LeClair's life is taken from articles in Bell's *Wind River Mountaineer,* vol. 5, no. 1.

89   revised allotment process: Loretta Fowler's *Arapaho Politics, 1851–1978: Symbols in Crises of Authority* (University of Nebraska Press) describes the impact of the federal policy on the sale of allotment lands (p. 129) at Wind River. For an overview of the devastating impact in Indian Country of the Dawes Act of 1887 (creating the allotment system) and the Burke Act of 1906 (speeding the sale of allotments to non-Indians), check R. Douglas Hurt's *Indian Agriculture in America* (Kansas), pages 151–53, or the *Encyclopedia of the American Indian* (Todd Publications), page 27.

90   Edmo LeClair and his family: The description of the original ditch and the quotes from Edmo LeClair are from a 1926 interview with LeClair, part of the records assembled by the U.S. Bureau of Indian Affairs in 1975 in an attempt to clear up the question of how much the LeClair irrigators still owed the federal government for construction of their project.

The description of the party at the LeClairs came from the newspaper *Riverton Review,* Nov. 18, 1918.

91   repayment is owed: Information on federal funds invested in LeClair came, once again, from Molly Hoopengarner's unpublished research into non-

Indian irrigation development within the reservation's boundaries ("To Make the Desert Bloom").

92   an army reconnaissance journalist: William Jones's *Report Upon the Reconnaissance of Northwestern Wyoming* (1873) was published by the Government Printing Office in 1875.

Chapter 6: On the Riverbanks

95   "I had lots of brothers": Merle Haas's only siblings were sisters, but in Arapaho families, cousins and other male relatives are considered brothers.

97   Loss of indigenous language: The data on languages spoken in pre-European North America is from Peter Farb's *Man's Rise to Civilization* (Dutton). Farb explores some of the popular myths about Indian history, and I found his thoughts about the brevity of Plains Indian culture persuasive. The information on Native American languages today came from a *Washington Post* article by John Schwartz, "Speaking Out and Saving Sounds to Keep Native Tongues Alive," March 14, 1994.

99   the population of North America: The debate over the population and civilizations of pre-Columbian America goes on and on. How many Indians were here before Europeans arrived, where were they, what sort of government and culture had they developed? Alfred Kroeber, an anthropologist who studied the Arapaho early in this century, contends there were about 1 million humans in North America before 1492. Recent scholarship (summarized in David E. Stannard's *American Holocaust* [Oxford University Press], p. 267) suggests as many as 20 million. Alfred W. Crosby's *Ecological Imperialism* (Cambridge University Press) argues that the diseases that came with sailors from Europe, for which Native Americans had no resistance, may have rushed inland ahead of settlement, decimating native populations even before the settlers made their way West.

99   Arapaho roamed: The migrations of the Arapaho are described in Zdenek Salzmann's *The Arapaho Indians, a Research Guide and Bibliography* (Greenwood Press), page 4.

     Finn Burnett, Frontiersman (A. H. Clark) was ghosted by Robert Beebe David in 1936.

99   Arapaho alphabet: Much of my material on the Arapaho language came from a class taught by Dickie Moss at Wyoming Indian High School in 1991, supplemented with material in various anthropological papers and Alfred Kroeber's 1904 book, *The Arapaho*. Then Sara Wiles, who has worked with Dickie and Alonzo Moss on several Arapaho/English translations, looked it over and told me most of it was wrong. For her help I'm grateful, but neither she nor the Moss brothers should be held responsible for the results. The difficult job of transforming an oral language into a written one—especially a language spoken fluently by only a declining number of people—has been ably undertaken by Zdenek Salzmann fairly recently, and

one might expect further fine tuning in spellings and definitions. The Shoshone are in the midst of a similar effort to save their language, but their task is even more daunting. Few elders in the tribe are fluent today, and for several generations the language was withheld from outsiders. Only in the last decade have native Shoshone speakers begun working with a linguist to preserve the language in written form. The world of linguists and anthropologists has its changing fashions, too—I've been told I should change the spelling of the "tipis" in this book to "tepees" if I want to be accurate.

102 **the late Ralph Hopper:** Hopper, who passed on stories to Merle Haas, was crippled by a fire as an infant. Unable to play, he spent much of his childhood listening to tribal elders like Yellow Calf, his grandfather. Here's a translation from the Arapaho that gives a sense of how he told a story: "Sharpened Leg," from *Stories from Yellow Calf,* told by Ralph Hopper, collected by Frances Goggles, is described as a moral story, or parable.

> The next story I want to tell is about a man with a sharpened leg. There was a camp along a river and there was a man who used to sharpen his leg. He used to do that for a reason. One day he sharpened his leg and after he did this, he looked around and saw a buffalo herd. He looked for the fattest buffalo. He used his powers to get the fattest buffalo after he sharpened his leg. He used his leg and his power to get the buffalo.
>
> There was a white man who came along. He saw the man sharpening his leg. The white man kept watching him. The man put his leg on top of a log and he took a knife and sharpened his leg. The white man watched the other man get the fattest buffalo. The white man wanted power like that. He asked the Indian to give it to him, to give him his power, but the Indian refused. "I can't do that. It is impossible to do that."
>
> The white man kept begging. "I would like to have your power," but the Indian kept refusing.
>
> So many times, the white man asked the Indian. The Indian finally said, "All right, I will give you my power, but you must not overdo it. You are supposed to do things only four times and not over four times. I use it as my own power, but I will give it to you. If you overdo it, you are going to get yourself into trouble, and something is going to happen to you."
>
> The white man said he would respect the power and not go over four times. So the Indian had the white man put his leg on top of a log and the man took his knife and was ready to strike.
>
> The white man said, "Wait! Wait!" Four times he hollered

for the Indian to wait, but it was too late the fourth time. The man had already struck his leg and sharpened it.

"Now, you go. Do not overdo your power. I'm warning you, white man," the Indian told him.

The white man left. He looked around for a buffalo herd. White man chose the fattest buffalo. He used his power and killed the buffalo, but he did not touch the dead buffalo. He went on looking for more buffalo. He tried his power again and he done good. He went on again and just left the dead buffalo lying there. It was the third time he looked around for a buffalo herd. He found the fattest buffalo and killed it. The fourth time was the last chance for the white man. He used his powers and he killed the buffalo, but he did not touch the dead buffalo. He left to find more but he made a mistake. The fifth time when he struck the buffalo with his leg, his leg got stuck. The buffalo dragged and kicked the white man and he could not get loose.

This story says that we must not overdo things. Today, we say that people overdo things, but everything is limited. We can get into trouble. We have to go easy on what we do. The white man got himself into trouble in the story because he overdid his power.

Chapter 7: Ethete

115 "Genoa": For a more detailed description of the Indian boarding school in Genoa, Nebraska, see Albert Kneale's *Indian Agent* (Caxton Printers), page 168. Kneale explains the rationale and methods used at these schools, where he worked as a headmaster.

116 Reverend John Roberts: The letters and journals of the Reverend Roberts have been collected by his granddaughter, Beatrice Crofts, in her book *Walk Softly, This Is God's Country* (Mortimore Publishing). If you're interested in the radical differences between Arapaho and Shoshone languages, the book includes an appendix of Shoshone vocabulary.

117 St. Michael's Mission in Ethete: Information on Ethete and St. Michael's was gleaned from Works Progress Administration files stored at the Wyoming State Museum in Cheyenne; the St. Michael's Mission brochure was in collections at the Denver Public Library.

Chapter 8: Washakie Plunge

129 a more popular spot: The struggle between Washakie and the military over the hot springs was researched by Henry E. Stamm IV in the correspon-

dence and annual reports of the Commissioner of Indian Affairs and reported in his thorough book *People of the Wind River* (University of Oklahoma Press), pages 196–98.

131 Whether the story is true: I was unable to verify David Love's story among tribal members, but historian Todd Guenther of the Fremont County Pioneer Museum believes the tar-pit claim is recorded in the records of the Shoshone Mining District, at South Pass City, Wyoming.

133 Imagine this scene: The transcript of the 1911 meeting was found in the Wind River Agency records stored at the National Archives office in Denver.

136 oil companies allegedly stealing: The story of the tribal investigation of oil thefts was pieced together from interviews with John Washakie, Wes Martel, other tribal members, and BIA officials. I also relied on a fine book about various tribes' efforts to regain control of the natural resources of reservations, *Breaking the Iron Bonds* (Kansas), by Marjane Ambler. The inefficient management of tribal resources by federal "trustees" has been investigated and reported by both the Interior Department's inspector general and Congress's General Accounting Office, but the Bureau of Indian Affairs has been unable to reconcile accounting records for as much as $500 million in trust funds held by the federal government for various tribes. In 1999 a federal district court judge in Washington, D.C., cited Secretary of the Interior Bruce Babbitt for contempt for not providing BIA records to the court. According to the 15 March 2000 edition of the South Dakota newspaper *Indian Country Today*, the judge called the government's recordkeeping "fiscal and governmental irresponsibility in its purest form."

Chapter 9: Fort Washakie (Part 1)

144 parts of the U.S. Constitution don't apply: Because many North American tribes entered into treaties with the U.S. government as sovereign nations, the U.S. Supreme Court ruled over a century ago that they could govern themselves without being subject to Constitutional rules like the Establishment Clause (separation of church and state) or the Fifteenth Amendment, which bans discrimination on the basis of race. In the 1960s, the U.S. Congress passed the Indian Civil Rights Act to give Indian citizens basic Bill of Rights protection within the reservation (they already had such protection elsewhere, as U.S. citizens). The act leaves a few things out—Indian courts don't have to provide lawyers for indigent defendants, for instance, and they can still exclude non-Indians from voting in tribal elections. For more information about the legal particulars of Indian government, see the American Civil Liberties Union's *The Rights of Indians and Tribes* (Southern Illinois University Press).

144 history of Native American governance: My source for most of the information on historic forms of tribal government is Sharon O'Brien's *Ameri-*

can Indian Tribal Governments (Oklahoma), in addition to some information from DeLoria and Lytle's *The Nations Within* (Pantheon).

145 Joint Business Council: Transcripts of Joint Business Council meetings were found in the Wind River Agency files at the National Archives branch in Denver.

148 Loretta Fowler: Fowler's *Arapaho Politics, 1851–1978* (University of Nebraska Press) gives a detailed and insightful history of how tribal political institutions evolved from the mobile warrior society to modern reservation life. It's an anthropologist's book, but not laden with jargon; the balance of anecdotal history, selected government records, and subtle analysis makes it a valuable book. From 1908 on, according to Fowler, tribal leaders adjusted their government institutions to the expectations of the federal Indian Office, hoping they would be granted more control if they appeared "progressive." They formed an Arapaho Business Council, and wore "white men's clothes" to the meetings. But among tribal members, councilmen were called "Six Chiefs." Fowler's book describes this sensitive dance between tribal leaders and paternalistic federal overseers, pages 128–287. While I understand, with Fowler's help, the complexity of these relationships, the institutions of the tribal General Council and business councils, as well as the federal Bureau of Indian Affairs, do not appear to me to function well at this time.

150 FBI prepared charges: The information about the embezzlement charges came from an FBI agent formerly stationed in Riverton, Wyoming.

150 1991 General Council: The description of and quotes from the 1991 General Council meeting come from a transcript obtained from an Arapaho tribal member.

152 A dinner more than a century ago: The dinner attended by Washakie and Black Coal was described by Mary Katherine Jackson, the daughter of an army officer stationed at Fort Washakie. Her memoir was published in Tom Bell's *Wind River Mountaineer*, vol. 6, no. 2.

Chapter 10: Fort Washakie (Part 2)

156 engineers followed the water: This information comes from Marc Reisner's *Cadillac Desert* (Penguin), pages 474–75. Reisner's book is the definitive history of water development in the American West.

Shards of Shoshone-style prehistoric pottery: The information on widespread Shoshone artifacts came from *Shoshone Indians* (Garland: American Indian Ethnohistory), evidence compiled by the Indian Claims Commission, page 9. The Claims Commission was created in 1946 to field tribal claims against the federal government. The claims had previously gone to the U.S. Congress.

157 They differed physically: John Roberts's observations about the two Wind River tribes were reprinted in the *Riverton Ranger*, October 9, 1969.

158 Shoshone were quick to adapt: Exactly where and how the Shoshone obtained horses is unrecorded, but in the early eighteenth century they were among the first tribes on the northern plains to ride, and it gave them a powerful, if brief, advantage over enemies like the Blackfeet. The Spanish explorers who traveled North America in the sixteenth century rode only stallions; it's now generally accepted that the first reproducing horses to fall into Indian hands were captured by Indians during the Pueblo uprising of 1680, in New Mexico. Shoshone bands in the Great Basin would then have taken horses north. (It's worth noting that the ancestors of the horse roamed North America millions of years before, and before becoming extinct, probably crossed the land bridge to Asia, where they spread west and evolved into the animal brought back to North America by the Spaniards. Perhaps that's why Mark Soldierwolf insists with a glint in his eye that his people had the horse long before Europeans arrived.) More information on the role of the horse in Indian culture is found in Herman J. Viola's *After Columbus* (Smithsonian Books) and Peter Farb's *Man's Rise to Civilization* (Dutton).

159 By the late nineteenth century: Much of the history of the Eastern Shoshone from the nineteenth century forward is taken from *The Shoshonis, Sentinels of the Rockies* (Oklahoma), by Virginia Cole Trenholm and Marine Carley. The story of the battle at Bear Lake is on pages 196–97.

160 daughter of one of the officers: This recollection of life at the fort is by Mary Katherine Jackson, "Recollections of an Army Girl," reprinted in Tom Bell's *Wind River Mountaineer*, vol. 6, no. 2.

161 their very own farmer: The memories and opinions of early attempts at farming are from *Finn Burnett, Frontiersman* (A. H. Clark), by Robert Beebe David.

164 a glowing report: Found in federal files by Henry E. Stamm IV and quoted in his *People of the Wind River* (University of Oklahoma Press), pages 104, 112–13.

165 "The white man kills": Washakie's speech was quoted in a letter from Wyoming governor John Hoyt to the Secretary of Interior, 17 July 1878, and reproduced in Trenholm and Carley's *The Shoshonis*, page 280.

165 Washakie: There are many biographical sketches of Washakie, from Hebard's biography to long sections in Trenholm and Carley's *The Shoshonis* and chapters in books such as *American Indian Leaders* (Nebraska), edited by R. David Edmunds. I've also used contemporary reports from the Utah Superintendency of Indian Affairs, edited by Dale Morgan and published in *Annals of Wyoming*, and some of the papers of Swedish anthropologist Ake Hultkrantz. There are numerous descriptions of Washakie's funeral, but it was Hebard who described the pile of sagebrush.

Chapter 11: The Courts

173 the media were all over the story: In this I include myself. I was running a bureau in Fremont County for the *Casper Star-Tribune*—the only Wyoming newspaper that circulated statewide—and the reservation was my primary beat. In fact, I'd been covering the water rights dispute since the early 1980s, when I did a piece about it for the *New York Times*.

174 more than $60 million: The state of Wyoming has to report how much it spends each year to the state legislature. As for the rest, federal government costs are folded into much larger budgets, and each of the twenty thousand water rights holders in the basin have probably had to consult lawyers to a greater or lesser degree. I think $60 million is a conservative estimate.

177 prior-appropriation doctrine: Of the many papers and books that tell the history of the prior-appropriation doctrine and Wyoming's role in Western water policy, Donald Worster's *Rivers of Empire* (Oxford University Press) was most useful to me. It's history told with literary flare and includes an insightful brief biography of Wyoming's most famous water engineer, Elwood Mead.

177 the state team tried a preemptive strike: The many volumes of documents and transcripts in the attic at the Washakie County courthouse are no longer in perfect order, but most of the testimony recounted here is from those archives, supplemented by interviews with most of the principals in the courtroom, including Special Master Teno Roncalio and several of the judges who heard the case. Roncalio's 451-page Special Master report ("In re: The General Adjudication of All Rights to use Water in the Bighorn River System and All Other Sources, State of Wyoming") is a surprisingly lively read.

187 famous Indian-law decisions: Various lawyers talked to me about significant cases in the evolution of Indian law, and the specifics of the cases and opinions come from *Documents of United States Indian Policy* (University of Nebraska), edited by Francis Paul Prucha. Marc Reisner's *Cadillac Desert* (Penguin) includes a pertinent discussion of *Arizona v. California* on page 270, and for more about *U.S. v. Sioux Nation*, the Black Hills case, see *Killing the White Man's Indian* (Doubleday), by Fergus M. Bordewich, page 230.

Chapter 13: Diversion Dam

204 John Truhero: This version of Truhero's vision comes from *Yellowtail, Crow Medicine Man and Sun Dance Chief* (University of Oklahoma Press), as told to Michael Fitzgerald. There is a much more political description of Truhero's rise as a Sun Dance chief in Fred W. Voget's *The Shoshoni-Crow Sun Dance* (University of Oklahoma Press). Though other sources say Truhero was revered among the Shoshone, and never overbearing about his spiritual role, Voget describes Truhero's involvement in the Crow Sun

Dance in part as an escape from lack of acceptance by and completion with other Sun Dance chiefs at Wind River. Voget goes so far as to say that some at Wind River "doubted his veracity and ridiculed his pretensions" (page 185).

207   *"Tam Apo,* here we are": There are many records of the Sun Dance ritual and its meaning, most of them by non-Indian anthropologists. This prayer from a 1948 Shoshone Sun Dance was included in an essay by Ake Hult-krantz, "Religious Belief Among the Wind River Shoshoni," on page 204 of the publication *Ethnos* Nos. 3–4, 1956. His report is among several stored in the collections at the American Heritage Center at the University of Wyoming in Laramie; there is also a detailed description of Shoshone Sun Dances in 1966 and 1967 by Thomas H. Johnson, a participant.

208   The Indian Office outlawed the Sun Dance: The Indian Office's Circular #1665, 26 April 1921, gives some idea of how the bureaucrats in Washington—in this case, Commissioner Charles H. Burke—viewed traditional Indian ceremonies:

> The sun-dance and all other similar dances and so-called religious ceremonies are considered "Indian offences" under existing regulations, and corrective penalties are provided. I regard such restriction as applicable to any dance which involves acts of self-torture, immoral relations between the sexes, the sacrificial distruction [sic] of clothing or other useful articles, the reckless giving away of property, the use of injurious drugs or intoxicants, and frequent or prolonged periods of celebration which bring the Indians together from remote points to the neglect of their crops, livestock, and home interests; in fact any disorderly or plainly excessive performance that promotes superstitious cruelty, licentiousness, idleness, danger to health, and shiftless indifference to family welfare.... It seems to me quite necessary to Indian progress that there should be no perversion of those industrial and economic essentials which underlie all civilization, and that therefore meetings or convocations for any purpose, including pleasurable and even religious occasions, should be directed with due regard to the every-day work of the Indian which he must learn to do well and not weary in the doing, if he is to become the right kind of a citizen and equal to the tests that await him.

211   some remedies: My information on medicinal plants came from a variety of sources, and so includes some terms and spellings with which others will take issue. The information comes from an uncredited list given to me by an Arapaho source, as well as from D. B. Shimkin's *Childhood and Development Among the Wind River Shoshone,* Jack Weatherford's *Indian Givers* (Fawcett), Alfred L. Kroeber's *The Arapaho,* and interviews with Millie Guina, a Shoshone.

215 Marc Reisner's monumental *Cadillac Desert* (Penguin) tells this story about passage of the reclamation law on pages 115–18.

Chapter 14: On the Wind

222 turbidity studies: The figures on turbidity above and below Diversion Dam are taken from a study by David Vogel for the U.S. Fish & Wildlife Service completed in October 1980, titled "Instream Flow Recommendations for Fishery Resources in the Major Rivers and Streams on the Wind River Indian Reservation, Wyoming."

224 Most of the damage: The material about non-Indian landowners' attempts early in the twentieth century to avoid paying construction costs of the irrigation systems they had inherited from former Indian landowners is in the form of agency reports and letters in the Indian Service historical materials stored in the National Archives in Washington, D.C., and Denver.

226 embarrassed by articles: The most damaging of the newspaper stories was an article by Andrew Melnykovych in the *Casper Star-Tribune*, 13 March 1988, detailing the failure of Midvale to repay the building costs of the project, amounting to a federal subsidy of millions of dollars annually. The following year I went to work for the newspaper and over the next two years wrote a number of articles about Midvale.

228 Fish and Wildlife Service planted . . . fingerlings: At the time of the conflict over fish-planting, I was working for the *Casper Star-Tribune*. I obtained the various memos from the FWS and interviewed the participants.

Chapter 15: Courts Redux

232 "a positive result": Proceedings of Reid Payton's article, "Indian Water Rights After the Wyoming Decision," was published in the *1989 Proceedings of Harvard Indian Law Symposium*.

232 scurrying back to the courts: Events in the courtrooms in Worland and Cheyenne are well documented, though much of that documentation is now stacked in boxes in the attic of the Washakie County Courthouse. In addition, I interviewed judges, attorneys, and other participants. Here's the citation for anyone interested in searching for the opinions and other documents in the case: In re the GENERAL ADJUDICATION OF ALL RIGHTS TO USE WATER IN THE BIGHORN RIVER SYSTEM and All Other Sources, State of Wyoming, State of Wyoming; Midvale Irrigation District; G. A. Brown Testamentary Trust through Langford Keith, Co-Trustee; LeClair Irrigation District; Riverton Valley Irrigation District; and James R. Allen, et al., Appellants (Plaintiffs).

Chapter 16: Bahwitchyagaqt

245 Shoshone was not a written language until very recently, and so you find many different spellings of commonly spoken words, as you do with Arapaho. I began with *Pah gwe che yah gah* as a spelling for the Shoshone name for Bull Lake, which I found in the book *Walk Softly, This Is God's Country* by Beatrice Crofts, Elinore Markley, and Reverend John Roberts (Mortimore). Readers had raised many questions about my spelling of Arapaho words, so I called the Shoshone Tribal Cultural Center to check this one. They were as unsure as I was, and left the phone for a few hours to consult books and experts. *Bahwitchyagaqt* is what they came up with, although I have no doubt that someone is going to tell me that's wrong.

246 There are many versions of the Crowheart duel. This one is taken from accounts in Grace Raymond Hebard's book *Washakie* (University of Nebraska Press) and a Works Progress Administration report from 1936 by A. F. C. Greene, "Shoshone History and Legends," in the Wyoming State Museum in Cheyenne. I've also discussed the story with various descendants of Washakie and made some modifications based on their comments.

A Note on the Type

This book was set in Monotype Dante, a typeface designed by Giovanni Mardersteig (1892–1977). Conceived as a private type for the Officina Bodoni in Verona, Italy, Dante was originally cut only for hand composition by Charles Malin, the famous Parisian punch cutter, between 1946 and 1952. Its first use was in an edition of Boccaccio's Trattatello in laude di Dante that appeared in 1954. The Monotype Corporation's version of Dante followed in 1957. Although modeled on the Aldine type used for Pietro Cardinal Bembo's treatise *De Aetna* in 1495, Dante is a thoroughly modern interpretation of the venerable face.

Composed by Creative Graphics, Allentown, Pennsylvania
Printed and bound by R. R. Donnelley, Harrisonburg, Virginia
Designed by Anthea Lingeman